"Christians can profit from Professor De Young's investigation of the basic moral questions of citizenship. He illustrates his points with ample citation from Scripture, history, and contemporary scholarship."

—Tom A. Coburn, M.D.
U.S. Senator

"'Timely' is one description of this book, but 'essential' is more appropriate. Major national issues are raised and discussed with clarity from a strong biblical perspective. Universal principles are shown in historical setting with gripping true stories bringing those principles to life. Careful study of this work lays a foundation for further thinking, and necessary action. The author has aptly summed up, 'In short, how does the Christian balance his earthly and heavenly citizenship?'

"After the 'balance' is found, what should we do?—in light of his challenging statement: 'The (contemporary) revolution in law which rejects all absolutes is a revolt not only against biblical authority, but also against conscience, reason, general revelation, and history.' This book must inform the Christian public."

—Donald K. Smith, B.S., M.S., M.A., PhD., Litt.D.
Founder of Daystar University, Nairobi, Kenya, and formerly Distinguished Professor of Intercultural Communication at Western Seminary, Portland, Oregon

"For 2000 years Jesus' followers have sought to work out, in theory and in practice, what it means to 'render unto Caesar what is Caesar's, and unto God what is God's.' How does one go about reconciling these seemingly conflicting loyalties? Such questions become acute in times of rapid social, economic, moral, and political change, such as the world is experiencing today on a perhaps unprecedented scale. James De Young offers here his timely analysis of the challenges facing our world today, and draws principles for a Christian response from key texts of Scripture. Readers may differ in their understanding of current events, and in the interpretation and application of the biblical texts treated here. Yet those who seek to be at once a human being, a patriot, and a Christian will do well to consider again these passages, which form important building blocks for the construction of a social ethic and political theology that is both rooted in Scripture and critically engaged in today's world."

—Joel Burnell, PhD.
Author of *Poetry, Providence, and Patriotism:
Polish Messianism in Dialogue with Dietrich Bonhoeffer* (Wipf & Stock, 2009)

"In this timely book James De Young deals with such important moral issues as homosexuality and gay rights, abortion, revolution, and war, but he deals with all of these and more in the context of the issue of obeying government. What does the Christian do when the state demands allegiance to it rather than to God? De Young provides seven biblical guidelines to help Christians in cultures from both the East and the West to decide this question. He introduces each chapter with a true story from Church history of those who have resisted the state and paid the cost for doing so. In this era of revolution and terrorism, De Young's book provides a welcome, encouraging, and inspiring resource for all Christians to read and to study."

—ENOCH WAN, PH.D

President, Evangelical Missiological Society (www.EMSweb.org); Founder/editor, multilingual online journal www.GlobalMissiology.org; and Research Professor of Anthropology and Director, Doctor of Missiology Program, Western Seminary.

To Submit or to Rebel against the State?

To Submit or to Rebel against the State?

Seven Biblical Principles to Guide Christians Everywhere During an Age of Revolution and in the Struggle for Religious Freedom

JAMES B. DE YOUNG

WIPF & STOCK · Eugene, Oregon

TO SUBMIT OR TO REBEL AGAINST THE STATE?
Seven Biblical Principles to Guide Christians Everywhere
During an Age of Revolution and in the Struggle for Religious Freedom

Copyright © 2012 James B. De Young. All rights reserved. Except for brief quotations in critical publications or reviews, no part of this book may be reproduced in any manner without prior written permission from the publisher. Write: Permissions, Wipf and Stock Publishers, 199 W. 8th Ave., Suite 3, Eugene, OR 97401.

Wipf & Stock
An Imprint of Wipf and Stock Publishers
199 W. 8th Ave., Suite 3
Eugene, OR 97401
www.wipfandstock.com

ISBN 13: 978-1-62032-441-7
Manufactured in the U.S.A.

All scripture quotations, unless otherwise indicated, are taken from the Holy Bible, New International Version®, NIV®. Copyright ©1973, 1978, 1984 by Biblica, Inc.™ Used by permission of Zondervan. All rights reserved worldwide.

This book is written in appreciation for all those Christians who have gone before who have been steadfast in their witness for Christ, even at the cost of their lives. They continue to speak to us today.
Hebrews 11, especially verses 39–40.

Contents

Preface xi
Introduction—The Purpose and Plan of This Book xiii

PART 1   THREE REVOLUTIONS STALK THE EARTH   1
The Revolutions in Government, Law, and Morality

1   The Revolution in Government   3
   The Threats of Islamic Terrorism and Anarchy

2   The Revolution in Law   19
   The Demise of Natural Moral Law

   Addendum—*Additional Principles from the Declaration of Independence*

3   The Revolution in Morality   50
   The Rejection of the Judeo-Christian Ethic

   Addendum—*The Myth of Moral Pluralism*

PART 2   TO SUBMIT OR TO REBEL AGAINST THE STATE?   69
Seven Biblical Principles to Guide Christians Everywhere During an Age of Revolution and in the Struggle for Religious Freedom

4   The Source of Government   71
   The Martyrdom of Ignatius

   Principle 1   Christians Should Submit to Government as Established by God *(Romans 13:1–2)*

5   The Purpose of Government   85
   The Martyrdom of Polycarp

   Principle 2   Government Should Promote Good and Punish Evil
   (Romans 13:3–7)

6   **The Limitation of the Authority of Government** 106
    The Martyrdom of William Tyndale

    Principle 3   Allegiance to Government Is Not Absolute
    (Matthew 22:17–21; Acts 5:29)

7   **The Relationship of Law to Morality** 127
    Isaac Backus: Champion of Religious Liberty in Early America

    Principle 4   Morality Is Legislated *(1 Timothy 1:8–11)*

8   **The Standard for Law in Government** 149
    Christians Aid the Collapse of Communist Governments

    Principle 5   The Standard for Law Is Divine Revelation
    (1 Timothy 1:8–11)

9   **The Christian's Unique Role in Government** 168
    Only True Christians Can Save Their Country
    —Diognetus, Sharp, Wilberforce

    Principle 6   Christians Must Pray for Leaders of Governments
    (1 Timothy 2:1–2)

10 **The Limitation to Liberty: Is it Right to Rebel?** 191
    An Afghan Woman Finds Jesus

    Principle 7   Liberty Is Not License *(1 Peter 2:13–17)*

    Conclusion   In an Age of Terrorism, What Does the Future Hold?
        —Facing the Coming Unrest and Revolution 215
    Epilogue   The Great Hymns of America 229
    Appendix 1   The Founding Fathers Support Natural Moral Law
        and Religion in America 232
    Appendix 2: The Reformers on Revolution 237
    Bibliography 244

Preface

Jesus warned that it was necessary to read the signs of the times that point to his Second Coming and the end of the world (Matthew 16:3; 24:3–14).

ONE OF THOSE SIGNS is unrest, including war, among nations. Another sign is the persecution of his followers. Such a time of tumult seems to be more worldwide than ever before. In such a time what do Christians do? When their government fails them, when it institutionalizes evil more and more, what recourse do Christians have? When the State turns against Christians and persecutes them, even forbidding them to worship their Lord and God, is resistance and rebellion the only choice?

It is with these concerns that I've written this book.

I'm convinced that the Bible provides guidelines and principles that will empower Christians to make correct decisions for these times of tumult and revolution. I'm also convinced that such matters are not new, that Christians have faced them for two millennia, and that we can learn from the past.

It has always been the case that Christians submit to the authority of Jesus and his Apostles for all things, including their view of the State and its legitimate exercise of power. "In Jesus Christ are hidden all the treasures of wisdom and knowledge" (Colossians 2:3).

Introduction

THE PURPOSE AND PLAN OF THIS BOOK

There is a rising world conflict that threatens to engulf the world's nations in a war on a scale not seen before. Instant communication and globalization inflame this conflict. The stakes are so high that failure to prevail in this clash could mean the end of civilization as we know it.

Christians especially need to have clear guidance regarding this conflict, and their relationship to their particular state or government. It is not too much to say that upon Christians rests the salvation of the world.

In the following pages, I set forth seven principles to guide Christians in their relationship to the state. These principles comprise Part 2, the last seven chapters of this book. Together they describe the core teaching of the Bible on this issue.

To lay the groundwork for the urgency of these principles, the first three chapters (otherwise known as Part 1) alert the reader to the revolution that has already begun taking place in government, in law, and in public morality. They describe the revolt and terrorism attacking the long held ideas of nationhood, universal law, and public morality. These first chapters also argue the case *for* nationhood, Universal Moral Law, and the essential place of the Judeo-Christian ethic; and the case *against* the touted pluralism crippling our nation today.

In addition, I've begun each chapter of Part 2 with a short vignette, taken straight from actual history. Each is a true story of how Christians have supported (or defied) their state in order to obey a higher law: the law of God. These stories span two millennia, from the first Christian martyr after the New Testament, the godly Ignatius, to the most contemporary examples today, Christians in the Islamic state of Afghanistan who have paid a tremendous price to follow Jesus Christ. These stories

Introduction

give precedence, encouragement, and guidance to meet the inappropriate demands of the state.

THE RISE OF ISLAMIC FUNDAMENTALISM CREATES URGENCY FOR THIS BOOK

An undercurrent running through this book addresses the threat that extremist Islam poses to the survival of governments in the East and the West. Extremist Islam is committed to the destruction of all governments that do not conform to Islamic law, in which Allah has absolute sway over all institutions and life. The imposition of Islamic law would mean the end of the freedoms that the Constitution of the United States guarantees to its citizens.

The contemporary war on terrorism gives added urgency to the understanding of the Christian's relationship to the state. The terrorist attack on the United States on September 11, 2001, changed forever the focus of this country. No longer are we invulnerable as a nation, separated from other continents by two great oceans. With modern technology and the impetus of globalization, weapons of mass destruction are no longer restricted to rogue nations. Islamic extremists, and others, are capable of bringing to our shores the means to wreck unspeakable havoc on the citizenry of this country. Innocent civilians are susceptible to biological weapons, chemical weapons, and even nuclear weapons. The prospect of experiencing one or more of these kinds of assaults on our country is almost certain. Intelligence agencies give the probability of such attacks as more than 50 percent.

Moreover, such prospects are not limited to the United States. In the last few years, virtually every Western nation has been terrorized in one form or another. Holland, Spain, France, and Great Britain are those that have experienced some of the more virulent forms of destruction. Israel and Lebanon confront terrorism head on daily. And the threat has arrived in South America, Asia, and even in the largest Muslim nation of Indonesia. Christians in Nigeria suffer increased persecution and death arising from the strife between its Muslim north and Christian south. During the year 2011, several states in North Africa (Tunisia, Algeria, Libya, Egypt, and Sudan) experienced revolutions. Syria and Iran are state sponsors of terrorism, with Iran seeking nuclear weapons!

Introduction

The enemy of freedom-loving people is not limited to a rogue nation bent on subduing its neighbors. The enemy is now scattered around the world, hiding in legitimate states, but waiting for the appropriate hour to strike against innocent civilians. Not since the rise of communism has there been such a foe to peace, stability, and freedom. This enemy is not motivated by desires for wealth, natural resources, or even by freedom. Rather, Muslim terrorists are motivated by an extreme interpretation of their faith. They seek to glorify Allah and extend his rule around the world.

National boundaries are meaningless compared to the brotherhood shared by Muslim fundamentalists and their commitment to universal Islam.

A DIFFERENCE OF WORLDVIEWS

At issue is the matter of worldview. The West, particularly the United States, embraces a worldview that derives from the Old and New Testaments. It views reality as consisting of visible and invisible realms—the reality of earthly and physical matter and the greater reality of God, heaven, and his kingdom. It views God as revealed in Scripture as the source of truth and morality. It views the coming of Jesus Christ as the greatest event in all of history. The basic Christian view in the West embraces Jesus Christ as the special, divine Son of God whom the Father sent as Savior of the world. Also, Christians confess the Holy Spirit as the third member of the Trinity who is active in the world today.

Islam embraces a deceptively similar but crucially different worldview. It adds the *Qur'an* as an additional and final source of revelation, surpassing the significance of the Bible. It rejects the Trinity, and rejects Jesus Christ as the divine Son of God. Islam makes Jesus a mere man who could not be a Savior, since there are no sins needing atonement and forgiveness. His was not a special resurrection. Indeed, Jesus probably did not die on a cross. Islam embraces Muhammad as God's final, superior prophet, even though he did not claim to rise from the grave to be alive forevermore.

The practical difference between these worldviews is that Christians are called to be disciples of Jesus and what he taught. In the Sermon on the Mount, Jesus calls his followers to love their enemies and to forgive

Introduction

them. Following Jesus, his apostles similarly taught Christians to love their enemies and not seek personal vengeance (Romans 12:9-21). They instructed the first Christians to submit to human, secular government (Romans 13:1-6), and to exercise their heavenly citizenship in tandem with their citizenship in an earthly nation. In so doing, Christians follow the teaching of Jesus regarding their allegiance to God and to the state (Matthew 22:15-22).

Islam challenges its followers to extend Allah's realm throughout the earth by conversion, tribute, or sword, till all the world embraces Islam. The law of *sharia* implants the rule of the *Qur'an* and accompanying tradition (*hadith*) as the law and culture on all nations. Given this approach, all governments would become theocracies. There is no place for secular government. Fundamentalist Islam resorts to any means, including war (*jihad*) and terrorism, to bring this to fruition. The current struggles in Iraq and Afghanistan represent the unveiled face of extremist Islam.

THE SPECIAL CHALLENGE TO CHRISTIANS

In an age of terrorism, what are Christians to do? Contemporary terrorism makes even more strongly and urgent the case for a sound view of what government is and can do, and what citizens should do. More precisely, what should Christian citizens do? Are Christians to take up arms and overthrow rogue nations? Should governments do so? Is it correct to engage in war? What is a "just" war? What about capital punishment? Is there biblical support for any of this?

Other questions arise: Should Christians submit to governments which fail to guarantee liberties at one time granted by their constitutions? Do Christians have to respect the law? What limits are there, if any, to our patriotism and to our submission to authority? In short, how does the Christian balance his earthly and heavenly citizenships? In an age of terrorism, where can the Christian find guidance, peace, and justice?

The approach of this book is to discover and interpret Biblical teaching from the New and Old Testaments in an attempt to arrive at a cohesive understanding of the purpose and role of government and a Christian's civic responsibility. I also appeal to Natural Moral Law, as revealed in history and in creation. I use these two sources, the Bible and Natural Moral

Law, as the final authorities on which every Christian should form his beliefs and practices regarding the state.

This book unfolds the nature of the current revolutions taking place and reveals how Christians can in fact be biblical in their civic involvement. This approach incorporates applications throughout, and concentrates on several major moral-political issues, especially abortion, homosexuality, war, the death penalty, civil disobedience, and the terrorism current today.

THE FOUNDATION FOR THIS BOOK

The central message of this book is based upon the words of Christ in Matthew 22:21, which were spoken during a time that saw an unrest and revolution not much different from what we see now. Jesus said, "Render to Caesar the things that belong to Caesar and to God the things that belong to God." The belief underlying this statement is that both government, with its necessary accompaniments of law and morality, and God's realm have legitimate claims on the individual. The statement implies that both the state and the church are institutions designed by God, and both command proper spheres of allegiance. How to discern and define these "proper spheres of allegiance" is the concern of this book.

I will show that Jesus' words form the greatest statement about statecraft in the history of humanity. The impact of them is so far reaching that they became the basis for the American experiment in democracy and are at the heart of contemporary constitutional debates in our country and throughout the world.

The benefit of this book will be its use as a guidebook or primer for addressing both the general conflict in society (between church and state) and the particular moral and social issues at hand. It will be useful internationally and cross-culturally as a help to Christians in both revolutionary and non-revolutionary societies today. Throughout I have kept transcultural settings in mind.

THE REASONS FOR THIS BOOK

My reasons for writing on this topic are threefold. First, my own experience in social and moral issues has forced me to examine carefully the

Introduction

issues facing every Christian. As any good citizen should, I have followed the political issues of this and other countries. While I am not a political scientist, I majored in history in college and studied the Civil War in particular. I have voted regularly. My wife and I have been precinct committee chairpersons; we went door-to-door to help elect Ronald Reagan as President. For several years, I participated in a Christian think tank, the SaltShakers, which sought to bring Christian values to moral issues in the Portland, Oregon, area; I also edited our newsletter for eighteen months. I have participated in peace conferences. I have given testimony before state legislative committees, have had opinions published in the *Oregonian* (the state's major newspaper), have written on many moral issues, and have participated in televised Town Hall broadcasts and numerous radio interviews on a host of issues.

I have published a book on how to interpret the Bible, a book on Greek syntax, and a book on one of the most urgent moral issues of our day—homosexuality and gay rights, including gay marriage. I have also published a book dealing with the beliefs of Islam and the challenge of Islamic fundamentalism: *Islam, Terrorism, and Christian Hope: Reflections on 9-11 and Resurging Islam*. The impetus for this book were the events of 9-11 and my two visits to Afghanistan (2003, 2005). I've written other books, including one on the role of women in ministry, and another, an exposé of the popular novel, *The Shack*. My book is titled *Burning Down the Shack: How a "Christian" Bestseller is Deceiving Millions* (2010). In that book, I expose one of the major deceptions in the Christian faith today: universalism.

I have a doctorate in theology. I have taught theology, Bible, biblical interpretation, early church fathers, and the biblical languages for forty years in a Bible school and seminary. I mention this theological training and teaching because past generations believed that Scripture is the foundation of *all* civilization and law. And, as a Christian, I believe that it still is. In the following pages I attempt to prove this as I set forth seven universal principles to guide Christian citizens.

The second reason for my writing this book is my perception of a need for a work that goes beyond addressing the particular social-moral issues confronting us today (such as abortion, euthanasia, war and peace, submission to government, homosexuality, the lottery, drugs, etc.). Instead, I explore general biblical guidelines that can instruct Christians on any issue. Based upon a biblical understanding of the origin and nature of government, law, and morality, Christians should be able to work through the appropriate response to the many challenges and conflicts that arise in the realm of their civic responsibility.

Rather than concentrating on one issue or several separate issues, this book seeks to deal with the big picture of Christian accountability to God and to the state. Hopefully, this book will give guidance to Christians of any culture on such questions as: Is it ever right to violate the law (engage in civil disobedience)? Can a government become so oppressive that Christians are justified in taking up arms and revolting?

The third impetus for writing this book is the arrival of terrorism on America's shores. While terrorism, especially in the form of Islamic fundamentalism, is not new to many other countries, its devastating arrival here makes such a work as this especially urgent. While I began this book during the later years of the Cold War, during the 1980's, I sense that terrorism in the name of religion now exceeds the challenge posed by communism. The latter is on the way out and terrorism is on the way in. The war on terrorism is the first war of the 21st century. And it is a world war that will probably outlast the 21st century. My visits to Afghanistan have reinforced this observation.

The year 2011 saw the rise of the Occupy Movement, which espouses revolution in the form of the end of capitalism and the redistribution of wealth among all the people. Just where this movement will lead no one knows. No doubt it derives its inspiration from President Obama, when during his campaign he called for the redistribution of wealth.

The way in which governments respond to current terrorism raises other concerns, such as the extent that civil liberties should be suspended in the war, the role that private citizens should play in assisting in the war (spying on neighbors, etc.), and the use of religious organizations in gathering intelligence information to assist the war effort. Another danger is that government, in its zeal to thwart terrorism, becomes terrorist itself. Or, terrorism could become a cover under which government will grow in power to hamper constitutional rights or limits, especially those of conservatives, under a new, liberal president and Congress. Through this book, I am determined to set forth the proper role of government, even in times of war and terrorism, as found in Scripture and in history.

Scattered throughout the chapters of this book are significant quotes from the founding fathers of the United States, from Abraham Lincoln, and from our founding documents, along with their modern interpreters,

Introduction

which focus on the role of religion in shaping public morality and law. In the Appendices, I quote the inspirational leaders of our past, and also give expanded treatment of how the Reformers (such as Martin Luther, John Calvin, and others) dealt with a Christian's relationship to the state. These quotations are themselves a special resource for the Christian citizen.

BROADER QUESTIONS ADDRESSED AND ANSWERED

We live at a time when there is much confusion and misunderstanding regarding the Christian's relationship to the state. Many questions confront the sincere Christian. In this book, the reader will find answers to the following larger questions, among others.

- Where did the idea of the state or nationhood come from, and why did it originate? (Chapter 1)
- What is the purpose or role of government and/or the state? What danger do empires pose? (Chapters 1, 6, and 7)
- Why is a multitude of individual states preferable to a one-world government? (Chapter 1)
- Where does law come from and what is its relationship to the state? How is law changed? Why does the Declaration of Independence refer to "natural law"? (Chapter 2)
- What is Natural Moral Law? What does the Bible say about it? What does history teach? (Chapter 2)
- What is the relationship of religion, morality, and law? (Chapter 4)
- Why is the contemporary pursuit for pluralism inherently flawed? (Chapter 3)
- Where does government get its authority? What does the Bible mean when it calls on Christians to "submit" to the government? (Chapter 4)
- How does government fulfill its purpose? (Chapter 5)
- What did Jesus say regarding the state and allegiance to it? (Chapter 6)

Introduction

- Are there any limitations to a Christian's allegiance to government? If so, what are they and how do Christians recognize them? (Chapter 6)
- Can Christians demonstrate against the state and still be good citizens? Do they have to submit to evil governments? (Chapters 6 and 10)
- Can Christians participate in revolution to change a government? Can they lead a revolution? If so, under what conditions may they do so? (Chapters 6 and 10)
- Can morality be legislated? Should it be legislated? (Chapter 7)
- What is the standard for law or legislation? Where should legislators go to find the standard for right and wrong? (Chapter 8)
- What is the Judeo-Christian ethic? Why should it have precedence in society? (Chapter 8)
- How is prayer for leaders and rulers the special task and privilege of the Christian? What are the Old Testament precedents? What should they pray for? (Chapter 9)
- What can contemporary evangelicals contribute to the moral, legal, and religious crisis facing their countries? (Chapter 9 and the Conclusion)
- What does Christian freedom mean? Being citizens of heaven, do Christians really owe any allegiance or submission to an earthly state? Is the state inherently diabolical? (Chapter 10)
- What did the Reformers (Luther, Calvin, Knox, and others) have to say regarding revolution? (Chapter 10 and Appendix 2)
- Why is a spiritual renewal in the West needed? How can it come about? (Conclusion)

ADDITIONAL AND MORE NARROW QUESTIONS

In each chapter, the answers to these larger questions will stimulate more specific questions on current issues facing Christians. The following are addressed:

Introduction

- Should a Christian be patriotic? (Chapters 1 and 4)
- How are communism and radical Islam alike? (Chapter 1)
- What is the source of our liberties, or inalienable rights? (Chapter 2)
- Where does public morality come from? (Chapter 3)
- What is civil religion and why is it wrong? (Chapter 1)
- Can a person be a conservative in theology and a liberal in politics? (Chapter 2)
- Should the Christian say the Pledge of Allegiance to the flag of the United States? Should Christians in any land pledge allegiance to the state? (Chapters 4 and 6)
- Should Christians pay taxes, even when the state funds abortions and promotes other evils (such as slavery, euthanasia, the lottery, etc.)? (Chapter 5)
- Is war justified? What are the criteria for just war? Where did the criteria come from? Is the use of weapons of mass destruction ever justified? (Chapter 5)
- Is a preventive first strike against a hostile nation a justified act of war? (Chapter 5)
- Is the death penalty a just act applied by the state? (Chapter 5)
- Can Christians break the law in order to obey a higher law? When should they do so? (Chapter 6)
- What is the biblical position on slavery and abortion? (Chapter 7)
- What is the biblical position on homosexual behavior? Should the state limit it? Should the state legalize homosexual marriage? (Chapter 8)
- Should there be prayer in public schools? What is "separation of church and state"? What did Jesus contribute to this contemporary discussion? (Chapter 9)
- What is liberation theology? How does it violate the gospel? (Chapter 10)

Introduction

While the reader may disagree with my answers to these questions, my hope is that this book will become the basis for further informed discussion of great issues, which have great significance.

If there looms on the horizon the threat of a clash of civilizations, between the Christian West and the Muslim world, then we would do well to pray and work for spiritual renewal. This is the focus of the last chapter of the book (the Conclusion). As I show, Christians play the pivotal role for the survival of our republic.

In the following pages, I invite the reader to take a journey with me into the land of faith and politics, into the realm where great issues are debated, determined, and even fought over. It is a journey that has no final end but there are many guideposts along the way that will illuminate the journey itself. May God, the Ruler of the nations, guide us on our way.

PART 1

Three Revolutions Stalk the Earth
The Revolutions in Government, Law, and Morality

Introduction

THREE REVOLUTIONS STALK THE peace of the world: the revolution in government or the state, the revolution in law, and the revolution in morality. These revolutions threaten the existence of civilization itself.

I have written the following pages to arouse the reader's awareness of how pervasive these revolutions are. These pages lay the foundation for the following chapters in part 2 that set forth the principles that will rescue and restore a Christian vision of the state.

In this first chapter, I seek to show what the Bible says about the origin of the state and its nature and its purpose. Should modern circumstances, such as nuclear war, global politics, and religious fanaticism, alter the biblical witness? How does the witness of Scripture correspond to the witness of history regarding these issues?

1

The Revolution in Government

That is why it was called Babel—because there the Lord confused the language of the whole world. From there the Lord scattered them over the face of the whole earth.
—*Genesis 11:9*

These are the clans of Noah's sons, according to their lines of descent, within their nations. From these the nations spread over the earth after the flood.
—*Genesis 10:32*

The God who made the world and everything in it is the Lord of heaven and earth and does not live in temples built by hands. And he is not served by human hands, as if he needed anything, because he himself gives all men life and breath and everything else. From one man he made every nation of men, that they should inhabit the whole earth; and he determined the times set for them and the exact places where they should live. God did this so that men would seek him and perhaps reach out for him and find him, though he is not far from each one of us.
—*Acts 17:24–27*

WORLDWIDE REVOLUTION

Throughout much of Latin America, Africa, Asia, and the Middle East, the winds of revolution have blown like a hurricane. Colonial rule is a thing of the past and people are seeking their own indigenous form of government. In some countries, this has taken the form of violent, armed rebellions. Communist totalitarian regimes usurped control in various states, and still hold it in Viet Nam, China, North Korea, and Cuba. Extremist Islamic states have been established in Afghanistan and Iran, and threaten Iraq, Egypt, Algeria, Libya, Sudan, Turkey, Syria, Lebanon, Nigeria, and Indonesia, as well as other countries. In the Philippines, revolt led to democratic government. It is usually the "oppressed classes" who call for reform and revolution. And often it is religious people taking a leading role in espousing the revolution in government.

WHAT IS A REVOLUTION?

The dictionary defines revolution as "a total or radical change . . . a fundamental change in political organization . . . the overthrow or renunciation of one government or ruler, and the substitution of another by the governed." A revolution may not be an armed uprising; indeed, the dictionary makes no mention of armaments but does mention a "revolution in thoughts."[1]

The central issue in a revolution is the goal, not the means of bringing it about. For many revolutionaries, the end justifies the means. It may take the forms of violence and war, the abrogation of personal rights, the destruction of certain institutions (for example, the church, the government, the family), but revolutionaries are willing to embrace all these means as necessary and acceptable if the desired end is achieved.[2] Revolutionaries seek a change in the very nature of government itself. Nationhood would dissolve into international-hood (i.e., internationalism) of one form (religious) or another (secular). One government for the world is the goal.

Across Western civilization, there is a growing peace movement seeking to bring about a one-world government. Even now, after the acts of terrorism in the United States on September 11, 2001, there are many who demonstrate on behalf of peace and disarmament, especially in the form of nuclear arms. All of this is happening at a time when many warn that rogue nations, such as Iran and North Korea, part of President

---

1. *Webster's New Collegiate Dictionary*, 726.

2. Even the popular novel, *The Shack*, because of its opposition to these institutions is revolutionary (see my book *Burning Down the Shack*, ch. 6).

George Bush's "axis of evil," are pursuing nuclear arms. President Obama has expressed his concern for the spread of nuclear weapons.

THE RESURGENT CONFLICT BETWEEN THE CRESCENT AND THE CROSS

The association of religion with revolution is demonstrated in another way that could not have been imagined a few years ago. It can be said, without overstatement, that not since the time of the Crusades has the potential for conflict between Islam and Christianity (or Judaism) been greater.

This conflict has risen to the level where radical Islamists have targeted governments around the world to overthrow them and bring them all into compliance with religious Muslim law, known as *sharia*. The goal is to extend the universal rule of Allah across all national boundaries.

The most obvious example is the conflict between the Islamic Arab nations and Israel. The conflict with the Hezbollah in Christian Lebanon showed the extent to which terrorists will go. In addition, such countries as Egypt, Algeria, Sudan, Nigeria, Kenya, and Indonesia have experienced ongoing conflict between their Christian and Islamic citizens. The goal of radical Islam is to create theocracies (Islamic states), as has been done in Iran.

The hostility has reached a new level of intensity since the events of September 11, 2001. Arab extremists, seeking to bring religious war (*jihad*) to America's shores, died as martyrs, according to their understanding of Islam. This marked the greatest attack on America's shores, and signaled the beginning of the "war against terrorism." Only time will tell how far reaching this struggle will be and what will be the outcome. Al Qaeda and other extremist groups have as their goal, in the words of one observer, "the absolute destruction of America as we know it."[3]

THE ORIGIN AND PURPOSE OF GOVERNMENT

Nationhood is God's idea. Nations have a key role to play in the rule of morality and law in civilization. With their diverse languages and cultures, nations are ordained by God to restrain the power of evil in the earth.

3. As quoted in *USNWR*, 27.

To Submit or to Rebel against the State

God rules over all (Daniel 4:35), and on earth he exercises his will and program in a significant way through human governments. Scripture first mentions the existence of nations in Genesis 10. Apparently only families and clans and cities prevailed (Genesis 4–5) before this. Prior to the Flood there was a kind of collective evil that called forth judgment. The Bible records that "the wickedness of people was great on the earth, and ... every intent of the thoughts of their hearts was only evil continually" (Genesis 6:5; author's trans.). After the Flood, the same evil began all over again. A common universal language facilitated the political and religious unity of mankind to join in a united rebellion against God.

The descendants of Noah and his three sons—in point, all of humanity—had been commanded to fill all the earth (Genesis 9:1), to populate it abundantly, and multiply in it (Genesis 9:7). God had made a promise, an everlasting covenant, to all people that he would never again destroy the earth with water. In return, human beings were to exercise justice and punish evil, particularly murder, on behalf of God in order to restrain greater evil (Genesis 9:9–17). The universal scope of this covenant cannot be denied. It is implicit, if not explicit, in almost every verse of Genesis 9.

Yet people refused to disband and instead organized a conspiracy against God and his purposes (note Genesis 11:4b). The rebellion against the command to disburse is clear: "Come, let us make for ourselves a name; lest we be scattered abroad over the face of the whole earth." The people were gathered into one city and began to build a tower to reach heaven and dethrone God.

This rebellious action brought forth God's judgment. When the people built the Tower of Babel, Genesis 11:5–9 (TNIV) records:

> But the Lord came down to see the city and the tower they were building. The Lord said, "If as one people speaking the same language they have begun to do this, then nothing they plan to do will be impossible for them. Come, let us go down and confuse their language so they will not understand each other."
>
> So the Lord scattered them from there over all the earth, and they stopped building the city. That is why it was called Babel—because there the Lord confused the language of the whole world. From there the Lord scattered them over the face of the whole earth.

Because God confused human speech and formed various languages (Genesis 11:1-9), people were dispersed over the earth in accordance with God's original command (Genesis 9:1, 7), and national boundaries were formed (Genesis 10:5, 20, 31-32).[4] Each entity was characterized by families or clans, language, land, and nationhood (see Genesis 10:31-32). Hence the nations mentioned in Genesis 10 came into being only after the dispersal due to the confusion of languages described in chapter 11. In other words, the multiplicity of languages that arose in chapter 11 is the cause for the beginning of nations described in chapter 10.

The Tower of Babel symbolizes collective rebellion on the earth against God in heaven. Dispersal at the Tower represents the means whereby to limit this rebellion. So while the dispersion was commanded in the Noahic Covenant (Genesis 9:1, 7), and is anticipated there (9:19), only in Genesis 11:1-9 is it accomplished. The dispersion resulted in the formation of nations. Their formation represents the restraining of greater collective rebellion.

THE PURPOSE OF GOVERNMENT: RESTRAIN EVIL

One of the chief components of the Noahic Covenant, fully in keeping with the institution of nations, is the institution of the death penalty. This is to be exercised by human beings collectively, in nations, not individually (Genesis 9:5-6). The death penalty has the symbolical meaning of expressing society's determination to exert justice—that is, to punish evil whether that evil is a lesser crime or a greater one demanding death.

In light of the foregoing, nationhood serves the purpose of curbing greater evil.[5] A nation may have an evil character and wicked designs, yet these remain limited as far as global evil is concerned. When nations are joined with others, as, for example, in the formation of empires or international confederations, the potential for evil becomes much greater.

---

4. As far as I'm able to discover, no other ancient literature gives an origin for the divergent languages of the nations of the earth.

5. Ross, "Dispersion," 120.

THE WITNESS OF THE NEW TESTAMENT

The New Testament reaffirms God's ordination or establishing of nations. In Acts 17:26, the Apostle Paul tells the Greeks of Athens that God made all nations from one and determined their appointed times of existence and their geographical boundaries. In a very pagan setting, Paul declared that God " . . . made from one every nation of people, that they should inhabit the whole earth; and he determined the times set for them and the exact places where they should live. God did this so that people would seek him and perhaps reach out for him and find him, though he is not far from each one of us" (translation mine).

When Paul later writes to the Romans (13:1–7), he makes the divine source and sovereignty over governments or nations an essential part of his teaching about government. In the chapters that follow, I will deal more fully with this passage.

SATAN'S ROLE

The more limited a nation is in its political organization, or the greater separation of nations there is in the world community, there is a lesser potential for doing greater evil. The potential for evil is proportionate to the power of nations.

The evil nature of international confederacies during the present age can be seen from another perspective. The Scriptures teach that Satan is the ruler of this world (John 12:31; 14:30; 16:11; 1 John 5:19), and the god of this world (2 Corinthians 4:4). The world is characterized by darkness (Ephesians 6:12), and by evil desire and pride (1 John 2:16) that reflect the influence and nature of Satan (John 8:44; 1 John 2). The primary means by which Satan intends to thwart God's rule in the earth is to lead the nations in confederate rebellion against God. Such a pattern of rebellion has occurred in the past and is prophesied for the present and the future (as shown in Psalm 2:1–3; with Satan's role as instigator given in Revelation 12:17; 13:4, 7, 14; 16:13–14; 17:17; 19:19; 20:8, 10). At the end of this age, Satan will employ the Antichrist to head up the final confederacy of nations. Satan is the great *deceiver* of nations and seeks to employ governments in his evil design. In his First Epistle, John again links the Evil One with *deceivers*, the world, and antichrists who have already begun to arrive.

Yet Satan's role in a confederacy of nations with its potential for evil must be seen from the standpoint of God's sovereignty. All that takes place is included within God's plan, and he allows evil to exist—even the activities of Satan behind a united humanity disposed to evil. He allows Satan to work behind and within nations, against individuals (Job 1:12, 21; 2:3–10), and against rulers (1 Chronicles 21; 2 Samuel 24). Through it all, God uses these means to accomplish his sovereign will throughout Heaven and Earth (Daniel 4:35).

THE WITNESS OF HISTORY

Both biblical and secular history tend to bear out the greater evil posed by nations joined together. When Israel, loosely joined together under temporary judges, asked for a king to rule them, the request was a rejection of God's best for them (1 Samuel 8:7–8). It meant conscription in peace and war, increased taxation to support the military and throne, and confiscation of property (1 Samuel 8:11–18). Israel was a theocracy, both when ruled by judges and by kings, but the potential for oppression, totalitarianism, and loss of individual rights (e.g., possession of personal property) became far greater when the monarchy replaced the looser confederation under judges. While the threat from without was lessened under the monarchy, the threat from within was increased.

Yet Israel was never allowed to become an empire. From the beginning God limited Israel's boundaries, even when the powerful reigns of David and Solomon could have enlarged them.

There is the precedent of secular history as well, as reflected within the Bible.[6] According to the perspective of Scripture, only six world empires existed until the time of the New Testament (Daniel 2 and 7; Revelation 17:10ff.). These have opposed the God of the Bible and sought to destroy God's plan for mankind, which he has designed to bring to pass through the nation of Israel.

---

6. Regrettably, there is little concern in most circles of America today for the record of the past, and this attitude often characterizes the church as well. For the Christian, it means that he could never identify "the Christian position" on many issues. Joseph Sobran addressed this apathy toward the past by referring to the philosopher of history, Eric Voegelin, who suggested that those who are in revolt against the past may actually be "in revolt against the terms of creation and the permanent conditions of our existence." This position is untenable for Christians. (Sobran, "National," 7:44.)

To Submit or to Rebel against the State

Egypt, the world's first empire, kept Israel in bondage for 430 years (Genesis 15:13-16) and has repeatedly attacked Israel. Historians agree that Egypt under Thutmose III was the world's first nation to rise to empire status.[7] And then Assyria arose and captured the ten northern tribes (721 B.C.) and almost destroyed Judah (701 B.C.). After that, Babylon captured the two southern tribes in 606 B.C. and destroyed the temple, enslaving multitudes. Media-Persia followed and continued the enslavement of Jews until God moved the king to allow the Jews to return and rebuild the Temple and Jerusalem. Even this empire, however, had its wicked opponent: the Prince of Persia (Daniel 10:13), who sought to stop God's program. The Empire of Greece, begun by Alexander the Great, also had its wicked angelic prince (Daniel 10:20). His human counterpart, Antiochus IV, almost obliterated the Jews by forced secularization (Daniel 8). Such tyranny sparked the Maccabean revolt in about 165 B.C. To this day, when the Jews observe the feast of Hanukkah, they celebrate their liberation from this tyranny.

Finally, in 63 B.C., the last empire of biblical history, the Romans, conquered Palestine. In A.D. 70, the Romans destroyed the Temple and Jerusalem. After a second revolt (A.D. 132-135), the Romans forced the Jews into a world-wide dispersion that continued till 1948. The consequences of this dispersion remain to this day. Isn't it amazing that all of these six world empires engaged the tiny nation of Israel?

According to the perspective of the Book of Revelation, the seventh and final world empire under the Antichrist will be worse than all the preceding. It will once again seek to obliterate Israel (Revelation 12, 13, and 17; Daniel 8-9; Matthew 24:15ff.), and will nearly accomplish this before Christ, as the supreme warrior, intervenes on behalf of the nation of Israel and delivers her (Zechariah 12 and 14; Revelation 19; cf. Daniel 2). All the other empires that have appeared on the world's stage since the writing of the Revelation (whether Western, Eastern, etc.) are not relevant to God's timetable.

Psalm 2 outlines in broad strokes the whole course of human history with its collective rebellion and its culmination. The nations, unfettered by restraints which God has imposed, seek to control and rule the world according to their own evil designs (verses 1-3), rather than allow God's anointed, the Messiah, to rule from Israel. Yet God will not allow this to happen, for Christ will rule with a rod of iron during his visible kingdom

---

7. See Durant, *Civilization*, 1-3. For a list of Palestinian cities captured, see Aharoni and Avi-Yonah, *Bible Atlas*, 32.

(Psalm 2:4-9; cf. Revelation 20). Therefore, the inspired writer advises the nations to abandon their evil designs and submit in allegiance to the Son of God before he destroys them (Psalm 2:10-12).

EMPIRE-BUILDING AND UNIVERSAL GOVERNMENT

Yet the movement to dissolve national governments and form a universal government and police force has a far greater potential for evil than empire-building. In a world of fallen people and nations, this great leveling would do far greater harm than good. Recent history has shown that even meager attempts at universal government have not secured greater happiness, freedom, and peace for mankind. Indeed they often have contributed to greater poverty, war, and oppression. After WWI, the League of Nations may have actually contributed to the forces that led to the greater conflict of WWII. War had to rein in the evil of Nazism and imperialism.

Without an absolutely just ruler to guide the reins of world government, there is simply a greater potential for evil in one great government as compared to the evil that many competing lesser governments could achieve. It seems that nationhood is the best pattern for the present age.

NATIONALISM, PATRIOTISM, AND THE UNIVERSAL CHURCH

There is a direct application that flows from the place of nations in God's plan for humanity. Patriotism is the will of God. As the devotion to the welfare of one's country, the encouragement of nationalistic fervor and love of one's own country will work toward curbing evil posed by a collective union of nations. Certainly patriotism can be abused, but the extreme does not mitigate the fact that patriotism is God's will. Two voices from the past (Rev. Jonathan Mayhew and President Lincoln—see also Appendix 1) remind us of the importance of patriotism.[8]

---

8. It is unfortunate, indeed, how few symbols of patriotism remain in contemporary America, even after the terrorism of September 11, 2001. Let every Christian in every neighborhood be an unashamed patriot. In so doing, Christians will encourage the restraint of international rebellion and conspiracy. The words of Rev. Jonathan Mayhew, written in 1754, are still pertinent today, as given by Long (*American Yardstick*, viii).

> The very name of patriotism is indeed become a jest with some men; which would be much stranger than it is, had not so many others made

Patriotism also promotes the sense of community over individuality. It leads the citizenry to work for the greater good, and not just its own good. It represents selflessness and love of neighbor.

POTENTIAL CONFLICT OF ALLEGIANCES

Undoubtedly some will see a conflict between the Christian support of nationalism and their membership in the universal Church. Does not patriotism run counter to the community of faith, which transcends nationalities? Does the inauguration of the New Covenant mean that God is dealing with the nations on the basis of the Sermon on the Mount (we should forgive our enemies, turn the other cheek, etc.)? This apparent conflict is resolved by understanding that God is doing two works on the earth, with a specific purpose for each.

The Redemption Plan, Work One

One work is heaven-oriented and consists of God creating a new people, made from the people of every nation, bound together by redemption through the blood of Christ. All believers make up one body over which he is the Head. The mandate given to this body, the Church, is to reach all the world with the good news, to teach, and to baptize (Matthew 28:19–20).

---

a jest of the thing, serving their own base and wicked ends, under the pretext and color of it. But there will be hypocrites in politics, as well as in religion. . . . And those times are perilous indeed, wherein men shall be only lovers of their own selves, having no concern for the good of the public. . . . [A Christian lacking patriotism] . . . would be a reproach not only to his religion, a religion of charity and beneficence, but even to our own common nature, as corrupt and depraved as it is. But how much more infamous were this, in persons of public character? In those, on whom the welfare of their country, under providence, immediately depends?

Years later, at his first inaugural address, March 4, 1861, Abraham Lincoln spoke in a similar vein regarding patriotism. In light of the pending clash over slavery, he said: "Intelligence, patriotism . . . and a firm reliance on him who has never yet forsaken this favored land are still competent to adjust in the best way all our present difficulty."

The Kingdom Plan: The Final Act of the Play, Work Two

Yet there is another work of God that is earth-oriented. Christians live in nations all over the world and usually are the minority. The majority of the world continues to reject the gospel and reject its heralds, as the world rejected Christ (Matthew 7:13-14; John 15:18-19; 17:14-16). According to the parable of the tares (Matthew 13:24-30), Satan is sowing evil people in the world in an attempt to subvert Christ's work of sowing people who belong to the kingdom. Both grow together until the harvest, the judgment at the end of the age (Matthew 13:36-43).

This other work, this kingdom plan that God is doing in the world, is the preparing of the world theater for the final act of the play on the stage of history. The drama recounts the noble destiny of people on this planet to rule as vice-regents of God. Since people rebelled against this play and tried to rewrite the script in their own way, the Playwright masterfully included the institution of the state to coerce people to obey the will of the Playwright. Human governments are God's servants to force compliance. Satan, however, seeks either to destroy these institutions or to enlist them in his cause of opposing God's will. At the end of this tragedy, all the nations, except Israel, will throw their allegiance to the great deceiver, Satan (Revelation 13:2-8, 12-17; 16:12-16; 17:13-15; 20:3, 7-10).

The apparent conflict between these two purposes of God, represented by the Church and by the state, is alleviated when the Church, multiplying in a particular nation, reaches out to evangelize other nations. Nationalism is somewhat decreased, but this does not pose a threat. For where church unity promotes a decrease of nationalism there is less fear of satanic deception of that nation.

An enlightened and instructed Church should not confuse the separate roles of Church and state. It should not seek to make the state a church. When the Roman Catholic Church became involved in nationhood and formed the Holy Roman Empire in the Middle Ages, it had confused the respective responsibilities of the state and Church.

For the nations, the kingdom plan is basically concerned with justice and the restraint of evil. This is the emphasis that Paul, a minister of the New Covenant, makes in Romans 13:1-7. Individuals belong to the invisible kingdom of Christ and seek to extend its values in the visible realm by redemptive means. They seek to actualize the unseen realities of God's kingdom on the earth. Yet the parable of the wheat and tares (given by Jesus in Matthew

13:24–30; cf. Matthew 25:31–46) makes it clear that Christians leave judgment for God to carry out at the end of the age. During the present era, government is God's agent to maintain justice among the peoples of the earth.

DISTINCTIVE ROLES FOR CHURCH AND STATE

It is Jesus himself who affirms the respective and separate roles of the state and the church or religion. In Matthew 22, he instructs his hearers to render to Caesar what belongs to Caesar, and to God what belongs to God. Therefore the purposes of God are two-fold: to build a redeemed community out of every nation, and to secure his program to restrain evil within the nations until Christ comes again to rule his kingdom and enable humanity to achieve its prior calling of nobility and dominion over the earth. In the Messiah's actual rule on earth, there will be a coalescing of both purposes (redemption and rule) that will go on into eternity. Yet redemption enables nobility; only as redemption takes place is kingdom-living finally achieved. It cannot be the other way—that nobility is achieved apart from redemption. Liberal churches seek to reverse the order.

The apparent conflict, then, between the roles of the Church and the state is resolved by remembering that God has a defined purpose for both. A balance must be maintained between these two purposes. While the Church should influence the state toward the good, it should not seek to usurp the role of the state.

Yet one thing is clear from the preceding. It is the Church that must inform the state of its proper role, not the other way around. Redemption must occur before nobility is regained. Yet each has its proper sphere of influence and its role in the world.

THE PROMISE OF A NEW STATE, A THEOCRACY

Biblical history teaches the inability for virtue to rule, or the kingdom to reign, apart from redemption and grace. Under the Mosaic Law, Israel was a state and a church, seeking to provide or allow both nobility and grace. This was a theocracy.

And this theocracy required God's direct rule, and later, his indirect rule through kings, to bring a degree of measured success. The theocracy failed. However, its failure was due to faulty people, not a faulty plan.

"Finding fault with them" (Hebrews 8:8), God promised a new plan that would transform the people on the basis of redemption in Christ. This would enable them to achieve nobility (Hebrews 8:8-13 quoting Jeremiah 31:31-34). In this New Covenant, the people would be changed within—their very nature would be changed. They would have divine enablement to live righteously; and their sin would be removed in a final and complete way: "For I will be merciful to their iniquities, and I will remember their sins no more" (Hebrews 8:12, translation mine). This New Covenant has been inaugurated.

In the age to come, both the Church and the state will be dissolved in the New Jerusalem, the "new nation," where redeemed people rule in nobility over the vast creation of the new heavens and earth, apparently without national divisions. People will so reign only because God will dwell where they are: "And there shall no longer be any night; and they shall not have need of the light of a lamp nor the light of the sun, because the Lord God shall illumine them; and they shall reign forever and ever" (Revelation 22:5, translation mine; see also 21:1-3, 23-24). This is the fulfillment of the ultimate desire of the saints for God's very presence on Earth (see Hebrews 11:10, 16; 12:22; 13:14).

DISTORTION OF THE PURPOSES OF THE STATE AND THE CHURCH

Today, both the state and the Church are tempted to distort their God ordained purposes. The state attempts to bring in utopia or nobility apart from the provision of grace or redemption. In its worst forms, the state attempts to destroy human dignity. This distortion exalts the state unduly over the Church. Marxism (or socialism) and Islamism exemplify this distortion most clearly.

For the Church, the temptation is two-fold: Either (1) to follow the distortion of the state by trying to bring in nobility without redemption (so modern liberalism); or (2) to bring in grace or redemption without any thought for the nobility of people. The latter idea derives from the belief that there should be complete separation between the Church and state, that society should be divided between the sacred and secular. This distortion is also an idea totally foreign to a biblical worldview, and will be discussed in chapter 8.

To Submit or to Rebel against the State

Only one nation has had God's special ordination—and it is not America. Israel was distinctly established by God, and it failed. Israel served a special purpose.[9] Others, including the United States, serve other purposes.[10]

9. All nations are divinely ordained (Acts 17), but one nation, Israel, has a special divine ordination. God has sovereignly chosen Israel as a nation through which he will bless the rest of the nations (Gen. 12:1–3). No other nation, such as the United States, Great Britain, etc., can claim this special place. Through Abraham and his descendents, all the rest of mankind will be blessed. So crucial is Israel that all the rest of the world's nations are blessed and cursed in accordance with their treatment of Israel (Gen. 12:3). Several results issue from Israel's special ordination. No other nation can claim a relationship with God like Israel can (Deut. 4:7). Correspondingly, Israel is God's possession, purchased by him in redemption from Egypt (4:20), uniquely loved (7:6–10), and chosen and created (4:32–35; cf. Ezek. 16) by him. Israel was to be distinct and different from all other nations (Lev. 20:24, 26; Num. 23:7–10). God was the One who determined her prosperity (Deut. 8:17–20). Her unique purpose for existence, an immutable purpose (Num. 23:19–24), was to be a holy, separated nation (Lev. 19:2; 20:26), established to point others to the true God, and to be a source of blessing or cursing to the rest of the nations of the world.

Through Israel, all nations are able to find God and salvation (John 4:21–22). This is ultimately accomplished in the special Seed, namely Christ, promised to Abraham and his descendants (Rom. 1:3; Gal. 3:16, 19). In his first coming, Jesus provided redemption for all people, and inaugurated the New Covenant with its universal blessings of forgiveness and the Holy Spirit (Jer. 31:31–34; Matt. 26:28; Luke 22:20; 1 Cor. 1:25; 2 Cor. 3:6; Heb. 8:6–13). At his second coming, he will end the world-wide conspiracy of evil under Antichrist, and from Jerusalem will rule the world in universal peace and righteousness (Gen. 49:8–12; Num. 23:24; 24:7, 17; Ps. 2; Isa. 2, 4, 11; Rev. 12, 19). Israel will once again be restored to a place of blessing and favor among Gentile nations (Rom. 11:11–29), and the latter will fully participate in the time of restoration because of Israel.

Because of Israel's special ordination, she has a special calling or responsibility. She is to reflect her God, who called her by being holy (Lev. 19:2; 20:7, 24, 26; Deut. 7:6) and just (Lev. 19:15), by showing love (Lev. 19:18, 34; Deut. 6:4–5, 13–15), and by showing obedience (Deut. 7:11). Yet, by her disobedience in rejecting Jesus Christ as her Messiah, Israel has rejected her special ordination among nations. In a very real sense, the conflict of the ages between right and wrong, between God's way and Satan's way, is a conflict of nations. Our own nation owes much more to the Hebrews, i.e., to biblical Judaism, especially in her morality and laws, than it owes to the Greeks (Hellenism) or others.

Satan will continue to enlist any and every nation in continuous attempts to destroy, if possible, the nation and people of Israel. In destroying Israel, Satan would thwart God's plan of salvation for all the rest of the nations. Such is the suicidal nature of satanic deception!

10. What about the place of the nation of the United States? Does it have a special ordination in God's plan? Two opposing and extreme views are held which betray a distorted view of America's role in providential history. One view overemphasizes the role of this country in God's program, so that all of God's program is made to hinge on the success or failure of this nation. This fails to realize that God is doing great things in other

Several observations may be summarized here from the foregoing discussion.

1. The separation of peoples into national entities, divided by land and God's direct intervention (as exemplified by the Flood), is part of God's good plan for the world.
2. The state and the Church have distinct and legitimate roles.
3. Human government, as the collective expression of its inhabitants, will always have a tendency toward evil. Consequently, it is better for government to be limited than unlimited, for this will curb international conspiracy and rebellion.
4. There need be no conflict between patriotism and membership in the Body of Christ, which transcends national boundaries.

CONCLUSION: THREE DESTRUCTIVE FORCES ARE AT WORK

International communism and socialist opposition to capitalism, liberation theology, and Islamism are three powerful forces working toward a one-world government and the destruction of nationhood. Globalization of economics, culture and language, politics, and religion spur on this

---

countries and that his program for worldwide Messianic blessing will come through Israel, not the U.S. On the other hand, there is the view that fails to see God's special providence exerted on behalf of this land. This and all nations have a predetermined season and place (Acts 17:26). No nation should ever be abandoned to the forces of secularism or evil, especially one with our heritage. No other democratic nation in the history of the world was so founded on Christianity as was America.

This leads to the oft-discussed question regarding the specific role of America in the program of God. In addition to the obvious contribution this country has made to the evangelization of the world, something more should be said. Perhaps America's role among the nations of the world has been to restrain international empire-building, and thereby restrain a greater evil to come from a rebellious confederacy of nations. Of course, the preservation of Jews through America's participation in World War II is an obvious element in the preservation of God's program for that people in this age.

At present, it is the United States that is pursuing the war on international terrorism. Again she is acting in the role of preserving greater freedom in her pursuit of those who would destroy it and unite all under an Islamic culture and religion. Yet a sober word must be given here: The United States has departed far from her historical moorings, and freedom has given way to license. In doing so, America may well become the catalyst for the greatest evil in government—that of Antichrist.

movement, both leveling the differences among nations and stirring local pride (tribalism) and nationalism at the same time. The impetus for internationalism (or one-world government) has never been stronger. And the pressure for such will only increase as the world's economic woes continue, along with the depletion of natural resources and the destruction of the environment.

Today, the most virulent form of religious globalism is fundamentalist Islam. With "brotherhood" as one of its main tenets, Islam reaches across ethnic and national distinctions to bring about a universal rule under Islamic law called *sharia*. Such a form of Islam rejects the special distinctiveness of individual nations. Freedoms that Americans and people of all nations enjoy under their particular form of government would no longer be allowed.

All these movements encourage rebellions against God's plan. They fall into the snare of the deceiver (Satan) of the nations and promote the day of Antichrist.

2

The Revolution in Law

Then God said to Noah and to his sons with him: "I now establish my covenant with you, and with your descendants after you." —*Genesis 9:8–9*

Will not the Judge of all the earth do right? —*Genesis 18:25c*

For what great nation is there that has a god so near to it as is the Lord our God whenever we call on Him? Or what great nation is there that has statutes and judgments as righteous as this whole law which I am setting before you today?
—*Deuteronomy 4:7–8 (NAS)*

CHANGING LAWS

IN 1856, THE SUPREME Court of the United States interpreted the Constitution of this country to say that Black slaves were only property, not persons, and that they had no personal rights. Known as the Dred Scott Decision, this action affirmed the legitimacy of slavery. A few years later, the Civil War decided this issue in an opposite way: Black slaves were set free and the law of the land, the Constitution, was amended to prohibit slavery forever.

Throughout almost all of America's history, abortion was unlawful in all fifty states. Then, in 1973, the U.S. Supreme Court decided in *Roe v. Wade* that abortion was legal on the basis of a so-called "right to privacy." What was once illegal and deemed immoral became legal overnight. Its immorality remains. No amendment was made to the Constitution to legalize abortion.

In 1986, the same Supreme Court (in *Bowers v. Hardwick*) upheld the right of states to discriminate by law against homosexual behavior. That is, the Court found that the Constitution does not affirm an inherent right to practice same-sex behavior, even among consenting adults. However, in June 2003, the Court reversed itself, declaring that such a law in Texas and thirteen other states was unconstitutional. The six-to-three decision cited a right to privacy as the basis of its decision.

These cases raise significant issues regarding the source of law in general, as well as the relationship of law and morality. Several questions arise: How can law be dismissed so dramatically? On what basis is law changed? Are some laws unchangeable? What is the nature of law and how is it related to government? Is the legal thing always the moral thing? How is law related to morality?

In this chapter, I will describe how a revolution in law is taking place. This revolution is so far reaching and profound that it threatens the American experiment in government. In order to appreciate the scope of this revolution, it is necessary to survey the biblical and historical basis for law in any nation, and in the United States in particular.

LAW MUST NECESSARILY ACCOMPANY GOVERNMENT

When collective responsibility for dealing with murder was first enjoined in Genesis 9:5–6, the instructions to Noah showed that a law had been violated and a crime committed. Both God and people had been affected. With the beginning of national government came the beginning of the role of law in government also. Without law, there is anarchy, which is no government at all.

The only defense made in Genesis 9 for the kind of penalty assessed for the crime of murder, namely death, is that man is made in the image of God. This calls to mind Genesis 1:26–27 and the great theological truths of people being created in the image of God. People have a moral, spiritual nature to accompany the physical. Law, then, is related to behavior. The law in Genesis 9:5ff. assumes that a certain standard of behavior is acceptable and another is not. This is public morality.

Israel's laws are divine in origin (Deuteronomy 5:1–5). This imparts a special value to Israel's laws. Old Testament laws are essentially religious, because they affirm values that find their source in the nature and character of God. As Israel's God is special and unique, so are her laws and statutes. No other nation has laws as just and righteous as Israel's (as Deuteronomy 4:7–8 affirms—see the passage cited at the beginning of this chapter). Religion and law go together as special revelations made to the nation of Israel.

THE DIVINE SOURCE AND NATURE OF LAW

What about the source and nature of the laws of other nations? If Deuteronomy 4:7–8 is true, then, to the extent that any other nation's laws correspond to Israel's laws, such laws will be good and just (righteous). The laws of Israel given in the Old Testament, especially the moral laws, provide a model for other nations. Proof of this comes from the Old Testament itself: The Canaanites were judged for various sexual sins about which only Israel had been explicitly forewarned (Leviticus 18, 20). So while only Israel was "under the Law of Moses," all people and all nations are held accountable for adherence to certain universal laws.

The Epistle to the Romans gives two bases for this accountability. They are natural revelation—namely, the creation (Romans 1:18ff.)—and the standard of conscience (Romans 2). In addition, it may be assumed that oral tradition provided knowledge of God's will from the beginning onward. In the Noahic Covenant, God established his covenant with all people—all the descendants of Noah (Genesis 9:8–9).

Other nations prior to Israel had some of the same or similar laws as Israel had. The Code of Hammurabi and other ancient law codes contained much legislation similar to the Mosaic Law.[1] This universality suggests that such laws are due either to the created nature of people or to the divine order for society. Thus certain laws are divine in origin, are universally applicable, transcend all time, and are absolute.

Law is a timeless necessity. There were laws or prohibitions even in the innocent state of Eden. Law has always been an accompaniment of faith. Under the New Covenant, God explicitly gives the laws to be obeyed (Jeremiah 31:31–34; repeated in the New Testament in Hebrews 8:8–13). The difference between this and the Old Covenant of Moses is that there

---

1. Kaiser, *Ethics*, 73, 98–107.

is an accompanying enablement to obey the laws. In heaven itself, there are rules and standards that Satan violated and first transgressed.

Obedience to the Law meant favor; disobedience brought disfavor (see Deuteronomy 4:25–31). Prosperity, including long life and multiplication, was promised to Israel if she kept all of God's commands (4:40; 6:1–3). However, of primary importance was the heart attitude, which issued in the obedience. Note the yearning of God in Deuteronomy 5:29 (NAS): "Oh that they had such a heart in them, that they would fear Me, and keep all My commandments always, that it may be well with them and with their sons forever!"

PURPOSE OF LAW

This raises the question of the purpose for the Mosaic Law and for all law in general. It is clear that the law cannot justify the person who has violated it (so Galatians 2:16–21; 3:11, 21–22; 4:5; 5:4). One can be justified before God by faith alone. Law has a different function, as Paul writes: "Is the Law then contrary to the promises of God? May it never be! For if a law had been given which was able to impart life, then righteousness would indeed have been based on law" (Galatians 3:21, NAS). The "if" here introduces a contrary-to-fact condition. It means that no such law capable of bringing salvation had ever been given.

One cannot be sanctified or be made more holy by a code of laws. It cannot relieve the bondage of sin. It can only identify, confirm, and accentuate our bondage to sin (Romans 6:14; 7:1–6; Galatians 2:19–21; 3:1–5, 11; 4:21ff; 5:1–2, 18).[2]

What then is the purpose of law in general, law as commandment? What is its role in government? There are several purposes.[3] Law (1) can command and demand obedience (Galatians 3:12), as seen in the Ten Commandments; (2) it can pronounce approval and blessing upon conformity to its demands (Romans 7:10; Galatians 3:12); and (3) it can

---

2. Happily, believers have died to the Law of Moses (Rom. 7:3–6; Gal. 2:19) in the sense that they are identified with Christ in his death to the Law. Because Christ died to meet the Law's demands regarding full obedience to God, the Law has no further demand to make on the Christian. By faith, Christ's saving act is actualized in and for the believer (1 John 5:4–5). For the Christian, Christ is the end or fulfillment of the Law. The Christian is empowered to obey God by the internal constraint of the Holy Spirit.

3. Murray, *Romans*, I, 229.

pronounce condemnation upon every infraction of its demands (Galatians 3:10). Here it functions in its role as the restrainer of sin, as a custodian and tutor (Galatians 3:19, 23–25). Also (4) law exposes and convicts of the bondage of sin (Romans 8:8, 14).

Finally (5) law, rather than curbing sin, often excites and incites the sinner to more aggravated transgressions (Romans 6:19; 7:5, 8, 11, 13). For example, people may not consider trespassing until they come across a sign saying, "No trespassing." Thus law has several functions, but justification and sanctification are not among them.

If law can both expose and excite sin, and restrain it, then law, to some extent, determines moral behavior. This relation of the law to public morality (and of public morality to government) will be explored in the next section. At this point, it is sufficient to note that law and public morality are clearly interrelated.

The question simply stated is this: Is law divine in origin, therefore absolute and unchanging? Or, is it human in origin, therefore relative and changing? The focus of the modern debate in law centers around the concept of Natural Law.

BIBLICAL SUPPORT FOR NATURAL MORAL LAW

Does the Bible support Natural Law? The founders of our Republic believed in Natural Law, but what does the Bible say? The Christian needs to know what an extended and careful study of the biblical material reveals. After pursuing the biblical foundation for Natural Law, I will present arguments for Natural Law on the basis of natural revelation, the human conscience, and history.

I give to the term Natural Law the fuller title of "Natural Moral Law," because the latter title specifically points to the ethical norms inherent in Natural Law for judging a person's behavior. All of one's activities must pass the test of public morality or ethics.

There is a growing consensus by Roman Catholic and Protestant scholars that biblical warrant for Natural Moral Law exists. Still, some strongly oppose Natural Moral Law, insisting on biblical law alone. On the other extreme are those who exalt Natural Law, including reason as the final authority.[4] What does the Bible teach?

---

4. See Johnson, "Biblical Warrant," 185–199, for a discussion of many biblical passages supporting Natural Moral Law.

SUPPORT FROM THE OLD TESTAMENT

Passages which support Natural Moral Law from the Old Testament include the following: Job 31:13–15, where Job recognizes the equal standing before God of himself and his slave; Amos 1–2, where commonly agreed upon moral standards for warfare are assumed; cases in Genesis 20:1–18 and 26:6–11, where people outside Israel practice standards of morality; passages in Isaiah (2:7; 3:10–31; 28:1) where sins are listed that do not occur in previous biblical prohibitions; and the passages of Amos 6:12, Isaiah 5:8–10, and Ezekiel 18, where practices contrary to nature or common moral principles are described.

Of the Old Testament passages supporting Natural Law, those from the period before the giving of the Mosaic Law are especially instructive. They reflect a universal understanding of absolutes or norms, which only later came to be represented or stipulated in the Ten Commandments and other legislation from Moses. Three passages are especially noteworthy, the last being found within the Mosaic Code.

The Covenant Made With Noah After the Flood

First, the Covenant made with Noah after the Flood is universal. The passage specifying it (Genesis 8:20—9:17) has many references to universality (e.g., terms such as "all flesh," "every living thing," and "the earth" occur in practically every verse) and timelessness ("you and your descendants after you," "never again be cut off," "for all successive generations," "the everlasting covenant," and "while the earth remains . . . shall not cease"). In addition, the main principle or moral statement, which concerns capital punishment, is couched in terms of generality in the third person, rather than the more specific direct terms of the second person, which permeate the rest of the passage. Genesis 9:6 reads: "Whoever sheds the blood of man, by man shall his blood be shed; for in the image of God has God made man."

I've already cited this verse as supporting the inauguration of human government with law as its accompaniment. However, as a support for Natural Law, I emphasize that the institution of capital punishment for murder does not rest upon some specially revealed law as such. God is not depicted as Law-giver but as Creator. Appeal is made to the *nature* of human beings as made in the image of God. This is an appeal to some universally recognized implicit understanding of both the nature of people and the nature of God. Explicit in the context is recognition of the inherent difference between the nature of people and animals.[5]

This has pertinent contemporary application. Presently, in the face of terrorism, many nations in Western civilization are debating the virtues of the death penalty. In a subsequent chapter dealing with Romans 13:1–7, I will discuss this issue more fully.

Genesis 18:25 and the Destruction of Sodom

Genesis 18:25 is one of the strongest passages supporting Natural Moral Law. It has implications for the issue of sodomy and gay rights. The latter half of the chapter (18:16–33) gives the account of Abraham's petition to Yahweh (the LORD) to spare Sodom for the sake of fifty, then forty-five, then thirty, twenty, and ten righteous people living there. In this manner, Abraham intercedes on behalf of his nephew Lot and his family living in Sodom. To each of Abraham's requests, Yahweh responds favorably. Although Sodom is destroyed (because there are fewer than ten righteous), God still delivers Lot and his family (because they alone are righteous) (cf. 2 Peter 2:6–9). However, the conflagration overtakes Lot's wife because her heart is still in Sodom.

In petitioning for the righteous people living in Sodom, Abraham based his entire intercession on a Universal Moral Law that all people immediately recognize, namely, that the wicked and the righteous should not be judged or punished the same way, i.e., be treated the same. Note the words found in Genesis 18:23, 25:

---

5. This is clearly seen in many verses. For example, animals are sacrificed, not people (Gen. 8:20). The ground will never again be cursed on account of human beings, not animals (8:21). It is the intent of a *person's* heart that is evil from one's youth (8:21). Mankind is blessed and told to exercise dominion over the animals, which are actually given for the benefit and service of people (9:1–3). People are said to be made in God's image; animals are not (9:6). Finally, the covenant is directly spoken to human beings, not to animals (9:9). Evidently human beings are the direct partners of the covenant, not animals.

In many ways, this passage reflects the Genesis creation account where the distinctive nature of human beings is both explicitly (Gen. 1:24–30), and implicitly taught—no animal was a suitable mate for Adam (Gen. 2:18–24). The assumption in these passages is that the moral law regarding murder is universally applicable and absolute, because everyone is able to recognize the distinctive nature of human beings, the distinctive nature of God, and the distinctive nature of animals.

To Submit or to Rebel against the State

> Then Abraham approached him and said: "Will you sweep away the righteous with the wicked? . . . Far be it from you to do such a thing—to kill the righteous with the wicked, treating the righteous and the wicked alike. Far be it from you! Will not the Judge of all the earth do right?"

The significance of these words must not be missed. Abraham is saying that even the Judge of all the earth is bound to act according to his nature, his character. Abraham knew this character of God because he, like all other humans, was made in God's image. All of God's creatures recognize a moral standard according to which the Judge will deliver justice. God must act in agreement with laws of morality as certain and absolute as he himself is.[6]

The implications of this passage are significant. If God judged righteously, acting consistently with a Natural Moral Law, then all should recognize the rightness of his destruction of Sodom because of its sodomy. This is the sin highlighted in Genesis 19:1–9, which confirmed the great evil of the place (18:20–21; note 13:13). In other words, sodomy is sin according to an implicit Natural Moral Law, and this is proven by God's special revelation in the form of intervention and destruction of the place. Through judgment, special revelation adds its witness to that of Natural Moral Law. Sodomy violates the created order and all people understand this. Punishment of sodomy proves that Natural Moral Law exists.[7]

The Holiness Code of Leviticus 18–20

Finally, in the book of Leviticus, Moses sets forth the moral code required of Israel. In two significant chapters (18, 20), this code speaks particularly of sexual sins. In both chapters, God (through Moses) warns Israel not to commit such sins because they have the lessons of the past that teach them how much God abhors such practices. He has judged the Egyptians and the Canaanites (Leviticus 18:3) for doing such deeds. All such

---

6. Indeed, our justification by faith in Christ rests upon the very same moral absolutes. We who have been saved are rescued from an eternity of separation from God because God has followed the same standard in the death of Christ. In our place, Jesus Christ took our sin, became guilty and worthy of damnation, and was judged for sin in our stead. We experience forgiveness, mercy, and grace because the requirements of justice have been satisfied by Jesus Christ.

7. See De Young, *Homosexuality*, ch. 1.

nations have been defiled by these deeds and, therefore, deserve punishment (18:24–25, 29). The text reads:

> Do not defile yourselves in any of these ways, because this is how the nations that I am going to drive out before you became defiled. Even the land was defiled; so I punished it for its sin, and the land vomited out its inhabitants. . . . Everyone who does any of these detestable things—such persons must be cut off from their people.

It seems clear that the Egyptians and the Canaanites were violating a moral code superior to their own (which allowed many of these sinful practices; Leviticus 18:3; 20:23), and one that they were nevertheless responsible to obey. They were to reject the allowances in their own law code.

This responsibility could only be established if there was some basis for it, and the only basis possible was a Natural Moral Law. Their own moral code was defective and they were accountable for the universal one, although it had never been given to them directly, as Israel had been given the Mosaic Law.[8] They were held accountable to live rightly, according to a Natural Moral Law.[9]

It is significant that these very chapters are used in the New Testament to express universal truth. Jesus and his disciples make the command, "love your neighbor as yourself," the second great commandment (Matthew 5:43; 19:19; 22:37–40; Mark 12:31, 33; Luke 10:27; 2 Corinthians 6:14ff.; 1 Peter 1:14–16; Romans 10:5; 13:8–10; Galatians 3:12; 5:14; James 2:8). Even Paul's catalogue of vices (1 Timothy 1:8–10; 1 Corinthians 6:9–11) parallels the vices of these chapters. All of these reasons support the universality of many of the moral standards in these chapters.

These three passages (Genesis 9; 18:25; Leviticus 18–20) argue strongly for the existence of Natural Moral Law and its place in the Bible. People are culpable for the standard of ethics embodied in the Ten Commandments, whether or not they have received such a standard directly. No one who submits to the authority of the Bible can dismiss these chapters as irrelevant to modern culture.

---

8. The Canaanites' culpability was first hinted at in Gen. 15:13–21, where the practice of the inhabitants of the land is termed "sin." By Moses' time, the sin had become full and judgment—the loss of their land and death—followed.

9. Which sins of Lev. 18 and 20 are universally wrong? See my book *Homosexuality*, chapters 1 and 5, where I discuss this question in full. To begin with, those sins in Lev. 18–20 that correspond to the laws of the Decalogue in Exod. 20 and Deut. 5 would be wrong.

SUPPORT FROM THE NEW TESTAMENT

From Christ

Natural Moral Law is likewise supported by the New Testament.[10] Our Lord appeals to the nature of created human life in finding divorce wrong (Matthew 19:4ff), and to a common moral sense of the difference between doing good or harm on the Sabbath (Mark 3:4; cf. also John 5:28–29; Romans 2:6–11). Also, Christ appeals to the nature of human beings in order to demonstrate that the true source of moral evil is the heart and not food entering the stomach (Matthew 15:10–20). The former recognizes an internal and universal standard of what is wrong, while the latter defines the wrong by an external, localized code of tradition. Even the Golden Rule, "Whatever you desire that men would do to you, do so to them," is an appeal to a common moral awareness of what is good.

The parables exemplify this common standard of morality. In the Parable of the Good Samaritan (Luke 10:29–37), the priest and the Levite, who knew the written Law, did not aid their neighbor. But the Samaritan, who did not interpret the Law correctly, did show mercy. He acted out of a common sense of obligation to love a fellow human being. It took one who is a neighbor in heart to discover a neighbor outside of himself. In all of his parables, our Lord appeals either to human nature or to a sense of what is right and just in determining commonly accepted behavior in society.[11]

From the Apostle Paul

Elsewhere in the New Testament, support for Natural Moral Law comes most clearly from the Apostle Paul.[12] In Romans 1:18–32, Paul describes the universal culpability of the world before God. He writes (1:20): "For since the creation of the world God's invisible qualities—his eternal power and divine nature—have been clearly seen, being understood from what has been made, so that they are without excuse."

---

10. Johnson, "Biblical Warrant," 191ff.

11. Similarly, in the parable of the Laborers in the Vineyard, the land owner has the moral right to be generous as he exercises the moral obligation to do right in paying just wages mutually agreed upon. Also, the ignorant servant is punished more lightly than the servant who knew his master's will but disobeyed (Luke 12:47–48).

12. Johnson, "Biblical Warrant," 194ff.

The Revolution in Law

This culpability is valid only if the whole world has some basic, essential knowledge of God and his will, apart from direct revelation from the Bible. Paul particularly designates sodomy (same-sex behavior) as "against nature" (Romans 1:26–27) and says that unbelievers "*know* God's righteous decree, that those who do such things deserve death" (Romans 1:32).

In Romans 2, several references to Natural Moral Law occur. Paul appeals to the fact that God's judgment will be based on either good or evil deeds, not according to one's ethnicity (2:9–11). Verses 14–16 identify the Gentiles as pagans who are capable of living according to the requirements of the Law, which they have not received, by obeying precepts written on their hearts:

> Indeed, when Gentiles, who do not have the law, do by nature things required by the law, they are a law for themselves, even though they do not have the law, since they show that the requirements of the law are written on their hearts, their consciences also bearing witness, and their thoughts now accusing, now even defending them. This will take place on the day when God will judge the secrets of people through Jesus Christ, as my gospel declares.

This linking of Natural Moral Law with the standards of the gospel is done by Paul elsewhere in Scripture. In 1 Timothy 1:8–11, Paul advances from the Law of Moses to legislation, and then to the gospel, as presenting a harmonious, universal norm or standard for all classes of people. I will return to this crucial passage in chapters 9 and 10.

If government has been ordained to punish evil behavior and promote or approve good behavior, then there must be some universal standard which is apparent to all men for which they can he held accountable. This standard will be in harmony with the revealed will of God. I devote two chapters to the pivotal passage of Romans 13:1–7.

From Other Passages

There are other passages in the New Testament that support a Natural Moral Law (e.g., 1 Corinthians 10:32; 2 Corinthians 8:21; Philippians 4:8; 1 Thessalonians 4:12; James 3:9; 1 Peter 2:12, 3:16). Clearly the principle in Galatians 6:7 ("Whatever people sow, this they will also reap") is universally recognized (cf. Galatians 5:9).

In addition to these passages, the repeated phenomenon of a "catalogue of vices" (or sins) argues for Natural Moral Law (cf. Romans

1:28–31; 1 Corinthians 6:9–11; 1 Timothy 1:8–11; Galatians 5:19–21; Mark 7:20–23). These lists probably arise from the Old Testament (cf. Leviticus 18, 20) but were also a common literary device among the Chinese, Greeks, and Romans.[13] The early Christians continued such lists of sins.[14] The commonality of the contents of these lists argues for a moral code that all people recognize.

In addition, in the last book of the Bible, John writes that in the new age to come, in the new heavens and the new earth, there will be no place for these sins (Revelation 21:8, 27). Such behavior never finds approval. Thus, when nature is perfected, that which is unnatural will cease. For example, John employs the term "abomination" to point to the sexual sin of sodomy. The Greek term employed by John is the verbal link to the Greek translation of the Old Testament (the Septuagint, or LXX) at Leviticus 18:22, describing the same sin (sodomy is an "abomination").

SUPPORT FROM CHURCH HISTORY

There has been consistent support of Natural Moral Law through the ages of Christianity. The early church made use of the concept by appealing to the creation order.[15] Later, at the Reformation, Luther, Calvin, Melanchthon, and Zwingli all held to the concept.

For example, Calvin emphasized conscience rather than reason as the organ of Natural Law.[16] He also appealed to "the perpetual role of love" as a universal obligation for all people. In addition, Luther regarded the Ten Commandments as a divinely given summary of Natural Moral Law known to all men. Johnson cites him as having written: "Verily the Decalogue is lodged in the conscience. If God had never given the Law by Moses, yet the mind of men naturally has this knowledge that God is to be worshipped and our neighbor to be loved."[17] These words come from

---

13. Deissmann, *Light*, 315–318.

14. For example, *The Didache*, 2. 2–7. Also see *The Didache*, 3. 1–6; 5. 1–2; 16. 3–4; 16; *Epistle of Barnabas*, 19. 3–12; 20. 1–2; *Apocalypse of Peter*, 8.

15. Johnson, "Biblical Warrant," 185. For example, 1 Clement finds support for the reality of the resurrection by appealing to the course of the sun and moon, the growth of crops (planting and harvest), and the story of the Phoenix bird.

16. Ibid., 190.

17. Ibid.

The Revolution in Law

one who emphasized justification by faith. With Paul the Apostle, Luther saw the proper place of law (cf. 1 Timothy 1:8ff).

HISTORICAL PRECEDENT FROM THE DECLARATION OF INDEPENDENCE REGARDING NATURAL MORAL LAW

At this point, it is necessary to consider what history teaches us regarding the matter of Natural Moral Law. For this, I turn to the period of the founding of the United States, when so much discussion occurred regarding the nature and origin of law. What do we learn from this period?

There are explicit statements in the founding documents of the United States that embrace absolute or "natural" laws that find their source in God. The foremost example of this is the Declaration of Independence. This document comes very close to the biblical view of the relationship between religion and law. Some consider the Ten Commandments and the Declaration of Independence to be the two greatest documents of civilization. It is instructive to quote here the first paragraph and part of the second of the Declaration of Independence:

> When in the course of human events it becomes necessary for one people to dissolve the political bonds which have connected them with another, and to assume among the powers of the earth, the separate and equal station to which the Laws of Nature and of Nature's God entitle them, a decent respect to the opinions of mankind requires that they should declare the causes which impel them to the separation.
>
> We hold these truths to be self-evident, that all men are created equal, that they are endowed by their Creator with certain unalienable Rights, that among these are Life, Liberty, and the pursuit of Happiness. That to secure these rights, Governments are instituted among Men, deriving their just powers from the consent of the governed, that whenever any Form of Government becomes destructive of these ends, it is the Right of the People to alter or to abolish it, and to institute a new Government, laying its foundation on such principles and organizing its powers in such form, as to them shall seem most likely to effect their Safety and Happiness ...

Near the end of this document, appeal is made to "the Supreme Judge of the world for the rectitude of our intentions," and "to a firm reliance on the protection of divine Providence." In light of the context of these statements, there can be no doubt that these are references to the God of the Bible, and to none other than he.

In light of the above observation concerning the close relationship of religion, morality, and law in Israel and elsewhere, it is evident that the contemporary call for pluralism in social ethics ultimately requires a pluralism in religion and law. Yet no such attitude captured the mind and imagination of our founding fathers.

America may be pluralistic in regard to the peoples and cultures that make up this nation, but it should not be such regarding religion and morality. To be pluralistic in religion and law has perilous consequences. The addendum to chapter 3 shows the destructive effects of pluralism.

There are two essential principles among others that our forefathers embraced. They concern the basis and justification for the American Revolution in government and law. They are that belief in God is basic; and that natural law is unchangeable.

Theism is Basic

First, it assumes the existence of God; it is a theistic document. God is referred to as the Creator of men, the Bestower of rights, the God of Nature, the Supreme Judge (cf. Genesis 18:25), and the divine Provider. This recognition of God makes its governmental philosophy an essentially religious one. It leads one writer to assert that, of twelve basic American principles, the first and foremost one is that the spiritual is supreme.[18]

Belief in the divine origin of human beings asserts likewise that a human being is a spiritual being and as such is of supreme dignity and value. This leads to the self-respect of the individual and also mutual respect among individuals. This principle runs counter to the concepts of evolution, agnosticism, atheism, and secular humanism, or any form of economics or government structure, such as communism, which denies the spiritual nature of human beings. While not all of our founding fathers were Christians, some were (such as John Witherspoon). While others were deists, and a few were atheists, the majority of them recognized a Creator as the Bestower of inalienable rights. They believed that the Declaration of Independence is also a Declaration of Dependence.

18. Long, *Yardstick*, 7ff.

The Revolution in Law

Almost a hundred years after the Declaration, the divine origin of people was reaffirmed by Abraham Lincoln in his Gettysburg Address of November 19, 1863. He asserted: "Four score and seven years ago our fathers brought forth, upon this continent, a new nation, conceived in liberty, and dedicated to the proposition that 'all men are created equal.'" More recently, President Ronald Reagan (1980–1988) called upon this nation once again to affirm her belief in the divine origin of people and their accountability to God. President George W. Bush (2000–2008) continued this emphasis, reminding Americans that spiritual and moral values are crucial in the war on terrorism.

In 2009, President Barak Obama avoided joining in the national Day of Prayer, a tradition that dates back to President Truman in 1952. In recent years he has kept to this tradition.

If our founding documents were simply read in public and believed, I'm convinced that much progress would be accomplished toward ending the revolution in law and restoring to this land a respect for God and for people.

Natural Law is Unchangeable

The second essential principle, assumed in the reference to the "Laws of Nature," is that there is a higher law, Natural Law, which sets forth a moral code. This asserts that there are moral absolutes that are binding upon all mankind. Just as there are physical laws governing the universe (inactive life), there are laws governing animate (vegetable and animal) life and human beings. The Laws of Nature are the expression of the will of God. They are divine.[19]

19. Poythress, "Scientists," 111–123. The author shows that all scientific laws are universal; that is, they have the divine attributes of omnipresence and eternity. Thus he shows that the very existence of scientific laws argues for their being divine. Scientific laws possess all the attributes of God himself. Scientific law is immutable, immaterial and invisible, infallible, omnipotent, both transcendent and immanent, personal (law implies a Law-giver, is rational, and can be expressed in language, like a human utterance), knowable and incomprehensible, divine (law is God speaking, acting, and manifesting himself; law is divine in "power, authority, majesty, righteousness, eternity, and truth") (117), good, beautiful, fitting (demonstrating rectitude and righteousness), trinitarian (involving a plan, an expression of the plan, and a response to the plan as willed), revelatory, etc.

In addition, Poythress argues that scientific law lies in the background of modern technology, so that the latter itself witnesses to the presence of God who cares for his

To Submit or to Rebel against the State

Natural Law was widely accepted at the time of the founding of America. Sir William Blackstone wrote of Natural Law in his *Commentaries on the Law of England* (1803). It is upon his work that the American legal system was built. The chief points made by Blackstone are that this law derives from God, and judges do not make law but merely find and declare it. According to Herbert Titus, Blackstone said:

> This will of his Maker is called the law of Nature. For as God, when he created matter, and endued it with a principle of nobility, established certain rules for the perpetual direction of that motion; so, when he created man, and endued him with free-will to conduct himself in all parts of life, he laid down certain immutable laws of human nature.... These are the eternal, immutable laws of good and evil...[20]

Blackstone saw the universal aspect to such law and wrote:

> This law of nature being coeval with mankind, and dictated by God himself, is of course superior in obligation to any other. It is binding over all the globe, in all countries, and at all times: no human laws are of any validity if contrary to this; and such of them as are valid derive all their force and all their authority mediately or immediately, from this original.[21]

In addition to the two principles above, there are additional, vital principles that one can derive from the Declaration of Independence. At the end of this chapter, in an addendum, I discuss these and their implications.

The chief point to note from the above discussion is how entirely religious the philosophy underlying the American system of government and law really is. It is anchored to the Judeo-Christian revelation about both general and special revelation. There is no place here for the revolution of pluralism, which demands equal time for Islam, polytheism, pantheism, agnosticism, or atheism. Adherents of all religious persuasions that are not Judaic or Christian will find a haven of protection in America under the Constitution, but they should find no sympathy for changing the American philosophy or broadening its base.

---

creation. The attributes of eternity and omnipotence are visible for all to see. The practicality of this is to trust God in the daily practice of living (123).

20. Quoted by Titus, "Blackstone," 1:6.
21. Ibid.

People of any belief may find refuge here, but their ideas should be subjected to the scrutiny of these great principles. A society has the right to protect itself, to self-preservation. Perhaps this was best expressed in the personal affirmation of Thomas Jefferson: "I have sworn upon the altar of Almighty God eternal hostility toward any form of tyranny over the mind of man."

THE REVOLUTION IN LAW

If law is unchanging, universal, and derived from God, then it is impossible that judges could make law. Rather, they only find or discover it. What then is the current understanding of the nature of law that judges and legislators have?

Contrary to Blackstone, the jurist who influenced American law in significant ways and whom I cite in the addendum below, many today view law as a fluid mix of established principles and changing social values. They view judges as those who make law by creating new principles.[22]

How can this shifting view of law be explained? It is not due to some new discovery of scientific fact. Rather it is a moral and theological development. As Christian lawyers make clear, modern legal scholars have rejected Blackstone's views "because they have rejected his faith in God and his reliance upon the Genesis account of the creation and origin of man and the universe."[23]

As in many other disciplines, including theology and sociology, the main contributor to this changed view of law is the concept of Darwinian evolution. While evolution remains an unproved theory in science, Titus points out that "in law it has become an incontestable presupposition."[24]

Now some would say that Blackstone did not know any better; he wrote before the "discovery" that Darwin made. Yet it is *not* anachronistic to affirm that Blackstone in the 18th century rejected an evolutionary concept of the universe when he asserted that "we keep constantly in mind that the universe was not the result of pure chance."[25] Centuries before Christ came, Aristotle, the Epicureans, and others adhered to an

---

22. Titus, "Blackstone," 1:6.
23. Ibid., 7.
24. Ibid.
25. Brabner-Smith, "Prudent Pursuit," 1:8.

evolutionary concept of the universe. But even then there were those who opposed naturalism. Cicero (106–43 B.C.) is an example of one who argued for a divine origin.[26]

THE PERILOUS CONSEQUENCES FOR REJECTING NATURAL LAW

This changed attitude today toward our origins is a perilous threat to the survival of this nation. Just as the violation of physical law brings disaster, so does violation of natural law. Again Blackstone said it: "'The Law of Nature' is a supreme, invariable, and uncontrollable rule of conduct to all men; . . . because its violation is avenged by natural punishments, which necessarily flow from the constitution of things and are as fixed and inevitable as the order of nature . . . "[27]

Is not AIDS, common to those who engage in homosexuality and prostitution, one of the "natural punishments" that Blackstone referred to, which flows "from the constitution of things"?

Today many understand law as a matter of politics or social science rather than universal principle. Regarding the *Roe v. Wade* decision allowing abortion in 1973, authors Woodward and Armstrong, in their book, *The Brethren*, called the decision an absurdity as far as a constitutional matter is concerned. Some clerks called it Harry Blackmun's "abortion."[28]

REVOLUTIONARY JURISPRUDENCE

In light of the preceding historical and biblical data, modern jurisprudence and legislative decision-making constitute nothing less than a revolution in law. Modern jurisprudence has become pluralistic and often reflects nothing more than the changing standards of society. If the chief effect of pluralism is to deny the existence of the absolute, there can be no one true religion, no one unchanging standard of morality, no absolute or Natural Law.

---

26. Rehwinkel, *Creation*, 27–28, 129–130, 137.
27. Titus, "Blackstone," 7.
28. Ibid.

Natural Moral Law views law as having a fixed, absolute quality. It does not have to be made, but only discovered. As in theology, the key term is revelation, not creation.[29] These laws are as immutable as the law of gravity or the equation that *pi* equals 3.141592. It is as reprehensible for human beings to change Natural Moral Law or the standards of right and wrong as it would be for some mathematician to decide to round off *pi* to 3.0.

THE EFFECTS OF PLURALISM IN LAW

In the last sixty years, the effects of pluralism are seen with grave consequences in the decisions of the U.S. Supreme Court. The majority of the highest court of this land no longer interprets the Constitution in its literal, historical sense, based upon Natural Law. Instead, jurisprudence is now viewed as societal—as determined by contemporary standards of society.

Its decision to find a right to abortion violated two thousand years of Christian conviction and two hundred years of American precedent.[30]

---

29. Titus, "Blackstone," 4ff., shows how this position was represented by Justice Marshall, President Coolidge, and others.

30. That the framers could have excluded the unborn from this truth is impossible. Abortion has been known and practiced for millennia. It has no support in Scripture; on the contrary, the Bible treats human life as beginning at conception. The Old Testament empire of Assyria not only considered abortion a crime, but it also treated women having an abortion to an ignoble, humiliating death. See Kline, "*Lex Talionis*," 20:200–201.

The one Old Testament passage (Exod. 21:22–23) touching on the matter of abortion explicitly makes it clear that even the careless though accidental aborting of life is a serious matter. When human life is in view, any harm, including possible premature death, is to be punished appropriately by the law of *lex talionis* ("an eye for an eye . . . life for life").

In addition to this passage, there are numerous places that teach that life before birth is sacred, dignified, and accountable to God, and these argue implicitly against abortion (Ps. 51:5; 139:13–16; Jer. 1:5). Even Christ was already identified as the Son of God, conceived by the Holy Spirit while yet in the womb of Mary (cf. Matt. 1:18, 20; Luke 1:35, 43). Likewise John the Baptist was considered to be a son and responsive while yet in the womb (Luke 1:36, 41–44).

In the era immediately after the New Testament, early Christian writings list abortion among other heinous sins. For example, *The Didache*, 2.2, reads in its list of vices, "You shall not procure abortion, nor commit infanticide." In the *Apocalypse of Peter*, 8, the mothers who have procured abortions are seen as undergoing the torments of hell, while their children, alive, are seen in paradise under the care of a special protecting angel called Temlakos. There is and has been a Christian position on abortion for two thousand years, stemming from the fact that life is made in the image and likeness of God (Gen. 1–2).

To Submit or to Rebel against the State

Its first decision to uphold laws limiting homosexual behavior, while the right decision, was based on the wrong reason: societal standards. And its decision to prohibit Kentucky from posting the Ten Commandments in the public schools (1980) was inconsistent with its own Jewish and Christian heritage from which it derives the basis for its own existence and jurisprudence.[31]

Sociological jurisprudence has won the day in our court system, from the Supreme Court on down. The origin of this concept of law can be traced to Justice Oliver Wendell Holmes, who, after the Civil War, encouraged "a view of law that was rooted in sociology, not in nature, and certainly not in the Bible."[32] The formal introduction of this concept of law into the Supreme Court occurred during the year 1908. By the time Louis Brandeis was confirmed on the Court in 1916, it was officially recognized as part of constitutional law. Nederhood quotes Henry Steele Commager as saying:

> Anticipated by Holmes, championed unceasingly by Brandeis, supported by the muscular Harlan Stone and the eloquent Benjamin Cardoza and the learned Felix Frankfurter, sociological jurisprudence became, after the great struggle of 1937, the all but official doctrine of the Court.[33]

According to Francis Schaeffer, Holmes maintained that the "life of the law has not been logic: it has been experience." These words suggest that law can waver from one experience to another. Also, according to

---

The founding fathers of the United States did not hold another view, and included both the unborn and born under the protection of inalienable rights. Does not this universal rejection of abortion argue that it is a Natural Moral Law to preserve all life in the womb? Does not the nature of men and women, and the care by which we bring new life into the world, argue for Natural Moral Law? The innate conscience of humanity says that it does. Abortion is part of the age-long conflict between right and wrong, which every generation must wage. It is clear that while the courts may decree something legal, this does not make it moral.

31. The inconsistency of the Court is also seen in its ban of virtually all Christian expression in public schools, and yet its retention of the words "under God" in the Pledge of Allegiance. This latter act was justified by Justice William Brennan, because such expressions and exercises "no longer have a religious purpose or meaning." It will be interesting to see how the more recent challenges to these words in the Pledge will be handled by the Court.

32. Nederhood, "Justice," 1:11. For a similar indictment of the court system, see Brimelow and Markman, "Supreme Irony," 16–21.

33. Ibid.

The Revolution in Law

Schaeffer, Holmes then came to the conclusion that law is "the majority vote of that nation that could lick all others."[34] These words of a Supreme Court jurist are diametrically opposed to the position of the founders of this nation. The latter viewed law and the Constitution as a protection of the minority from the majority. It is cultural relativism.

Such a change in jurisprudence shows how pervasive the cancers of America really are. If the laws of this or any other land are evil, then evil living and wickedness will prevail. If America is to survive in this age of terrorism, nothing short of another revolution of renewal will be necessary to stop the present drift and return us to our heritage. In the first years of the twenty-first century, President George W. Bush made several conservative judicial appointments. President Obama has already acted to reverse this trend.

DIMINISHED RESPECT FOR LAW VIOLATES LINCOLN

With the foundation of Natural Law diminished, denied, and even destroyed, and with consequences such as AIDS, is it any wonder that disrespect for law is increasing? Lincoln, who read and even memorized portions of Blackstone and held to the same theological starting point, argued persuasively for reverence for the law. He said:

> Let every American, every lover of liberty, every well wisher to his posterity, swear by the blood of the Revolution never to violate in the least particular, the laws of the country; and never to tolerate their violation by others. As the patriots of seventy-six did to the support of the Declaration of Independence, so to the support of the Constitution and Laws, let every American pledge his life, his property, and his sacred honor; let every man remember that to violate the law, is to trample on the blood of his father, and to tear the character [sic for charter?] of his own, and his children's liberty. Let reverence for the laws, be breathed by every American mother, to the lisping babe, that prattles on her lap—let it be taught in schools, in seminaries, and in colleges; let it be written in Primmers, spelling books, and in Almanacs; let it be preached from the pulpit, proclaimed in legislative halls, and enforced in courts of justice. And, in short, let it become the *political religion* of the nation; and let the old and the young, the rich and the poor, the

---

34. Schaeffer, *Manifesto*, 26–27.

grave and the gay, of all sexes and tongues, and colors and conditions, sacrifice unceasingly upon its altars.

While ever a state of feeling, such as this, shall universally, or even, very generally prevail throughout the nation, vain will be every effort, and fruitless every attempt, to subvert our national freedom.[35] (Italics mine.)

Of course, legislators make new laws all the time. But we must distinguish universal laws from those that are not.

Again Blackstone saw the difference. He clearly distinguished the relationship between law as justice (Latin *jus*, what is just or right) and law as the rules of a political society (*lex, legis*, the legislated law).[36] The latter is derived from the former. This distinction is reflected in Lincoln's designation of "courts of Law" as courts of Justice.[37]

Paul the Apostle recognizes this distinction in various places. For example, in 1 Timothy 1:8–11, he first refers to the Law of Moses (which is absolute and divinely revealed) as good (1:8). Then he asserts that law or legislation is made to control or prohibit wrong behavior and thereby encourage good (1:9–10). In a later chapter, I will fully discuss this passage, which is so significant to the discussion of legislating morality.

THE SEPARATION OF CHURCH AND STATE? STRIKING A BALANCE

The current push by many individuals and groups (for example, the American Civil Liberties Union) for a secular society under the guise of "the separation of church and state" is grossly misguided. There is no such separation espoused anywhere in the founding documents of the American Republic.

The framers of the Constitution made it clear that government was to have no power within religion. They applied this principle by not permitting government to possess any such power. They made this explicit in the first amendment by expressly prohibiting such power: Congress could

---

35. Basler, *Lincoln*, 1:112.

36. Brabner-Smith, "Prudent Pursuit," 43. Blackstone also wrote that the "principal objects of the law are Rights and Wrongs."

37. Ibid.

make no law "respecting an establishment of religion, or prohibiting the free exercise thereof."

There is a delicate balance to be observed. While our government is not to establish a state church, and is to be neutral or secular with respect to an institutionalizing of Christianity, it is also founded on great religious principles and should defend these principles. While Christianity should not be institutionalized, it should pervade our institutions with the government's encouragement.

THE CONSTITUTION ONLY PROHIBITS A STATE CHURCH

The Constitution does not affirm a complete separation of church and state or a secular society. The words "an establishment of religion" were intended to mean specifically and only a church organization established and supported by the national government.[38] At that time, several of the states had established the Church of England or some other as their state church. Established churches were prevalent in Europe. It was this kind of institution that the Constitution prohibited, and only for the national government. At the time, several state churches existed and were not disestablished in Connecticut until 1816, and in Massachusetts until 1833.[39]

Clearly, new laws that would enforce secularism in this country constitute a revolution in law. The first amendment does not assert a secular society or atheism. While the *institution* of the government of the United States is secular, the government is to encourage and promote a religious society. The goal is a secular state but not a secular society.

38. Whitehead, "Secularizing America," 18–21. Whitehead affirms that the First Amendment was intended to encourage both *denominational* pluralism and Christianity. The First Amendment was not an attempt to level all religions and make the state indifferent to religion, as even the Unitarian Justice Joseph Storey (1811–45) acknowledged. See Horn, "God to Court," 24–27, for a review of cases where Christian expression is under attack. He argued then that such discrimination marks the court to be no longer of "benevolent neutrality," and is a dangerous step toward totalitarianism. See also Bird, "Freedom of Religion," 5:1–52.

39. The proponents of secularism today have no historical base for their claim. It was the Constitution of the former Soviet Union, article 124, that explicitly affirms the separation of church and state. According to Schaeffer, *Christian Manifesto*, 112–113, the section reads: "In order to ensure to citizens freedom of conscience, the church in the U.S.S.R. is separated from the State, and the school from the church. Freedom of religious worship and freedom of anti-religious propaganda is recognized for all citizens."

CIVIL RELIGION: GOVERNMENT DEIFIED

There is a delicate yet clear line between a biblical view of government and civil religion. Civil religion would make our national founders into founders of a new religion, with our institutions and documents having religious authority. Yet while we should disavow the tenets of civil religion, we must be very careful to affirm several significant truths: God is sovereign over all nations and has ordained America's (and any other nation's) time and boundaries (Acts 17); religion is fundamental and basic to morality and law; America has uniquely recognized the source of its rights in God and sought to guarantee these in a written constitution; and Judaism and Christianity have contributed the religious base and ethical standards to the form of government in this land. Christian ideals, while perhaps not the sole force in America's founding, were "vital to the American experiment in government."[40] Without these, America would not be America.

AVOIDING TWO EXTREMES: DEFYING AND DEIFYING THE STATE

Therefore, a proper view of the American system of government must avoid two extremes. On the one hand, pluralism in religion, morals, and law must be rejected in order to remain consistent with the ideals set out by the framers of liberty and God's plan for the role of faith in daily life. The call for a secular society pursued by a thoroughgoing pluralism must be scorned as un-American. A biblical ethic and the American system are absolutely linked.

On the other hand, civil religion is equally cancerous. It has an idolatrous view of the role that government, especially American government, has in society and history. *Government is to be neither defied, nor deified.* What a difference an "i" makes!

In summary, Jesus and Paul both acknowledged that the state is secular or neutral, and had a particular place in God's program to regulate morality and law. On the other hand, the state is to promote what is good, moral, and lawful, providing what is conducive to religion and human dignity (Matthew 22; Romans 13:1–7; 1 Timothy 2:1–2). I substantiate

---

40. Minson, "Ordered Liberty," 38:55.

these important points in the following chapters, especially when I discuss the all-encompassing words of Jesus in Matthew 22.

NATURAL LAW AND SPECIAL REVELATION

Many think that there is an inherent contradiction that arises when one affirms both the place of Natural Moral Law and the place of special revelation. Can those who base their morality on God's revelation be members of a modern democracy?[41]

In reply, I note again that a distinction can be made between a secular government or state and a secular society. Government in its forms and many of its laws must be secular or non-religious while promoting a religious society.

Natural Law, as the words indicate, is rooted in an order that "transcends civil society." Novak concludes: Natural Law arises not so much out of what is rational but out of the theological—"out of the doctrine of creation and the wisdom of God."[42]

Thus Christians need not shrink from acknowledging that their own understanding of Natural Moral Law arises from theological understanding. As people of faith, they make a contribution to society that the secularist cannot. They, not secularists, are the foundation and source for both the religious and secular aspects of a state. They have divine revelation for how both the religious and secular aspects of a state should work. The secularist has none of this.

I've devoted Appendix 1 to a sampling of the voices from among America's founders who believed that Natural Moral Law is inherent and necessary in the American philosophy of government. They are an ongoing inspiration for modern states. Not surprisingly, many of those who supported Natural Moral Law and its significance for government were ministers.

IMPLICATIONS OF NATURAL MORAL LAW

There are some rather acute implications that flow from the biblical and historical defense of Natural Moral Law. First, it seems to be a valid

41. Novak, "Moses, Nature," 48.
42. Ibid.

deduction that man-made laws that conflict with Natural Moral Law are not valid law. They must be changed, and will be, as more and more people become aware of the inconsistency.

Second, Natural Moral Law provides a standard by which to judge all human institutions—the home and family, the business, the church, and the government. For example, the family has divine sanction. It is a universal norm. Hence caution must be exercised in a society so as not to destroy this plan. There are many implications of this standard, for adultery and divorce, family planning, gay rights, adoption, welfare payments, the roles of the sexes in society, dress codes, etc.

Third, we need to see evolution for the great evil that it is. Atheistic evolution seeks to destroy the very base of Natural Moral Law, the existence of God who has established the order of people, society, and the creation. If there is no divine Creator there can be no Natural Moral Law. There is Law because there is a Law-giver. Christians should seek to check the insidious cancerous blight of atheistic evolution on the minds of young and old alike.

Fourth, there is a necessary connection between law and morality. It is not by accident that Natural Law is termed Natural Moral Law, for it specifically points to ethical norms for judging a person's behavior. All of one's activities must pass the test of ethics. In the following chapters, I pursue in depth this connection between morality and law.

Fifth, we must all clearly understand that Natural Moral Law should be judged by revealed law, by revelation directly revealed (as in Scripture). Natural Moral Law (or "Creation's Moral Law") is inadequate to point people to a Redeemer, because people themselves are fallen creatures and reject or dispute the revelation of Nature (Creation) (Romans 1:18ff.).[43] It is by special revelation that we know with certainty that there is Natural Moral Law, as well as its consequences.

---

43. De Young, *Homosexuality*, ch. 4. One of the revelations of Scripture is that the term "nature" is never found in Old or New Testaments as a reference to the physical creation (sometimes popularly referred to as "mother nature"). Rather, this is an idea derived from the Greeks who, with the Romans, went so far as to deify nature as the source of all (so Marcus Aurelius) and affirm the eternality of nature. The biblical terms are "creature" and "creation," because these point to the Creator and his eternality. So Natural Moral Law is truly better titled as "Creation's Moral Law."

WHY DOESN'T EVERYONE ACCEPT NATURAL MORAL LAW?

If Natural Moral Law is so "natural," or easily perceived, why do not all recognize it? The reason is that depravity—the sins of people—raises an imposing barrier to the recognition of Natural Moral Law. This blight on understanding is universal and pervasive. All people are born in and commit sin (Romans 3:9–26). It is part of a biblical worldview of reality that affirms that not only does God's realm of love and holiness exist, but so does Satan's realm of hatred, deceit, and sin (see 1 John 2–4).

Christians have entered into this understanding of reality, morality, and truth. They have come to know the true God as revealed in Jesus Christ and dwell in him. They affirm that the true Light of the gospel has come into the world to enlighten everyone more and more (John 1:4–5, 9).

CONCLUSION

In summary, there is a consensus regarding Natural Moral Law. It is biblical and held by the church throughout history. This witness agrees with the view of many historians and lawyers, statesmen and common people, past and present. It was the guiding principle for the founding of this nation as a nation of law.

The revolution in law, which rejects all absolutes, is a revolt not only against biblical authority, but also against conscience, reason, general revelation, and history. The revolt in law, along with the revolt in government (discussed in chapter 1), pose a grave danger to civilization.

Yet another revolution commands our attention, for it is intimately linked with the revolutions in government and in law. It is the third revolution—that of immorality.

Addendum

Additional Principles from the Declaration of Independence

There are other principles that may be derived from the Declaration of Independence in addition to the two already discussed above (that theism is basic, and that natural moral law is unchangeable). The third principle is that the claims are universal in scope. All people are created equal and are endowed with the same inalienable[44] rights. This must flow from the preceding point. If there is an absolute such as Natural Law, then it is binding upon all people everywhere, at all times, in all situations. The magnificence of the Declaration is that it gives hope and support to struggling peoples in the East and the West, in Central America and Africa, wherever mankind longs for freedom.

It is especially relevant today for Muslim peoples, few of whom live in democratic states. Indeed, fundamentalist Islam would impose *sharia*, Islamic law, in every nation where Islam could command a majority. The freedoms contained in our first ten amendments, the Bill of Rights, would not be allowed in such states. This fact underscores again the serious threat to freedom everywhere that fundamentalist Islam poses to the world. Equally, fundamentalist Christians, who would impose a "Christian" government in all the specifics of the Old Testament, make the same error.

The fourth principle is that all people are created equal. They are equal before the law, and have equal opportunity to pursue freedom. This describes equality in the sight of God and before the law. It does not mean that all are equal in economic status, means, office, or other matters. Nor should they be. These latter ideas were abhorrent to our founding fathers.

Fifth, the rights are endowed by God, not by human beings. By contrast, the French Revolution of 1789 set forth a different base, namely that rights derive from people, not from a Supreme Being. A godless

---

44. The preferred spelling today is "inalienable"; the original has "unalienable."

philosophy was the basis of that revolution. The difference means that if a person bestows the rights, a person can take them away. Only rights derived from God are "inalienable."

Until the American Revolution, no other people have based their government on a philosophy like that of the Americans. Even in England, the power of the Parliament is considered absolute and final and can change any law it desires, including so-called "constitutional" laws. The American declaration that rights are God-given reflects the proper relationship of religion to law. God bestows laws. This crucial distinctive gives hope to all oppressed peoples everywhere!

Sixth, it is assumed that there are more "inalienable rights" than those cited. The three listed do not exhaust the list. These rights are secured to people by the institution of government. Government is not instituted to take away these rights. Indeed, whenever this occurs, people have the right (another inalienable right) to alter or abolish their government in order to institute another one, which will promote their rights of safety and happiness.

THE RIGHT OF LIFE

The first right enumerated is life. Government should do all it can to protect life and prevent its destruction. It is apparent that the act of murder or abortion of the pre-born is a direct violation of this inalienable right. The right of life is limitless in scope; however, it is not absolute. There may be times when life must be forfeited (e.g., capital punishment).

THE RIGHT OF LIBERTY

The next right, liberty, derives from the fact that people are created by God and owe their ultimate allegiance to him. Liberty is not license to do as one pleases; rather, the people relinquish the freedom to exercise their rights fully to insure that there might be greater enjoyment of all of them. George Washington said that " . . . individuals entering into society, must give up a share of liberty to preserve the rest."[45] The basic idea is freedom of choice (when this does not conflict with other rights). The idea that liberty is not license to do as one pleases is a biblical principle.

45. Long, *Yardstick*, 29.

To Submit or to Rebel against the State

Both Christian and Muslim fundamentalists deny this basic right when they seek to impose on all a religious requirement that all legislation must be based on special revelation.

THE RIGHT OF HAPPINESS

The third right, that of the pursuit of happiness, flows from the right of freedom, for one can hardly be happy without freedom. It is an ongoing aspiration of man and incapable of limitation, as is the right of life. This right was frequently substituted in early America by that of private property. In the "Declaration and Resolves of the First Continental Congress" in 1774, the phrase used to describe people's chief rights was "life, liberty, and property." These three terms occur together as guaranteed rights in the Fifth Amendment to the Constitution of the United States.

Blackstone, the jurist who gave us so much in our understanding of law, correctly saw the relationship among happiness, justice, and law. Ethics and Natural Law were practically one in his thinking. God "has so inseparably interwoven the laws of eternal justice with the happiness of each individual that the latter cannot be attained but by observing the former."[46] Thus the role of obedience to God's laws of nature is reduced to man's pursuing his own true and substantial happiness.

The pursuit of private property is considered an essential legal right and provides the support and security for freedom, liberty, and the pursuit of happiness. People must be able to be free economically in order to avoid governmental control. As Hamilton said: "In the general course of human nature, a power over a man's subsistence amounts to a power over his will."[47]

Contrary to many (if not all) other ancient religions, the way to salvation in Judaism was not found in asceticism or the selling of one's possessions. Judaism was probably the most materialistic of all the ancient religions. God was the ultimate owner of the land and all the Israelites were only stewards of it (Leviticus 25:23–24). Nevertheless, the possession of each family's parcel was a sacred right and so protected that no matter what might have happened in the meantime, the land returned to the original owner every fiftieth year—the Year of Jubilee (Leviticus

---

46. Brabner-Smith, "Prudent Pursuit," 44.
47. Long, *Yardstick*, 98.

25:8–22). The priests had their own lands and could take no other. As revealed in the New Testament, Christianity continued this respect for private property and its place in orderly society.[48]

These rights are inalienable or inviolable. Neither government nor any individual may take them away. They can be interfered with and, by force, denied, but they can never be abolished or destroyed. These are not only rights but also capacities possessed by all people. All have the capacity to reason and to be self-governing, and to have life, liberty, and happiness.

A final observation can be made regarding the intrinsic relationship of law and government. The purpose of government is solely to secure and protect peoples' inalienable rights. Government is not the giver nor the originator of such rights. Government must be limited to its "just powers." If government violates these essential rights, it is the right of the governed to change or abolish its government, as the Declaration of Independence states.

This too is in accord with Scripture. When government is ordained in Genesis 9, God does not ascribe to the institution of government the making of the law regarding capital punishment; that is, the law does not derive from the institution. Rather, the law is assumed to be "natural" and self-existent, derived from the nature of the Creator and the creaturely nature of human beings. Government and law are both derived from God by general and special revelation.

---

48. There is no basis for claiming that the early Church was communistic in its economic policy, as state communism is practiced today in a few countries. It is clear from Acts 4:32—5:11 that the land that was sold belonged to those selling it. They willingly and freely sold it in order to share the proceeds with those in need. This was not a mandated practice; there was not a community ownership of land or goods; there was no state involvement. But the early Church did manifest a care and concern for community that we in the West need to emulate.

3

The Revolution in Morality

> Furthermore, since they did not think it worthwhile to retain the knowledge of God, he gave them over to a depraved mind, to do what ought not to be done. They have become filled with every kind of wickedness, evil, greed, and depravity. They are full of envy, murder, strife, deceit, and malice. They are gossips, slanderers, God-haters, insolent, arrogant, and boastful; they invent ways of doing evil; they disobey their parents; they are senseless, faithless, heartless, ruthless. Although they know God's righteous decree that those who do such things deserve death, they not only continue to do these very things but also approve of those who practice them. —Romans 1:28–32

INTRODUCTION

TO DEMONSTRATE THAT THERE has been a revolution in morality is hardly necessary. The signs are all around us. The most obvious example of this is the sexual revolution. The recent rampages of herpes, acquired immunity deficiency syndrome (AIDS), and other sexually transmitted diseases (STDs) have led newsmagazines and other media to proclaim that "the sexual revolution is over." The completion of the revolution is arguable, but it is an implicit recognition of the sexual revolution itself.

MORAL RELATIVISM

The recent revolution in morality derives from the advent of "situational ethics" in the 1960s, and postmodernism at the present. The standard for right and wrong is no longer objective and unchanging, but egoism, utilitarianism, hedonism, etc., have produced a cultural relativism virtually without boundaries. This view of ethics (what we ought to do) rejects all norms and absolutes except the absolute that all behavior done in love is acceptable and normative. This fails to consider the fact that God's revealed law and Natural Moral Law are also part of our larger situation. Regardless of the immediate situation, some behavior is always wrong or immoral.

Postmodernism makes the majority vote of the community the determiner of what is right and wrong. Yet what if the majority is wrong? Nazi Germany illustrates how the majority can be deluded and deceived. The rest of the world had to resort to war to correct their view of morality. As related in Exodus 32–34, the majority of the Israelites were pursuing idolatry and gross immorality while Moses was on top of Mount Sinai getting the Ten Commandments from God. If a majority vote determines morality, we would not have the Ten Commandments (nor a civilization built on law and human dignity). We would have the "Ten Suggestions."

Another aspect of our moral relativism arises from pluralism and political correctness. Many assert that we live in a pluralistic society today; that is, pluralistic in peoples, races, backgrounds, customs, and languages. They further argue that this pluralism should extend to moral standards and religions. No one standard of values, morality, or ethics should be given prior place. This is radical and total pluralism—a revolution in morals. This revolution is being exported to countries around the world by American media. Apparently it is the view of President Obama.

Public morality is linked with reality (what is real) and truth as the basic issues that fill a person's worldview. Throughout time, both philosophy and theology have sought to deal with them. Since everything a person believes and does is determined by his worldview, our understanding of worldview is crucial.

To Submit or to Rebel against the State

CONSEQUENCES OF MORAL RELATIVISM

The consequences of moral relativism are mushrooming around us in the breakdown in moral values and in basic institutions. This has led to a significant rise in crime in recent decades. The failure of the home has lead to rampant divorce and remarriage. About 50 percent of all marriages end in divorce. The consequences of broken homes breed further ills for society. Sociologists on the West Coast have studied children from broken homes for a period of ten years. They discovered that fully two-thirds of such children never become reconciled to the divorced parents, and half of them remained actively hostile to the situation after a whole decade. What kind of society will these children mold in the future? Is it any wonder that several communities have seen outrageous crimes where young people killed classmates in their schools? Over one million men and women—about one in every three hundred Americans (including children)—are incarcerated! The collapse of businesses, such as Enron, because of fraud and corruption has resulted in the loss of retirement income to millions of Americans. Corruption in government, most notably the scandal of the Clinton presidency, has contaminated the whole realm of politics. The recent financial crisis began with greed, particularly in the funding of the housing market, the former chairman of the Federal Reserve, Allan Greenspan, asserted.

The revolution in morality is all-encompassing. Infanticide and abortion affect the very young; pre-marital sex affects teenagers; and euthanasia is a concern for the elderly. For the first time in the history of the United States, it is legal (first in Oregon, now in Washington state) for doctors to put the elderly to death if they desire to end their lives. Today there are unprecedented numbers addicted to drugs, alcohol, and gambling, while pornography enslaves many more.

Studies conducted by Judith Reisman have shown that for more than thirty years "soft-core" pornographic magazines (*Playboy*, *Penthouse*, *Hustler*, etc.) have promoted the sexual abuse of children, as well as other perversions of male-female relationships. There were more than 6,000 illustrations and cartoons of children (ages 6–11 predominate) in various sexual associations and activities, including bestiality.[1] No doubt the situation is worse now.

---

1. Beane, "Pornography," 106–110. In one and the same issue, a major West Coast newspaper (*The Sunday Oregonian*, June 7, 1981, A 20) carried two articles that support

SEEKING THE ANSWER TO MORAL RELATIVISM

Perhaps the most pressing issue for this society, and indeed all of Western civilization, is this question: What standard of morality is to prevail? The Judeo-Christian ethic is under attack everywhere, and Christians are being intimidated by a belligerent segment of society that asks: What right do Christians have to force their standard of morality upon the rest of us?

In attempting to answer these questions, several significant issues must be understood. One of the most important is to understand the relationship of public morality to religion and the law. This issue raises significant questions. Must public morality have a divine sanction (a religion) behind it? Can morality be legislated? Should pluralism prevail in standards of public morality? Is ethical pluralism of no greater consequence than pluralism in customs, cultures, and languages? Are the pluralisms different? Do absolute standards of morality exist? How essential is an unchanging standard of morality? Is there a subterfuge in the call for pluralism in ethics, which masks an actual revolution in morality? These questions are a vital concern to Christians, and to all those who desire an ordered and good society in which to live.

Christians—whether citizens of America or another country—cannot avoid the issue of public morality and their part in affecting it. They are citizens of both heaven (Hebrews 12:22–24; Philippians 3:30) and an earthly kingdom. They are called to be light and salt in a needy world (Matthew 5:13–16). Without them, the world would not survive; the onslaughts of evil and its consequences would doom it to extinction.

A proper understanding of how a Christian's earthly citizenship relates to one's heavenly citizenship determines the manner by which one effects public morality. The history of Christianity demonstrates how the church has erred by being too involved (or not involved enough) in its earthly identity. Control of the state by the Roman Catholic Church, known

---

the role of personal and public morality. Robert Coles, a distinguished child psychiatrist of Harvard and an author, had for twenty years missed the central point in children's lives. He acknowledged that that point was the moral life of children and involved their beliefs in ultimate reality. This professor finally came to realize that morality, moral notions, and moral life are the "central riddle" of children's lives! The second article in *The Sunday Oregonian* was a review of a science fiction book depicting life in the year 2025. The book claimed that America will abandon moral standards, and crime, sabotage, and fear will become so rampant that bus stops will have to be heavily protected by armed troops! These articles have a common theme: A standard of morality is essential to a society. It cannot function without it.

as the Holy Roman Empire, and by certain Protestant denominations has been one of abuse. On the other hand, asceticism and monasticism led the church to withdraw from the world. More recently, fundamentalism led many Christians to withdraw from American culture, and, hence, failed to influence it. On the other hand, the triumphalism of theonomy leads many to insist that our government strictly follow the cultural patterns of the Old Testament. All of these represent distortions of the relationship between a Christian's earthly and heavenly citizenships.

I am convinced that the correct balance of this dual citizenship is most clearly taught by our Lord himself. On two occasions, he was faced with the obligation of paying taxes—once as challenged by the Pharisees, and once by collectors of the temple tax. Regarding the former occasion, Jesus stated: "Render to Caesar the things that are Caesar's; and to God the things that are God's" (Matthew 22:21, NAS). The law demanded that the tax be paid, and the Lord respected this law as a citizen of Israel. Yet, on the other occasion, he told Peter that sons are free from paying taxes (Matthew 17:24–27). This suggests that the Christian, as a son of God and his kingdom, is ultimately free from paying all taxes. Somehow both the Christian's freedom and obligation must be harmonized so that neither one's obligation to God or to the state ordained by God is neglected.

In an amazing way, Jesus provided the basis both for living as a child of God's kingdom, and for the foundation of the secular state. Discovering and affirming the principle involved in this matter is one of the most crucial in developing a Christian attitude toward the state, law, and public morality.

The Christian then must be involved in society's pursuit for a standard of morality, as any other citizen must be. However, the Christian has an even greater stake in the standard of public morality, and he has a greater contribution to make. These points flow from the fact that Judaism and Christianity have provided the basic ethical standard for our society in the past. Both of these points will be demonstrated later.

The Bible makes it clear that there is both personal and national salvation. The former needs no substantiation. The latter is also distinctly taught. For example, when the collective sin of Israel became great, God allowed a pagan nation (Babylon) to judge and destroy its kingdom and to carry the people, both those engaged in idolatry *and* the faithful remnant, away as captives. Then, later, God judged the Babylonians (see Habakkuk 1–3). Countless references to non-Israelite nations that are accountable to

God occur in Scripture. This includes the Egyptians, Babylonians, Medes and Persians, Greeks, Romans, etc. (Read Genesis 19; Leviticus 18–20; Psalms 44:2, 11, 14; 72:11, 17; 79:1–10; Daniel 2, 7–10; Isaiah 13:4; 45:22; and Acts 17:26–31.)

Christians who fail to exercise their role in public morality will participate in the demise of their nation. While nations fall for various reasons, Scripture makes it clear that a primary reason is a lack of public morality (Leviticus 18:20; Proverbs 11:10–11, 31; 14:34). Has America's revolution in morality threatened her very survival?

UNIVERSAL MORAL STANDARDS

A newspaper columnist was once asked how she would convince someone who does not believe in God to practice a moral and ethical lifestyle. The columnist answered that morals usually are rooted in religion, and ethics (what we ought to do) are rooted in morals. She went on to say that we can be motivated to practice a moral or ethical lifestyle regardless of whether we have a religion as a foundation for it. The way children are taught to love, honor, respect, and—sometimes—fear God, they can also be taught to love, honor, respect, and fear humanity itself. Such teachings would guide human behavior. Any reasonable adult who desired the approval of his fellow man and woman would be motivated to do the right thing.

Yet one must wonder where "such teachings" come from. What if adults aren't reasonable? And how does one define "the right thing"? What makes it "right"? It seems that the columnist has not adequately dealt with the origin of morality or ethics.

Another error is to separate unduly science from religion. Stephen Jay Gould makes the assertion that science and religion are separate realms and should not be in conflict. Science concerns the "factual character of nature," and religion concerns "the need to define meaning in our lives and a moral basis for our actions."[2] As Fuller points out, this is similar to Hume's "naturalistic fallacy," that it is not valid to infer from a knowledge of what is any moral ought, since ought statements belong to another kind of discourse.[3]

---

2. Gould, *Rocks of Ages*, 175, as quoted by Fuller, "Critical Realism," 40.
3. Ibid.

To Submit or to Rebel against the State

When I speak of public morality, I have chiefly in mind what theorists usually call ethics (what people ought to do). Morals are usually limited to the rules about good and bad conduct. In this chapter, I am mainly concerned with the origin of the rules—where they come from. There are many theories about this.[4]

In summary, I believe that special revelation gives us some specific rules of conduct. In addition, general revelation through the creation, the conscience, reason, intuition, and even experience (history) informs us of universally recognized rules of conduct. General revelation is universal and ongoing. These all contribute to what we ought to do (ethics).

In earlier pages, I showed that diverse nations with their individual languages and cultures are ordained by God to restrain evil power in the earth. I have also presented the case for the universality and unchangeable nature of Natural Moral Law, drawn from the affirmations of Scripture, America's founding fathers, and the preponderance of similar law codes throughout time and geography. That same evidence supports the existence of universal standards of morality. In fact, no entirely new

---

4. Ibid., 39–45. Fuller summarizes the approaches to the nature and origin of ethics. The two broad approaches regarding the nature of ethics are the deontological (based on axioms assumed to be true; laws or rules which define ethical behavior) and the teleological (or consequentialist: actions are judged by the goals or consequences of the actions). The approaches regarding the origin of ethics include the realist (moral axioms exist, independently of time and place) and non-realist (axioms exist only for "the person or people who maintain their truth within a given, socially, historically, and culturally contingent context" [41]).

Fuller presents the major views of ethical theory. (1) Utilitarian ethics (teleological): Maximizing happiness for the maximum number of people. (2) Kantian ethics (deontological): One acts according to principles that are universal. (3) Social contract theories (both teleological and deontological): Ethical axioms are what society says they are. (4) Natural law theories (deontological): There are laws or human constructs that mean something deeper, what belongs to the essence of humanity. This leads to inalienable human rights. (5) Virtue theories: They focus on the character of the individual and ask, "What should I do ethically in order to shape and inform my own moral character?" (43). (6) Egoist ethics: A person willingly puts his or her own interests above everything else in considering how to act. It is "enlightened self-interest" (43). This might lead to the common good, at least in the economic sphere, as nations seek their own individual success. (7) Christian ethics: Some things have been revealed by God in the Bible as either good or evil; and God's will regarding the good is revealed in the Bible and lived out in community. There is an "indissociable unity between the theological and ethical aspects of Christian faith" (quoting S. Hauerwas, 43). "Ethical behavior *is* following the revealed commandments of God, and these may be discovered in Scripture and the teaching of the Church" (43). These may be deontological or teleological (not based in law but in values of the kingdom).

The Revolution in Morality

moral value can be invented, just as no new primary color can be imagined. These are "transcultural and transtemporal moral values," which are self-evident and objectively true.[5]

THE RELATIONSHIP OF LAW, MORALITY, AND RELIGION IN GOVERNMENT

Law and morality, whether good or bad, are intrinsic elements in government. There is also a clear, dynamic relationship among law, public morality, and government. Will and Ariel Durant, the secular and agnostic historians, searched through two thousand years of Western civilization to discover the basic and necessary elements for civilization to exist. They identify four interrelated elements.[6] Without any one of these, a society or nation or civilization has not existed and cannot exist. These four are (1) a form of government or political organization; (2) a system of economics; (3) the arts, including education; and (4) a standard of public morality. These four elements must be renewed by each generation, or a civilization will perish.[7]

5. Boa, "Behind Morality," 133: 154–156.

6. Durant, *Oriental Heritage*, 1–3.

7. It is helpful to review what forms these elements have taken in biblical and secular history. Governmentally, Israel moved from a theocracy to a monarchy to an oligarchy. The U.S. is a constitutional republic. Other forms of government include totalitarian dictatorships, socialist republics (the former Soviet Union and its allies; present day China, where the dictatorship of the proletariat is claimed), democracies, parliamentarian forms, etc.

Economically, private enterprise and ownership of private property characterized Israel, with one important stipulation: God was the real owner of all land and the inhabitants held it in stewardship for him. That is why all land reverted back to the original possessors in the fiftieth year, the Year of Jubilee, even if it had been sold in the interval (Lev. 25:8–23). In the U.S., a similar system of private ownership prevails, without the special limitations cited above. Other systems include socialism (state ownership), communism (all own all things in common), or Chinese communism (the state temporarily owns all until all the world is conquered, then pure communism can arrive).

The arts in Israel, including education, were centered in the home, the priesthood, and the prophets. Hence they were related closely to religion. In the U.S., the arts and education have also been closely related to the church, but recently they have become more and more secularized. There is a current resurgence of religious orientation to the arts and education. In totalitarian societies, such as the former Soviet Union and contemporary China, the state government controls all art forms and education. The same is true of states where fundamentalist Islam predominates.

Regarding the fourth element, God determined the standard of public morality in

To Submit or to Rebel against the State

So where does our morality come from? Theology always precedes (and is the basis of) moral behavior. The Bible tells us to give attention first to our duty to God—to love and fear him—then, second, to our neighbor. This is illustrated by the great Shema ("Hear, O Israel, the LORD our God, the LORD is one") passage (Deuteronomy 6:4–9), and elsewhere. Thus, fear of God precedes obedience, love, and service (Deuteronomy 10:12–13). So, too, the Decalogue (the Ten Commandments in Exodus 20) begins with one's relationship to God (the first four commandments), then proceeds to one's moral conduct toward others (the last six).

In the New Testament, Jesus similarly taught that there are two great commands (Matthew 22:36–40). The first is to have a proper response to God, which is to love him, as the Shema passage of the Old Testament declares. The second is to have a proper service to other humans, to love one's neighbor, which is derived from the Old Testament as well (Leviticus 19:2). Again, theology precedes and determines public morality.

The founding documents of the United States express a belief in God, and on our coins we profess trust in him. This should result in the practice of Judeo-Christian morality. In former Eastern Europe and Russia, atheism was the state's position. This is still the case in modern China. In such states, moral values have an altogether different standard theoretically, and the state seeks to destroy traditional values. Yet the existence of traditional moral values has continued, and has triumphed in the fall of communism in Europe. Traditional morality testifies to universal moral values by which all must live, as shown above.

Communism appears to be the first instance in the history of civilization in which an economic or political system has made atheism its base and deliberately tried to destroy religion, severing religion from morality. It has failed in Europe. It is not surprising that China and North Korea, with communism as their base, resort to lying to their own people, as well as to the international community, whether it concerns the military and nuclear weapons, the existence of disease (SARS and AIDS), the economy, or other matters. It will be surprising if such a system can

---

Israel, and this morality derived from Israel's faith. Perhaps Lev. 19:2 says it best: "Be holy because I, the Lord your God, am holy." When Israel's faith was vital and proper, her moral conduct was on a high plain. The whole message of the book of Judges reveals that when Israel forsook God, people then did what they thought to be right—there was no standard of public morality in force.

endure much longer in these countries. Because of the Internet and other mass communication, a people cannot be kept isolated and uninformed.

The relationship of morality to Christian faith is clearly understood from Romans 1, quoted in part at the beginning of this chapter. The rejection of a knowledge of God leads to immoral conduct.

Historians are in general agreement with divine revelation, that religion determines the standard of public morality. Will and Ariel Durant, throughout their massive ten-volume work, *The Story of Civilization*, constantly pose the question of whether morality requires a divine sanction. In a supplemental volume, *The Lessons of History*, they conclude that it does. They write that "there is no significant example in history . . . of a society successfully maintaining moral life without the aid of religion."[8] Without religion, civilization cannot exist. Even the Greeks and the Romans appealed to religion as providing the standard for their morality. All believed that law is derived from the gods.[9]

Take the example of homosexuality. According to the earlier writings of Plato, even homosexuality was justified because the gods Zeus and Ganymede engaged in it. Yet one is surprised to find that in the last work of his life, *The Laws*, Plato wrote that laws should be enacted to abolish incest, adultery, and homosexuality. He says that the justification for homosexuality, that it was practiced by the gods, was a fabrication coming from the Cretans (whom Paul also identifies as liars in Titus 1:12).[10]

THE GOLDEN TRIANGLE

The relationship among religion, morality, and law is best represented by a triangle. Faith (religion) forms the base; Morality rests upon this base; and at the apex comes Law. By Law, I mean jurisprudence, or positive law (that is, legislation).

---

8. Durant, *History*, 51. See also Toynbee, *Civilization*, 198–220, who argues for the essential role of religion in civilization.

9. Munoz, "Religious Liberty," 34. See also De Young, "Women in Ministry." I show that law, whether in the Old Testament or among the pagans, was considered authoritative because it came from God or the gods.

10. De Young, *Homosexuality*, 252–255.

To Submit or to Rebel against the State

LAW
MORALITY
FAITH

Although there may be shortcomings to this pattern, it is, in general, helpful for seeing important relationships. Within a nation, then, the religion of a people determines public morality, and public morality determines law. It follows also that if religion is supernatural, having tenets that are immutable and eternal, then there must be certain absolute standards of public morality, and certain laws regarding morality that are absolute.[11]

Another observation is that law is enacted morality.[12] Every law or piece of legislation reflects a standard of public morality, and standards of morality are appropriate concerns of legislation.

Morality is the bridge between theology and culture. The standards of morality are the means of bringing to daily life the tenets of theology. Even the atheist or agnostic must recognize certain standards in conduct and law that are necessary for the orderly functioning of society. Every society inculcates a moral code, and the unanimity by which the members of society practice the code "is quite as important as the contents of that code."[13] Indeed, there must be "a unifying moral code, some rules of the game of life acknowledged even by those who violate them, and giving to conduct some order and regularity, some direction and stimulus."[14]

Another observation on the triangle needs to be made. Although in general it is true that law will be the reflection and expression of the public morality practiced by the majority, there are cases where a certain law reflects only the moral standards of the minority. The genius of the Declaration of Independence and the Constitution of the United States

---

11. In Israel, law was specially revealed. Perhaps the order in the triangle would better be represented for her by the order of Religion, Law, and Morality. For all other nations, and for the legislation Israel formulated in addition to those divinely revealed, the order of Religion, Morality, and Law prevails. Also in the case of Natural Moral Law, law determines morality rather than being the reflection of morality. Yet even its observance depends upon peoples' morality formed by their religious beliefs.

The distinctive of the New Testament allows for law to arise from secular sources, from general revelation. Again, Jesus' unique recognition of the separate realms belonging to the state and to God is the basis for secular law.

12. Rushdoony, *Law and Liberty*, 1ff.
13. Durant, *Oriental Heritage*, 47.
14. Ibid., 3.

is that they protect the absolute rights of the minority from the majority. Thus, it is always wrong to murder, even if the majority should decide otherwise. Even if the majority should somehow legislate away absolute rights, the rights will still stand, for they are inalienable—given by God (so Natural Moral Law). In the latter case, the minority should insist on their rights, and are correct in doing so. The current morality may bring opposition and persecution, but the minority should be willing to endure such. There is a constant need for a society to review the reasons for its laws and argue them persuasively.

HISTORICAL PRECEDENT FOR THE GOLDEN TRIANGLE

As I've cited in appendix 1, historical precedent from the founding days of the United States supports the concept of Natural Moral Law. These same founders (and others) also believed that religion had to be the base for morality and law, and I've included a section in appendix 1 noting their statements. Their citations go far in showing just how extensive the revolution in morality has gone when many today no longer sympathize with such views.

CONCLUSION

The revolution in morality breaks through new barriers with every passing day. The media of film, print, television, and now the Internet are the major vehicles. This revolution is characterized by rejection of Judeo-Christian values, our national tradition of affirming Natural Moral Law, and the affirmation, "In God We Trust." In abandoning traditional values, this revolution defiantly substitutes an old immorality under the guise of the "new morality." The latest attempts to remove the words "under God" from our Pledge of Allegiance, or "In God We Trust" from our coins, are other symptoms of the rebellion against our morality, which has been founded on theology.

Pluralism in values is an evidence of the revolution in morality. Pluralism is a blight on our national life. Christians need to be aware of the meaning and significance of this moral pluralism, and how they can avoid falling prey to it. I discuss these matters in the addendum that follows this chapter.

To Submit or to Rebel against the State

How to renew the Christian vision of the state is the concern of the last seven chapters of this book. These chapters delineate seven principles that will recover the meaning of the American state in particular, but also serve as a guide for Christians as they face the possibility of revolution in whichever country they live.

Addendum
The Myth of Moral Pluralism

> In the past God overlooked such ignorance, but now he commands all people everywhere to repent. For he has set a day when he will judge the world with justice by the man he has appointed. He has given proof of this to all men by raising him from the dead.
> —Apostle Paul, Acts 17:30–31

RADICAL PLURALISM

Pluralism in ethics and moral law poses grave consequences to our way of life. Yet it seems that pluralism is becoming more and more acceptable. Probably the most obvious expression of the pluralistic view of morality is the oft-repeated question: "What right do Christians have to impose their morality on the rest of society?"[15]

Unfortunately, too many Christians view moral pluralism as a noble form of Christian toleration. Others believe that pluralism is inevitable, even desirable, especially if days of persecution for Christians lie ahead. Others are simply intimidated into silence by politically correct propaganda, and become apologetic for thinking to the contrary. Finally, many are simply apathetic and indifferent. Secularists pursue other things; and conservative Christians retreat from the world's "contamination."

By pluralism I mean moral or radical pluralism—pluralism in every area of life, including morality, law and values, even governmental

---

15. This attitude was best reflected, perhaps, by the vice-presidential candidate, Geraldine Ferraro, in 1984, when she said: "I am personally opposed to abortion, but I do not want to impose my moral standards on the rest of society." Many others have since followed her example.

structures or forms. This contrasts a tempered pluralism embodied and recognized by the founders of our country. They believed in a diversity of opinion and a cultural matrix. The new pluralism (moral or radical pluralism) is a smokescreen for an intolerant view that would drive traditional religious or moral values from the public arena, especially the public schools.

Moral pluralism is better termed decadence, because there is no normative standard left to which a society can be called. Hence, it is impossible to preserve or renew such a society, whether in culture, religion, morals, or laws. The only universal truth is that there are no universal truths; the only absolute is that all things are relative.

By considering values as objects of study rather than their rightness or wrongness, values are relativized and no value system is considered to be uniquely valid. In other words, when young people go to college and learn about values, they learn *about* them but are not instructed whether they are right or wrong. Values become denuded of any obligation to observe them.

The preceding pages showed that the founding fathers clearly chose virtue over self-interest. They realized that the American experiment bequeathed unprecedented liberty. Without virtue accompanying liberty and restraining it, liberty would lead to license, anarchy, and totalitarianism.

CONSERVATIVE VERSUS LIBERAL

The pursuit of virtue as our worldview is called conservative today, but, at the founding of our nation, it found endorsement from such liberal thinkers as Jefferson and others. Even though Jefferson could not be called a Christian (or evangelical), his worldview, at least in the area of ethics, made it possible for Christians to be allied with Jeffersonians in the election of 1800. Their common point centered on the inadequacy of self-interest to serve as the motivation in American polity. Instead, virtue must be the theme.

The humanist-materialist worldview has no ultimate point of reference, since humanity (or matter) is final, not God. This worldview is at odds with that of Christianity, and the two can never be reconciled. Classical liberal theology has drunk deep at the well of the materialist-humanist worldview. It is, as Francis Schaeffer points out, nothing more than humanism or materialism expressed in theological terms.[16]

It is probably not an overstatement to say that the revolution taking place in government, law, and morality is to be blamed upon liberal theology. Is there then a correspondence between liberalism or conservatism in theology and politics? In other words, if one is liberal in theology, should or would one be liberal in politics?

I believe that the answer to these questions is yes. In general, there is a correspondence between theology and politics, as far as liberalism and conservatism are presently defined. This may not always hold true in every particular, but observation supports a general correspondence. In addition, the reading of the past supports the same conclusion.

The moral pluralism espoused by many has two inherent and mortal flaws: (1) The call for pluralism is a smoke-screen for a new and radical orthodoxy that enthrones the heterodoxy of yesterday; and (2) Pluralism actually brings conflict, not peace and harmony, in society.

However, as the English historian E. R. Norman has observed, "pluralism" is a word society employs during the transition from one orthodoxy to another. In practice, it proves to be extraordinarily difficult to maintain genuine equality between "all points of view," even if it were possible to determine what "all" such points of view really are. A society cannot remain permanently fragmented with respect to values. Public policies of various kinds require decisions, which inevitably reflect values. Hence, value judgments must be made, whether or not this fact is publicly acknowledged. Each time such a judgment is made, one set of values is inevitably preferred over another set. Someone's beliefs are favored at the expense of someone else's.

While the call for "pluralism" is ostensibly merely a call for tolerance (a request that the reigning orthodoxy make room for newer "points of view"), in practice an orthodoxy that loses its authority has trouble even retaining the right of toleration. Although it is still extended bare legal toleration, in practice it finds itself more and more on the defensive, its very right to exist challenged in numerous ways.[17]

---

16. Schaeffer, *Manifesto*, 17–21.

17. Hitchcock, "Systems," 10, 2. The late William B. Ball, a nationally recognized constitutional lawyer, argued many cases before the Supreme Court. Ball points out that pluralism is only the ploy of humanism, whereby its voice is heard; but any voice from religion is rejected. See William B. Ball, *Moody Monthly* (July-Aug., 1981), 15.

Actually, pluralism is only a step in the larger movement to secularism. To remain neutral on strategic issues regarding the spiritual and moral life of a society is impossible. It is the myth of neutrality.

CHRISTIANS AND SOCIAL POWER

Rather than a system in which diverse groups mute their differences in the interests of mutual harmony, pluralism is a system in which diverse groups push their own interests strongly and persistently. In a pluralistic society, no group is taken seriously until it proves its ability to command social power. But social power is something many Christians seem to regard as inherently evil.[18]

Instead of retreating under a hail of threats, complaints, and innuendoes, the Christian should aggressively do battle in the public arena and insist on the Judeo-Christian ethic remaining in place. If all of life is sacred, then every area of life must be penetrated with the claims of Scripture regarding peoples' accountability to God above and their responsibility to live in a dignified manner.

Those of us who hold to the Judeo-Christian ethic have incredible repairs to make to correct the propaganda campaign that has overwhelmed our society.

Let Christians not be intimidated by the question, "What right do you have to force your standards of morality on society at large?" Christians have as much right as their opponents do in forcing a new, lower standard. Indeed, Christians have more right in the light of two thousand years of precedence in Western civilization and two hundred years of American tradition. Yet they have another right—they are committed to the universal demands of Scripture placed upon all nations to abide by God's standards based in Natural Moral Law.

The Christian must insist upon a Judeo-Christian ethic, and this insistence will bring conflict. Much of the present erosion of public morality is the direct result of "good men doing nothing." Too many evangelicals act as if God sovereignly controls the standard of public morality and he will either preserve it or not. It is not a realm in which the Christian should be engaged.

---

18. Hitchcock, "Systems," 10, 4.

But while God is sovereign, he has ordained the accomplishment of his plan through people. The incarnation itself attests to this, as seen in many passages of Scripture. The story of Esther is especially appropriate in showing both God's sovereignty and the responsibility he places upon people to act (4:13–14). Daniel's role in society is a similar case. He knew God's promise to end the exile, but he prayed for it nevertheless (Daniel 9:1ff.).

This is not a call for institutional imposition of Christianity upon the United States. This would violate the First Amendment and the teaching of Scripture about the special place God has given to government, even secular government. Instead, it is a plea for involvement of Christians in the articulation and defense of a Judeo-Christian ethic at all strata of society: government, law, business and economics, education, communication and media, art, concerns of welfare, labor, social affairs, military defense, etc.[19]

Albert Camers said that "the world expects of Christians that they will raise their voices so loudly and clearly and so formulate their protest that not even the simplest man can have the slightest doubt about what they are saying... We stand in need of folk who have determined to speak directly and unmistakably and, come what may, to stand by what they have said."[20]

Most historians agree that whereas Greece and Rome provided the governmental structure for the United States, it is Judaism and Christianity that have provided the pattern or structure, and content, for public morality. When Christians have concentrated on certain issues, genuine reform has come, as occurred in the days of William Wilberforce and Granville Sharp (Christians who spearheaded the abolishment of slavery from the British Empire). Sharp went so far as to purchase land in Africa as a new home for former slaves. This is the nation of Sierra Leone.[21]

Christians have also the obligation to speak out because of love. A love ethic considers first the needs of others, what is truly best for one's neighbor in light of God's plan, and best for the viability of a nation. Failure to speak out is not only a lack of courage, but a lack of love, just as one

---

19. Schaeffer, *Manifesto*, 63–71, 131–138. He repeatedly argues for the need to see the trend of society as a whole, and the responsibility that clergy, lawyers, and educators all have in resolving the issues.

20. Quoted by Emmerich, "Luther's World Ethic," 1:10.

21. Wallace, "Granville Sharp," 591–613.

who fails to discipline a wayward child fails to love. As Charles Emmerich writes:

> In the confrontation of societal issues such as abortion and euthanasia it becomes the church's duty to proclaim the Christian doctrine of life's intrinsic sanctity and dignity. Where materialism and utilitarianism cry out for abortion on demand and active euthanasia, the church and the Christian voice adamant disapproval. Silence in the wake of such ungodliness indicates a callousness not consonant with Christian love.[22]

Without a Judaic-Christian ethic and worldview, our freedoms would not exist. Secular humanism with its worldview would not and could not ever give us freedom. Secular humanism makes people the end and center of all, hence a high sense of human value could never have been formulated. Human worth is determined by the Creator of people, not by people.

CONCLUSION: RADICAL PLURALISM IS UNBIBLICAL AND UNAMERICAN

Radical pluralism violates biblical truth and American tradition. Every piece of our coinage proclaims on one side, *E Pluribus unum*, "Out of Many, One," and on the other side, "In God We Trust." Both of these maxims are necessary and related. They proclaim that the spiritual is supreme and that America deliberately committed itself to a single standard for morality and law: the Judeo-Christian ethic.

In addition to these significant phrases, the Great Seal on the currency of the United States bears the Latin Phrases, *Annuit Coeptis*—MDCLXXVI, and *Novus Ordo Seclorum*. These are translated: "He [God] has smiled on our undertakings—1776," and "A new order of [or for] the Ages." The founders had in mind the Puritan idea that Providence had given a world mission to the American nation.[23] There is no acceptance of pluralism in our wallets and purses. As Caesar's coin was used by Jesus to teach an important principle in his day, so our currency expresses an important principle for us today.

---

22. Emmerich, "Luther's World Ethic," 42.
23. Ahlstrom, *Religious History*, 383.

To Submit or to Rebel against the State

Moral pluralism blatantly advocates self-interest instead of virtue, contrary to our American heritage and biblical teaching. Pluralism is a smokescreen for a campaign of asserting secular-humanist values. Once they succeed, the plea for pluralism will cease.

The revolution in morality goes hand-in-hand with the revolutions in government and law. Pluralism simply hastens the revolutions taking place. What is the Christian to do in such a day of revolution as this? The chief concern of Christians should be that their conduct is based on biblical guidelines or principles. I've set forth these principles as the last seven chapters of this book.

PART 2

To Submit or to Rebel against the State? Seven Biblical Principles to Guide Christians Everywhere During an Age of Revolution and in the Struggle for Religious Freedom

THE WINDS OF REVOLUTION are in the air. The threat of terrorism based in fundamentalist Islam and other ideologies is real. Some historians warn of a clash of civilizations between the so-called Christian West and the Islamic world. We presently live in an age of rebellion, unrest, and uncertainty. Even among Christians there are voices calling for change, resistance, and, sometimes, disobedience to authority, when deemed necessary. What the future bodes is a matter of sober reflection.

As the fierceness of the pressures for change increases, there will be an accelerating attempt to fix blame for the misfortunes of society. It shouldn't surprise any believer if there is a deliberate, calculated attempt to fault Christians, to make them the scapegoat for the ills of society. Already in our pluralistic society, every form of diversity finds defense—only "restrictive" Christian morality is disapproved by the world community at large. Should Christians set out to resist the trend and disobey governmental authority, in the East or the West, there will be even greater attempts to fault Christianity.

In the preceding pages, I hope I've successfully impressed upon you what the real causes of revolution in government, law, and morality are.

To Submit or to Rebel against the State

The fault lies with those who reject what Christianity stands for and the impact a Christian worldview has had in society. In light of the winds of revolution, what should Christians do? This is a question especially pertinent for those living in totalitarian regimes, including countries where Islam predominates.

In the next seven chapters, I set forth seven principles that serve as guidelines for Christians all over the world in fulfilling their obligations as citizens of governments or nations. In addition, I seek to apply these principles to past, present, and future problems in this age of revolution.

Each chapter begins with a unique, real-life account of a specific Christian from the past who lived in a hostile state. Each vignette is applicable to the principle in its chapter and provides us an example of what Christians today may do in a situation similar to that in the story.

I've found the following seven principles in Scripture, in clear passages where Christian writers explicitly address Christian responsibility toward civil government. The key passages are Matthew 22:15–22; several references from the book of Acts; Romans 13:1–7; 1 Timothy 1:8–11 and 2:1–4; and 1 Peter 2:13–17. The last four passages receive extended, primary attention. I urge you to carefully weigh the interpretation of these passages for yourself.

I commend these universal principles to the discerning reader. They will do much in enabling the Christian and non-Christian alike to understand a biblical worldview that sees God as the personal Revealer of unchanging standards of law and morality for the preservation of society. The principles, if actualized, will renew the Christian vision of the state.

4

The Source of Government

THE MARTYRDOM OF IGNATIUS

IGNATIUS COULD HARDLY RESTRAIN himself. His joy was overflowing. At last he was reaching Rome's amphitheater, which was full of people by the sound of it. The Emperor Trajan himself would certainly be in attendance. Ignatius could not imagine a more glorious witness than this—his death for the sake of his Savior! Let the wild beasts come! The state would be defied. He had lived and would die for the kingdom of Christ.

He had been arrested several months before his long walk to the amphitheater. As he walked, Ignatius reflected on the great privilege that had been his to serve as the third bishop of Antioch. By the power of the Spirit, he had led the church through greater and greater expansion. He had faithfully served the gospel of Jesus Christ during his service; he had followed in an extraordinary line of bishops, which included the Apostle Peter and Euodius. And, as they had died the martyr's death, so he would now die. Peter had been crucified upside down; Ignatius knew his death would not be quite so glorious, but being eaten by lions would certainly carry its own special weight as a witness. No one would have to worry about burying his body, for that matter. The stomachs of the lions would be his tomb.

After his arrest, Ignatius had been escorted through various churches of Asia Minor. When he arrived in Smyrna, he felt compelled by the Holy Spirit to write letters to the churches of Ephesus, Mangnesia, Tralles,

To Submit or to Rebel against the State

and Rome, following the example of Paul. Later, when he reached Troas, he composed additional letters—to the Philadelphians and Smyrneans, and to Polycarp, the bishop of Smyrna.

Ignatius felt compelled to exhort the believers to regard their bishops and presbyters as they would regard the Lord himself. The Christians had no other authority than these godly men. They should keep the churches pure in their understanding of Christ—that he is both flesh and spirit. They should give no place to the insidious heresy of docetism, which asserted that the death of Jesus was only an apparition—that he wasn't truly God in a physical body, and that he didn't truly die. Ignatius desired to warn the churches that such heretical teaching would stab a dagger in the heart of Christianity.

He was especially concerned for Polycarp, who, Ignatius knew, would eventually be tested in his fidelity; the young bishop of Smyrna, "God's athlete," was especially vulnerable. The Apostle John's earlier letter had commended the church there for its strength and loyalty in the midst of horrible persecution—many had been imprisoned and been martyred for the Name. Would Polycarp be faithful to the end? Out of deep concern, Ignatius wrote him a personal letter.

Ignatius' heart was compelled by a deep love for the believers he would be leaving behind in Antioch. He exhorted the other churches to care for his people. When the people had named him Theophorus, the "God-bearer," he had simply responded that everyone who had Christ in his heart was worthy of this title. He was not someone great; he was only a prisoner for the Name. He was not yet perfect. Together he and the people he led were travelers, loving nothing but God alone. He exhorted the believers to be imitators of the Lord—to love one another with an undivided heart—because the end times were drawing closer.

Some considered intervening on Ignatius' behalf to deliver him from his military escort, but Ignatius would have none of this. His spirit was devoted to the Cross. Unless he willingly chose to die through Christ, with Jesus' same passion, then Jesus' life was not in him. If he did not die, how else could he be found to be a Christian in deed and not just be called one? As Ignatius faced his death, he recalled his bold words to the Romans:

I am writing to all the churches, and I give injunctions to all men, that I am dying willingly for God's sake, if you do not hinder it. I beseech you, be not "an unseasonable kindness" to me. Permit me to be eaten by the beasts, through whom I can attain to God. I am God's wheat, and I am ground by the teeth of wild beasts that I may be found pure bread of Christ. Rather, entice the wild beasts that they may become my tomb, and leave no trace of my body, that when I fall asleep I be not burdensome to any. Then shall I be truly a disciple of Jesus Christ, when the world shall not even see my body. Beseech Christ on my behalf, that I may be found a sacrifice through the instruments of these beasts. I do not order you as did Peter and Paul; they were apostles, I am a convict; they were free, I am even until now a slave. But if I suffer, I shall be Jesus Christ's freedman, and in him I shall rise free. Now I am learning in my bonds to give up all desires.

I long for the beasts that are prepared for me; and I pray that they may be found prompt for me; I will even entice them to devour me promptly; not as has happened to some whom they have not touched from fear; even if they be unwilling of themselves, I will force them to it. Grant me this favor. I know what is profitable for me; now I am beginning to be a disciple . . . Let there come on me fire, and cross, and struggles with wild beasts, cutting, and tearing asunder, rackings of bones, mangling of limbs, crushing of my whole body, cruel tortures of the devil, if only I may but attain to Jesus Christ!

The ends of the earth and the kingdoms of this world shall profit me nothing. It is better for me to die in Christ Jesus than to be king over the ends of the earth. I seek him who died for our sake. I desire him who rose for us. The pains of birth are upon me. Suffer me, my brothers; hinder me not from living, do not wish me to die. Do not give to the world one who desires to belong to God, nor deceive him with material things. Allow me to receive the pure light; when I have come forth, I shall become a man . . .

In the midst of life, I write to you desiring death. My lust has been crucified, and there is in me no fire of love for material things; but only water living and speaking in me, and saying to me from within, "Come to the Father." I have no pleasure in the food of corruption or in the delights of this life. I desire the "bread of God," which is the flesh of Jesus Christ, who was "of the seed of David," and for drink I desire his blood, which is incorruptible love.

I no longer desire to live after the manner of men, and this shall be, if you desire it. Desire it . . .

Principle 1
Christians Should Submit to Government as Established by God

> Everyone must submit himself to the governing authorities, for there is no authority except that which God has established. The authorities that exist have been established by God. Consequently, he who rebels against the authority is rebelling against what God has instituted, and those who do so will bring judgment on themselves. —Romans 13:1–2

INTRODUCTION

We've already learned that there is a revolution in the concept of government taking place today, which is far-reaching in its implications. The recent emphasis on globalization gives special impetus to internationalism. Global communication, transportation, and commerce have shrunk our world to limits never known before. This has led to the global sharing of ideas, economics, and political ideology.

The revolution in government takes three basic forms. They have in common an attack upon nationalism, or nationhood. One form of this revolution comes from those who advocate dissolution of all national governments in favor of a united, one-world government. If they were to achieve this goal, we would quickly see a dissolution of nationalism and national rivalries considered to be roadblocks to international peace and cooperation. Some argue that a one-world government would be able to bring world resources to bear on solving the world's ills in areas of hunger, finances, conflict, population, natural resources, pollution, health, global warming, etc.; just what form this new government would take is anyone's guess. However, with much of the world living under totalitarianism, the role of democracy is uncertain.

Another form of revolution seeks world union under one form of government, otherwise known as communism. This system would destroy all traditional institutions, including national government, the family, and the church, and would bring all under a totalitarian regime. Power and authority would be concentrated in the hands of a few who would rule with an iron fist. While communism has fallen in the Soviet Union and its satellites, its continued presence in China, Cuba, and North Korea poses serious challenges to world stability.

A more recent form of revolution is that advocated by extremist Islam. With the attacks on the United States on September 11, 2001, this country (and the world) went to war with a terrorism rooted in the religion of Islam. Extremist or fundamentalist Islam calls for a world united under Islamic law, called *sharia*, where freedom and democracy would be defined according to the Islamic holy book, the *Qur'an*. There would be no place for a secular government. The freedoms outlined in our Constitution's Bill of Rights would cease. Contemporary conflict with such Islamism appears in Nigeria, the Sudan, Indonesia, Iran, Iraq, Afghanistan, Somalia, and elsewhere in the Middle East and Africa. With about two billion people under the sway of Islam, its extremist proponents have a fertile field from which to find followers of one world united under Islam.

Yet there is another form of one-world government that is promised in Scripture. It is the time of Messiah's rule. All nations will be subjected to his rule as King of kings (take a look at Psalm 2 and Revelation 19). His reign will be characterized as one of perfect righteousness, peace, and justice. This is the basic message of the prophets of the Old Testament (consider Isaiah 40-66), and it is reiterated in the New Testament (Hebrews 1:8-9; Revelation 19).

This theocracy, however, does not come until a time of unprecedented evil overwhelms the earth during the reign of one who is opposed to God. The regime of the antichrist will be satanic in origin, power, and goal. This "man of evil" will seek worldwide domination, and use false religion to get it. While the reign of the Messiah will be one of peace and righteousness, that of the antichrist will be just the opposite. Since current moves toward one-world government are not based in allegiance to Christ as the One who brings peace and righteousness, they will more likely reflect the antichrist's rule.

New governments occur with frequency and by various means, including *coup d'etat*, revolution, and elections. There are also movements of protest within nations manifested by non-payment of taxes, recall elections, civil disobedience, and public demonstrations. Christians are more likely to be involved in these movements than in the more disruptive ones, such as riot, anarchy, or revolution. Yet the American Revolution, the Civil War, and the more recent collapse of Communism in Europe saw the significant participation of Christians. The rising discontent in China suggests a future involvement of Christians in revolution there.

What does Scripture say regarding the legitimacy of governments? Why do nations exist and what are they to do? Are they optional or necessary? Are there legitimate forms of opposition to civil government, and where does one draw the line? What should Christians do in carrying out their civil responsibility? Can they protest, lead a revolution, be anarchists? Can they demonstrate violently, bringing bodily harm to their opposition and destroying property? When can they join in a revolution?

This chapter demonstrates that civil governments are a necessary part of God's plan for the course of this age. God has established nationhood for the greater good. It is only when Christians are convinced of the divine design for government that they will be able to determine the proper attitude and conduct to follow in effecting change in their countries.

The earlier discussion of the institution of government or nations showed from the Old Testament that national governments or nation-states are part of God's plan. Various forms of government serve God's purpose of curbing the greater evil, which results when nations are in united confederation, as at Babel.

The New Testament concurs with the record of the Old. Romans 13:1-7 speaks more clearly of the divine ordination or establishment of civil government than any other passage in Scripture. In this chapter, I take a careful look at the first two verses of Romans 13, and then consider the remaining five verses in the following chapter.

THE POLITICAL SITUATION AT ROME AND ELSEWHERE

From Corinth, sometime in A.D. 56-57, the Apostle Paul wrote his epistle to believers living in Rome, most of whom were Gentiles. Many were probably Paul's own converts from other parts of the Roman Empire who had migrated to Rome. The churches there were probably started by Jews who became believers on the day of Pentecost (Acts 2). Paul's theme in the book of Romans is that the gospel of Christ reveals the righteousness of God (Romans 1:16-17). He argues for justification by faith (Romans 1-5), clarifies the meaning of holiness (Romans 6-8), deals with the situation of unbelieving Israel (Romans 9-11), and presents the implications of his gospel for specific areas of the Christian life, including obligations to the state (Romans 12-15). He then concludes his epistle in Romans 15:14—16:27.

Paul's teaching on government comes in the section dealing with the implications of the gospel of righteousness for various areas of life, including personal commitment (12:1-2), the body of Christ (12:3-21), human government (13:1-7), and relations toward others (13:8—15:13). Paul takes up the discussion of government at this point as another sphere of the believer's life where the good, acceptable, and perfect will of God (12:2) has to be done.

During the writing of Romans, there was an enormous urgency for Paul's message. Riots had broken out in Rome, and in Israel there was growing opposition to Roman control.

The central command that Paul is giving to his readers is that every believer must be in subjection to the governing authorities, namely rulers, because God has established the state. In Paul's time, this meant that all believers, whether Jewish or Christian, were to be in subjection to Gentile rulers. Of course, Paul's message also implied that all unbelievers were to be subject also.

This was a bitter pill for both Jews and Gentiles to swallow. The Jews, according to the New Testament, were concerned about the rights of the Roman government (as seen in Matthew 22:16-17, as well as in the other three gospels) and boasted of their independence (John 8:33). Revolutionary movements were prominent (Acts 5:36-37 and 21:38). The whole period leading from Jesus' death (around A.D. 30) until the destruction of Jerusalem by the Romans (in A.D. 70) was one of great struggle to be liberated from Roman control.

In the Law of Moses, the Jews are told not to put a foreigner over them who was not their brother (Deuteronomy 17:15). And Judas the Gaulonite, among others, viewed the condition of the Jews as downright slavery (according to the Jewish historian, Josephus, in his *Antiquities*, 16. i. 1.; 20. v. 1). Just a few years before, in A.D. 49, the Jews had revolted in Rome and were expelled from the city, Christians with them (Acts 18:2). The Jews' failure to accept the kind of teaching that Paul gives here eventually led to the destruction of Jerusalem and the dispersal of the Jews in A.D. 70. The Jewish state came to an end.

Paul also needed to correct Christian resistance to submission to the state that could have arisen in light of his teaching of freedom in Christ and his kingship. In particular, Paul, the "apostle of liberty," strongly condemns bondage to the law and legalism (see Galatians 4:21–5:1 and Colossians 2:8–23). Many of Paul's readers would be prone to think that spiritual and political freedom go together; even the gospel could be misunderstood as having purely materialistic aims with regard to a kingdom (Acts 1:6, 17:7). There was a need to delineate where loyalty to Christ superceded loyalty to the government, and where government had its rightful claim. Thus, both Paul and Peter elsewhere address these tendencies toward unrest among their followers, besides the teaching in Romans (1 Timothy 2:1–3; Titus 3:1; 1 Peter 2:13–17).

In addition, Paul had just written of the believer's need to love others, and not to take personal revenge when harmed (Romans 12:9–18). He writes that vengeance belongs to God; it's his prerogative (12:19–21). Yet a concern arises. If Christians are to love, how then is justice served, especially in the larger context of living in a community of non-Christians? What about crime, law, justice, and other such matters? This concern is directly addressed in Romans 13. Paul seeks to show that there is one who does avenge, that God exercises his vengeance during the present age by his institution of government (13:4). After addressing this concern, Paul returns to the personal ethic of love (13:8–10).

WHAT DOES PAUL MEAN FOR CHRISTIANS TO SUBMIT TO AUTHORITIES?

Romans 13 begins with a command that every believer must submit himself or herself to the governing rulers. The "governing authorities" to which Paul refers in verses 1 and 2 are literally the "superior authorities." This is not a reference to higher grades or levels of civil authorities as opposed to lower ones, but to all civil authorities who govern or rule over the Christians in Rome. Paul refers not just to the Emperor but to all civil or governmental leaders or rulers.

Paul's reason for his command to be in subjection arises from the fact that government is God's institution (Romans 13:1b): He established government and he gives it its power or authority. He delegates some of his power, as ruler over all, to human beings to rule over other human beings.

The verb form for the word "establish" means to "appoint," "assign," "order," or "ordain." Paul's words give emphasis to the direct work of God in establishing governmental authority. Paul makes it perfectly clear that authority is due to God directly. Whatever the existing forms of government may be, they are established or ordained by him directly.

The grammar places emphasis on the present reality of this ordination. That is, what God began in the past in establishing this role for government is still effective as Paul writes. There is nothing in this text, nor in others, that would qualify, limit, or abrogate Paul's words since he wrote them. Therefore, his teaching is still in effect. These words, then, are far-reaching and universal in scope. We'll take a look at whether or not they admit any exception when we begin discussing the next principle in the following chapter.

What Paul is saying in Romans 13:1–2 is that government is not a human idea but a divine idea. This agrees with the meaning of the events at the Tower of Babel, as seen in Genesis 9–11. The Genesis passage also shows that government is not solely a Christian idea—it long preceded the coming of Christ, the Church, or Israel. Government is part of God's plan for all the nations.

It's important to note that Scripture repeatedly affirms that the authority is said to belong to God, not Christ. When a person becomes a Christian, one's obligations and citizenship in the earthly kingdom, in the realm of government, continue. In violating the institution of government, the Christian sins against both God *and* Christ. This has led one writer to observe: "The state is the sum of divine institutions."[1]

ARE ALL GOVERNMENTS ESTABLISHED BY GOD?

Not only has God established human authority in the form of government in general, but he has also ordained and appointed every government that has ever existed. Paul writes: "The authorities that exist have been established by God." This latter thought, from the second part of the verse, reminds us of Paul's words in Acts 17:26: "From one man he made every nation of men, that they should inhabit the whole earth; and he

---

1. Stifler, *Epistle*, 214. The Jews believed that the Messianic promise was hostile to the claims of any pagan government. Perhaps this attitude is epitomized best by Eleazar, the defender of Masada (see Josephus, *Jews*, 8. 8, 9). According to this Jewish historian, Eleazar and his 960 followers finally committed suicide rather than be killed by the Romans in their conquest in A.D. 73. Some converts from Judaism may have brought their revolutionary attitudes into the church.

determined the times set for them and the exact places where they should live." Government is an aspect of the providential order, which God has established for the good of humanity. The extent and the time of every state is part of God's plan.

It is clear that Paul is referring to human powers or authorities alone here, and not also to angelic or demonic powers. Although the latter are called "authorities" elsewhere (for example, 1 Corinthians 15:24; Ephesians 1:21, 3:10, 6:12; and Colossians 1:16, 2:10, 15), submission to the demonic powers would contradict passages where they are described as opposing God's kingdom (2 Corinthians 4:4 and Ephesians 6:12) and as promoting only evil.[2]

Indeed, demonic powers attempt to usurp authority and distort the state (note Daniel 10 and Revelation 13:17), which acts as a restraint to demonic powers. Sometimes a state works within a demonic system. When the state is conquered by such evil, its authority becomes a force for evil.[3] The struggle in Daniel 10 implies that demons had almost gained control of Persia and Greece.

When Paul commands that everyone should be "in subjection," he is calling for obedience; yet the term "submission" is a better translation and is more inclusive than what obedience requires. "Submission" indicates a willing subordination, an active participation, in the duty of subjection, not just passive obedience.[4] It calls for willing compliance, not a grudging one. This clarifies Paul's command for us even more.

Abuse by human government is neither a necessary nor an ordained part of government. If abuse does occur, it doesn't invalidate government's divine charter or rob it of its sacredness, just as abuses of marriage do not. "Any government is preferable to anarchy, just as poorly enforced marriage laws are better than none."[5] However, along the same lines of thinking, it would seem that if the abuses become so wicked so as to end

---

2. See extended note refuting the idea of demonic angels for this verse in Murray, *Romans*, 2: 252–256; also Cranfield, *Romans*, 2: 656ff., retraces the arguments and rejects a reference to demons. See also the commentaries on Romans by Douglas Moo, Thomas Schreiner, Grant Osborne, and others.

3. Barrett, *Romans*, 249.

4. So Murray, *Romans*, 2: 148. The *huper* and *hupo* in *huperechousais* and *hupotassestho* are correlative. "Preeminence implies submission." So Liddon, *Romans*, 247. See also Cranfield, *Romans*, 2: 660ff.

5. Stifler, *Epistle*, 215.

a marriage, because of adultery followed by remarriage, or continuous sexual perversity (incest, homosexuality, bestiality), then also a government ceases to have authority to exist when it becomes so evil that it becomes the servant of Satan rather than God. Revelation 13 identifies such a government (that of Antichrist), one that is totally captured by Satan and his forces (a topic I will return to later in these pages).

WHAT ARE THE CONSEQUENCES OF RESISTING GOVERNMENT?

Romans 13:2 shows the logical and necessary result of rebellion to government that God has established. Paul writes that when one resists authority, it constitutes resistance to God's ordinance. Hence, those who do resist do so at their own disadvantage. They're held responsible for their actions and judgment is meted out because of this.

This judgment or condemnation is human since it comes through human agency, but remember that the judgment is also divine because the human government has its origin in God. Judgment is an expression of God's wrath and so has his sanction or approval. It's not a reference to eternal punishment but to retribution from the state.

The thought here reproduces our Lord's teaching in Matthew 26:52b: "all who draw the sword will die by the sword." The second mention of "sword" stands for the judgment of the government to come on them who resist government in a violent manner. However, some believe that divine judgment may be the meaning, perhaps because of the futuristic implication of "shall perish."

Paul is not endorsing an absolutist idea here of submission to government. He wouldn't have Christians act immorally because the state commanded it. As Stifler comments: "One can refuse to do wrong and undergo the penalty without resisting the power."[6] We take a longer look at this in chapter 6.

Romans 13:1–2 gives three aspects to the reason for submission to government. The human authority exists by God's authority; it's been ordained *by* God, and it's the ordinance *of* God.[7] The repeated emphasis on "ordained" (or "established") draws attention to the divine initiative in

---

6. Stifler, *Romans*, 216.
7. Murray, *Romans*, 2: 152.

the formation and purpose of government. A significant inference from these assertions is that it is sinful for a ruler to refuse to execute judgment against injustice, just as it is sinful for one to resist the ruler.

From this brief study of Romans 13:1–2, it's clear that Christians have an obligation to submit to human government. They cannot be part of a movement that would seek to overthrow all existing governments without defying God's order for human affairs.

Clearly Paul has Genesis 9 in mind, as well as our Lord's teaching on this matter, which will be discussed in another chapter. The exposition of Romans 13:1–2 gives us this important principle: Christians should submit to government as established by God. As we look at Romans 13:3–7, we will find two more principles to consider.

INFERENCES FROM THE PRINCIPLE

Before proceeding to the next principle, however, there are some key observations that can be drawn from Romans 13:1–2. The fact that authority exists by God, is ordained by God, and is God's ordinance supports the basic form and substance of the triangle illustration found at the beginning of this book, which shows the relationship of faith, morality, and law. Religion is the base upon which public morality is built—and then upon morality, law is built.

We have already observed from the Old Testament that nations are ordained by God, and nationalism serves as a curb on greater evil. Paul's words are consistent with this, for they contemplate or assume several rulers or authorities of several nations, not one ruler over all nations. This agrees with his words in Acts 17:26: "From one man [God] made every nation of men, that they should inhabit the whole earth; and he determined the times set for them and the exact places where they should live."

The idea of patriotism finds support in this passage. The Christian must obey the legitimate laws of the state. The "law-abiding citizen is the loftiest patriot."[8]

As we look closely at Romans 13:2, we make another observation: Murray states that governments derive their authority from God alone, and that this "excludes from the outset every nation to the effect that authority in the state rests upon agreement on the part of the governed or

---

8. Stifler, *Romans*, 218.

upon the consent of the governed."⁹ He believes that the verse does not encompass the idea of democratic or republic forms of government.

But I don't believe that Paul's words in Romans 13:2 exclude democratic republics and refer only to totalitarian regimes! Surely Paul was acquainted with history where various forms of democracy had reigned in Greece or Rome before his time. There are governments by *de facto* as well as by authority. All forms of government must come under the scope of Paul's words. Therefore, even those resting "upon the consent of the governed," such as the government of the United States, are established by God! How could this be denied for those forms of government (such as a republic) that acknowledge God as the supreme authority and affirm government to be his tool, which ours did and does?

Paul is arguing for government *per se*, and implies that a government must be true to itself (and not violate its own charter by which it is formed) and reflect God's will. No matter what the form, it is God's minister (Romans 13:4). Yet when government violates its responsibilities as a government, other considerations come into play.

The ultimate authority of government comes from God, however the exercise of that authority within a government is done. It may be done by various means, such as by a king or by the people in mutual agreement, as in a republic. The right of the latter kind of government to exist as much as any other form is guaranteed by God's authority.

It's clear then, as Liddon points out,[10] that Paul does not deal with the origin of a particular government, or its political form. He does not argue for the divine right of kings, the right of the people, or for any special kind of government. Rather, he argues for government and order.

Paul does not indicate when a new government becomes existent during the course of a revolution (note Romans 13:1), or when the old becomes nonexistent. He does not tell us when a government once illegal becomes legal. For the most part, these matters were of no practical value in the imperial Rome of Paul's day, or at least not his concern in this passage of Romans, although they are very important for our day. They have to be answered from the context of all of Scripture, and be derived from broader principles.

---

9. Murray, *Romans*, 2: 148.
10. Liddon, *Romans*, 247–248.

To Submit or to Rebel against the State

Paul's instruction in Romans 13:1–2 is clear; however, he raises all kinds of questions. What is the purpose for government? What should it be doing as God's established authority? What should people do when a government promotes evil or forces them to commit evil? Is submission absolute, or are there limitations? Is there ever a time to force a change of government? To what degree can the Christian engage in revolution?

I take a good look at these questions in the following chapters.

THE WITNESS OF IGNATIUS

We return to Ignatius in his conflict with the state. For him, the choice was clear. He could not compromise his submission to Christ with a submission to the state that involved idolatry. The state had declared that citizens of Rome should acknowledge the emperor as deity, and this Ignatius could not and would not do. Hearing the roaring crowds, Ignatius enticed the lions. It did not take long until he "attained unto God." One of the first martyrs of the Church, he went faithfully to his death in A.D. 108.

5

The Purpose of Government

THE MARTYRDOM OF POLYCARP, THE EARLIEST HISTORY OF A CHRISTIAN MARTYRDOM

IN THE MIDST OF his praying one day, Polycarp fell into a trance. In his vision, he saw his pillow on fire. This vision convinced him of his destiny. "I must be burned alive," Polycarp announced to his friends. Only three days later he was arrested.

Polycarp had never had such an experience of prayer before. For decades he had faithfully served the church at Smyrna. In his youth, he had known the Apostle John; later, his friend Ignatius, just prior to his own martyrdom, had exhorted him to be faithful to Christ. Now, in the year A.D. 156, he had become the focus of pagan opposition. The people had become incensed at the refusal of Christians to take the oath of allegiance to Caesar as Lord and to make sacrifices to him. They accused Christians of being atheists because they refused to worship idols. Christians were rounded up in the arena and submitted to torture, to fire, even to being torn apart by wild beasts. Some gave in to the torture and recanted, denying Christ.

As pastor and bishop of the Church, Polycarp symbolized the defiance of the Christians by his noble preaching, which resulted in both the Gentiles and the Jews turning against him and seeking his death. At the pleading of his friends, Polycarp evaded arrest for several weeks, only to have his location betrayed to local authorities by a slave. Polycarp did not resist his arrest.

The authorities tried to convince Polycarp, now quite elderly, that there would be no harm in confessing Caesar as Lord. But Polycarp wouldn't submit. The cavalry, under the command of one named Herod, took him to Rome. As he entered the arena where he was to be put to death, Polycarp heard a voice from heaven encouraging him: "Be strong, Polycarp, and play the man."

Recognizing how old Polycarp was, the Roman Pro-Consul sought to rescue him from certain death. He tried to persuade Polycarp to deny Christ and instead swear by the genius, the fortune of Caesar, and to denounce Christians as atheists.

But Polycarp would not compromise to swear by what Christians considered to be a demon in Caesar. It was the most horrible of all pagan oaths. It implicitly involved the recognition of Caesar as a god. Polycarp waved his hand at all the lawless heathen in the arena and looked up to heaven and said: "Away with the atheists."

The Pro-Consul pressed him: "Take the oath and I will let you go; revile Christ."

But Polycarp replied, "For eighty and six years have I been his servant, and he has done me no wrong, and how can I blaspheme my King who saved me?"

When pressed again, Polycarp answered: "If you are ignorant of who I am, listen plainly. I am a Christian. And if you wish to learn the doctrine of Christianity, fix a day and listen." When the Pro-Consul asked Polycarp to persuade the people, he responded by saying, "We have been taught to render honor, if it hurt us not, to princes and authorities appointed by God. But I do not consider these worthy that a defense should be made to them."

The Pro-Consul threatened to deliver Polycarp to wild beasts and to fire if he did not repent. Polycarp responded by saying, "Call for them, for repentance from better to worse is not allowed us; but it is good to change from evil to righteousness. Why are you waiting? Come, do what you will."

Principle 2
Government Should Promote Good and Punish Evil

> For rulers hold no terror for those who do right, but for those who do wrong. Do you want to be free from fear of the one in authority? Then do what is right and he will commend you. For he is God's servant to do you good. But if you do wrong, be afraid, for he does not bear the sword for nothing. He is God's servant, an agent of wrath to bring punishment on the wrongdoer. Therefore, it is necessary to submit to the authorities, not only because of possible punishment but also because of conscience. This is why you pay taxes, for the authorities are God's servants, who give their full time to governing. Give everyone what you owe him: If you owe taxes, pay taxes; if revenue, then revenue; if respect, then respect; if honor, then honor. —*Romans 13:3–7*

INTRODUCTION

The second principle to guide Christian citizens living in a revolutionary age also comes from Romans 13. In this chapter, we're going to take a closer look at verses 3–7, which will show that God's purpose for civil government is to punish evil and promote good.

Yet how should government exercise this power? Are there limits to its exercise of force? Is capital punishment a valid exercise of force? Is war a valid exercise of force? How does this principle relate to the Sermon on the Mount? Which view of war-making is correct, in light of Romans 13?

The United States has engaged in several wars in the nineteenth and twentieth centuries. Now at the beginning of a new century, it is engaged in other wars in its pursuit of the "war on terrorism" and militant Islam. Does this new kind of war (where no nations are directly engaged, but we are fighting an amorphous enemy scattered among several nations) pose a new challenge to the justification for war? May a government strike in a pre-emptive manner, to destroy an opponent before the opponent strikes?

To Submit or to Rebel against the State

THE MATTER OF WAR AND PEACE

Few issues have divided Christians for so long as has the issue of war and peace, or the exercise of force by governments. Throughout history, Christians have taken various positions on the right of government to bear arms, for example, to use force to punish evil at home as well as abroad. This issue is directly impacted by how one interprets the teachings of Christ.

Among Christians there have been two basic views regarding the use of force: the pacifist view and the just war view. The pacifist position teaches that it is unethical or immoral for government to resist evil. This view is based on Christ's words from the Sermon on the Mount, in which he exhorted his followers "not to resist evil" but "to turn the other cheek" (Matthew 5:38–39). This position would say that Christ rejects the law of *lex talionis* ("an eye for an eye, a tooth for a tooth") in the same verse and calls his followers to a higher ethic than that of the Old Testament. This view subjects Romans 13 (and all similar teachings in Scripture) on the use of force to the Sermon on the Mount (Matthew 5:9), as well as other passages similar to it (Matthew 26:52; Romans 12:17–21; Micah 4:3), and to the example of Jesus himself.

In general terms, the pacifist position holds that no Christian should participate in any form of military service; instead, all should be conscientious objectors. War, especially nuclear war, must be avoided at all costs and unilateral disarmament must be governmental policy. Nonresistance and nonviolence should be both personal and state policy. The same ethical standards should govern the church and the state.

However, this general pacifistic view is often nuanced. Some within the pacifist position hold that the government may exercise necessary force, but not the Christian. This historic pacifism bases its view upon a strong separation of church and state, which claims that it is upholding the view that the Christian church maintained for the first three centuries.[1]

More recently, radical pacifism has gained ground. It rejects governmental use of force and seeks to legislate pacifism as national policy.

---

1. Daly, *Military*, 1, 12–15, 29, 66. See also Swift, *Early Fathers*. Culver, *Peace Mongers*, identifies the early church as nonresistant, not pacifistic, and shows why they may have been wrong. Also helpful is Clouse, *War*. Each of the positions of nonresistance, pacifism, just war, and preventive war is explained by a proponent of the view. Herman Hoyt, defending nonresistance, strongly distances himself from pacifism (44–49).

The Purpose of Government

It would make nonviolence the position of the individual Christian, the corporate church, and the state. However, it would allow certain forms of resistance—nonviolent resistance, such as that practiced by Martin Luther King and Mahatma Gandhi—in order to change governmental policy.

As I mentioned before, the other major position regarding the use of force is commonly referred to as the just war position. It basically asserts that the exercise of force by the government is appropriate *when qualified by certain conditions.*

Today, within this broad approach there are at least four variations.[2] First, the nonresistance position supports the right of government to exercise force and allows Christians to support government, but it doesn't allow Christians to take the life of another human being. Therefore, Christians shouldn't participate in combat, but they may be involved in other forms of military service.

Second, the nuclear pacifist position holds common views with the just war position, but it draws the line at supporting a government's use of nuclear weapons to exercise force. This view generally supports conventional weaponry, but rejects the indiscriminate warfare that nuclear weaponry brings because it results in killing the innocent and the wicked alike. This view seems to come closest to the historic pacifist view. Today there are several kinds of weapons of mass destruction (WMDs). They are not only nuclear but also biological and chemical. Those who espouse the nuclear pacifist view are likely to embrace the same position regarding these other kinds of WMDs.

Third, the preventive war view, also known as the crusade, supports the government's right to exercise force and the Christian's involvement in combat service. This position allows government to use nuclear weapons, and, if necessary, to use them first to prevent use of nuclear weapons by others bent on aggression. It points to Israel in the Old Testament (and perhaps to the Crusades) as precedent for this view. The recent acquisition of nuclear and other WMDs by North Korea, Iran, Iraq, India, Pakistan, Israel, and others in the NATO alliance makes this view especially crucial and relevant.

And fourth, the traditional just war position does not go quite as far as the preventive war position. It allows the government to exercise force,

---

2. See Payne and Payne, *Just Defense*, 39ff.

even in the form of nuclear weapons, as long as such force meets certain guidelines or standards that make the use of force morally justifiable.

These guidelines have been presented in a new defense of the just use of nuclear weapons.[3] They include a just cause (defense), a just intent (to restore peace and protection for the innocent), a last resort (after all else has failed), a formal declaration of war by an authorized body, limited objectives (not total destruction), proportionate means (not unlimited warfare), noncombatant immunity (civilians discriminated from combatants), and a reasonable hope of success.

The guidelines for the just war position have evolved over the course of 2,300 years, yet there are seeds for them as early as 1500 B.C., as found in the Old Testament and among the Greeks and Romans. The writings of Augustine and Ambrose in the fourth century A.D. have made this the predominate view among both Catholics and Protestants for the last 1,500 years.

The rise of nuclear weapons has led many to reject the just war position. Others, however, have argued that limited use of nuclear weapons can be a legitimate use of force by a government, and an equally valuable means of deterrence.[4] Of course, only the United States has ever used nuclear weapons in combat. In 1945, the two bombs used on Hiroshima and Nagasaki in Japan brought the end of WW2 in the Pacific, saving far more lives than were destroyed in the bombing itself. It is estimated that an additional one million American lives may have been lost had these weapons not been used. From another perspective, the fire bombing of German cities and of Tokyo killed far more civilians than did the nuclear bombs dropped on Japan.

Capital punishment is another form of the exercise of force on the part of government. Do the words of Christ in the Sermon on the Mount abolish this form of punishment? Is it abolished if it is not carried out according to the patterns of the Mosaic Code? Is there a basis for it in Romans 13?

The issues of war and peace and capital punishment are complex, as the previous discussion shows. They are also urgent concerns for many nations where civil strife is rampant and where Christians are persecuted or caught between opposing forces, such as in Nigeria, Sudan, the

---

3. Payne and Payne, *Just Defense*, 42–43.

4. In addition to Payne and Payne cited above, see Swartzwalder, "Nuclear War," who holds to this view.

Philippines, India, Central America, and some of the former communist bloc of nations. In addition, the deliberate killing of about 3,000 American civilians on September 11, 2001, makes the criteria of just war especially relevant to Americans.

Romans 13:3-7 will shed much light on a government's use of force and the purpose for using such force. Let's take a closer look at this passage.

ROMANS 13:3—GOVERNMENT SHOULD PUNISH EVIL

Verse 3 of Romans 13 gives an additional reason for submission to government, in addition to the fact that God has ordained or established government as presented in Romans 13:1b. Paul now writes that Christians should submit themselves to government because rulers are a threat or terror or cause of fear to those who do evil, not to those who do good. This is probably the fear that is felt when a wrong has been done. It's the fear of the penalty rather than the fear itself that prevents wrongdoing, although both may be present.[5] Penal judgment has divine ordination—that means this: Not only is civil government ordained by God, but so is its power to cause terror in the evil person.

Paul writes in general terms and about general principles, as his use of the plural word "rulers" shows.[6] As I stated in chapter 4, Paul is not endorsing any particular state or any particular form of government, or the special conditions connected with it. He *is* arguing for the ideal of government and order. Generally it is true that governments exist for a beneficial end, meaning that they punish only evildoers.

Because government is generally on the side of good, Paul was able to find protection in Roman law, as the accounts of Paul's life in the Book of Acts show. Stifler believes that it is the so-called church rather than the state that has been the worst persecutor of men.[7]

---

5. Murray, *Romans*, 2: 150-151. The *gar* of verse 3 may introduce a reason for the immediately preceding statement that judgment will fall upon rebels, rather than giving another reason for the submission exhorted in verse 1.

6. So Sanday and Headlam, *Romans*, 369. Cranfield, *Romans*, 2: 664-665, believes that the promise of verse 3 is absolute. Rulers punish evil and reward good according to God's standard, whether they are conscious of this or not, or at least it will always turn out this way in the end.

7. Stifler, *Romans*, 216.

Paul says that those who do good have no need to fear authority. Indeed, this behavior will produce a positive reaction: praise and approval from the authority. In 1 Timothy 2:1, this behavior is characterized as leading a quiet and peaceable life in all godliness and dignity; we take a closer look at this in chapter 6.

This verse does not mean that government rewards the doing of good with the same fervor as it rewards the doing of evil. Doing evil brings a harsh reward, while doing good usually brings nothing but a smile, a passive acceptance, without formal acknowledgment from the governing authorities.

If the situation ever does occur where Christians suffer "because of righteousness," they are to consider themselves blessed. It's better to suffer for doing good rather than for doing evil (as 1 Peter 3:14, 17 affirms). Christians are not to compromise the good in order to escape persecution. The end does not justify the means. The persecution of the apostles in the early church, as revealed in the Book of Acts, illustrates this truth well. We'll explore this further a little later.

ROMANS 13:4—GOVERNMENT SHOULD PROMOTE GOOD

Verse 4 explains Romans 13:3. Christians need not fear authority when they do good, for God provides the ruler for the advantage of his people, "for a good end" or "to promote good."[8] The authority is "God's minister" for good to the Christian ("to you"). This again finds support in 1 Timothy 2:1–2, where Paul exhorts prayer for rulers so that they would promote a quiet, peaceful, godly, and dignified life. "The good the magistrate promotes is that which subserves the interests of piety."[9]

Romans 13:4 reveals the positive purpose of government—the well-being of society—while verse 3 gave the negative purpose. It would seem that any ruler promoting the opposite (revolution, chaos, aggressive war, national riot, unlimited immorality) is not a servant of God, but a servant of Satan.

---

8. Sanday and Headlam, *Romans*, 367.

9. Murray, *Romans*, 2: 152. It is what is morally good, good according to God's will (Cranfield, *Romans*, 2: 664, fn. 5), and that which promotes salvation (666).

The Purpose of Government

The antagonistic demonic forces behind Persia and Greece, as described in Daniel 10, exemplify what may lie behind the embodiment of evil. In the Greek king Antiochus IV (Epiphanies), we see a model of the antichrist (Daniel 8 and 11). He was determined to destroy the faithful Jews in any manner conceivable, including the outlawing of Judaism. In reaction to these laws, pious Jews sparked the Maccabean revolt, which restored a government that promoted godliness and dignity again. But in the end times, we can expect such evil again to be embodied in the government of the antichrist (Revelation 13:17). At that time, Satan (the red dragon) will be the one who inspires and empowers the human leader, so much so that it will hardly be possible to distinguish between the two (as shown in the book of Revelation, chapters 12–17).

Paul then expands on the negative purpose of the state—what it means for it to punish evil. The state, he says, is an avenger to execute or exhibit wrath, namely God's wrath, to those doing evil. As an "avenger," the state accomplishes the "vengeance" that God exercises on behalf of those who are persecuted (12:19). Vengeance is administered by the state as God's agent or minister of wrath and anger.

The two-fold use of "God's servant" or "minister" shows that both of these functions of the state are derived from God. These words have serious implications. Both the promotion of good and the check of evil belong to the purpose of government and come from God. There are both civil and religious aspects to both functions.

The word for "servant" is *diakonos* and has two different meanings in the New Testament. Usually it has the general idea of "servant," "attendant," or "minister," as we see in Romans 13:4. It's used in reference to the apostles (Matthew 20:26), servants to a king (Matthew 22:13), and servants of a household (John 2:5). It's also used of Paul and Apollos in 1 Corinthians 3:5, Christ in Galatians 2:17, and Tychicus in Ephesians 6:21. Paul designated himself a "servant of God" in 2 Corinthians 6:4, just as government is designated here. "Ministers of Christ" include Paul (2 Corinthians 11:23), Epaphras (Colossians 1:7), and Timothy (1 Timothy 4:6).

The technical usage of *diakonos* is for a church officer, or a deacon (Philippians 1:1; 1 Timothy 3:8, 12; Romans 16:1). While other terms of servitude (such as "bondman" or "attendant") imply relation to a person, *diakonos* relates the servant to his work. This distinctive is appropriate in Romans 13:4, where governmental rulers are servants because of both their positive and negative works.

The mention of the "sword," which the ruler does not bear in vain, is symbolic of "the executive and criminal jurisdiction of a magistrate," and refers to government's inherent power to punish evil.[10] The punishment they administer is the reason people should fear doing evil. Lesser penalties are applied for lesser crimes, but such power culminates in capital punishment, which we see granted to government in Genesis 9 to take away human life. Here Paul expressly vindicates "the right of capital punishment as divinely entrusted to the magistrate."[11]

The sword is the ultimate expression of a government's determination to carry out justice, to punish evil. All lesser punishments point to capital punishment and find their basis in it.

The "sword" is not a meaningless, empty symbol; it should provoke terror or fear in one who does evil. It becomes meaningless or "in vain" only when it is not wielded. The sword is a deterrent to evil.

CAPITAL PUNISHMENT

For some to deny that the death penalty is meant here is to refuse the evidence of New Testament usage. Often the sword is associated with death as the instrument of execution (Matthew 26:52; Hebrews 11:34, 37; Revelation 13:10). The magistrate has in his "sword" not only a sign of his authority or right, but the power to wield it as God's agent.

Those who oppose capital punishment out of concern for the offender do so only by opposing God himself, for it is God's righteous wrath that is in view. They are attempting to be more godly than God himself! Indeed, the death penalty wielded by government is an instrument of God's longsuffering. Through this partial demonstration of God's wrath, evil is restrained and the final judgment is deferred (2 Thessalonians 2:6ff.).[12] If the state refuses to exercise capital punishment, as do most of the nations of Western Europe today, evil increases and the judgment for it becomes more severe and terrible. By punishing evil, the state defers an even more severe judgment from God.

10. Sanday and Headlam, *Romans*, 367ff. The present tense of the Greek *phorein* points to the continued habit and is more expressive than the verb *pherein*.

11. Gifford, *Romans*, 212. Cranfield (*Romans*, 2: 667), who would not go quite so far, believes it is probably a general reference to military power. Yet this included the power of capital punishment. See also Sherwin-White, *Roman Society*, 8–11.

12. Barrett, *Romans*, 247.

ROMANS 13:5—MOTIVATED BY CONSCIENCE

Verse 5 is an inference made from the preceding verse, if not the whole passage. Christians should obey the state's rulers, not only because of wrath or fear of the sword, but also because of conscience (Romans 2:15, 9:1). It's morally right to submit to the state, whether or not it's expedient. This is so because Christians know that the state has a divine order and purpose as God's servant or minister.

The meaning of "conscience" is conscience toward God. It's a sense of obligation to God (consider 1 Peter 2:13, "for the Lord's sake"). This is an ethical demand (1 Corinthians 9:16) for subjection.[13] It's a moral necessity. It's morally right or just to submit. Implicitly, this compulsion by conscience invites Christians to stand for what is morally right. They have in these words the basis for their opposition to abortion, pornography, assisted suicide, homosexual behavior, and many other moral afflictions in society.

The fear of punishment has its proper place in public morality—it's a deterrent. But it's also a secondary motivation. The chief reason is the command of conscience.[14] It's crucial to remember this primary motivation in the debate over the death penalty. While arguments usually hinge on whether the death penalty is a deterrent, such a debate misses the primary motivation.

ROMANS 13:6—PAYING TAXES

Verse 6 confirms Romans 13:5. It's for this reason, because of conscience, that Christians pay taxes. Paying taxes recognizes the moral duty of submission to rulers. Because God has ordained government (that is, because it has divine sanction), taxes are therefore necessary to support it, so the payment of taxes is not a tyrannical imposition. Just as the preacher (a servant of God) receives just recompense for his labors on behalf of others (1 Corinthians 9), so does the state, when serving as God's servant.

The latter part of Romans 13:6 gives the reason for the payment of taxes: Rulers are the "servants of God, devoting themselves to this very thing." Here Paul uses a different term for "servant" (*leitourgos*) than that

---

13. Murray, *Romans*, 2: 154. A double moral necessity is indicated by the terms *anangke* and *suneidesin* ("it is necessary," "conscience"), according to Liddon, *Romans*, 249.

14. Shedd, *Doctrinal Commentary*, 378ff.

of verse 4 (*diakonos*). This term and its cognate word (*leitourgia*) may be used of secular servants (1 Kings 10:5 and Ecclesiastes 10:2). However, in the New Testament, the terms always refer to service for God and even ministry in the worship of God (Luke 1:23; Romans 15:16; 2 Corinthians 9:12; Philippians 2:17, 25, 30; Hebrews 1:7, 14; 8:2, 6; 9:21; 10:11). Thus the tax collector, generally unappreciated, is engaged in a dignified kind of ministry. Although we don't like to pay taxes, there is a divinely ordered place for them in this world.

For Paul, the Roman rulers were public servants of God, not of Rome, whether or not they realized it. Paul writes that they should persevere faithfully and devote themselves to their function, as ordained by God. They have a sacred obligation. They give "full time" to this governing. The words "this very thing," as the thing to which they are to be devoted, refers either to the exacting of taxes or the general carrying out of the purposes of government expressed in the previous verses. In either case, the idea in "devote oneself to" emphasizes this role of the state. It's not a secondary or optional purpose, and it's not to be neglected. Whether government promotes public works, provides for the homeless and the suffering, or does other works, it cannot neglect "law and order," or fail to provide the resources for this primary function.

Romans 13:6 has implications for the purposes for which taxes are collected; they're to be used for the purposes of government as described in Romans 13, not for abuses.[15] This is Paul's subtle reminder to the Rome of his day that there is another Ruler to whom account will be given.

ROMANS 13:7—OTHER OBLIGATIONS TO GOVERNMENT

Paul continues the discussion regarding obligations to government in verse 7, when he enunciates the kind of debts owed to government—he's not embarking on a new subject. The debt tax payers owe to the government embraces a broad spectrum. It's not only monetary, but it's also concerned with veneration and honor.

First, the debts are identified as taxes and custom (or revenue). "Taxes" relates to what is levied on persons and property in a nation (Luke 20:22; 23:2). The term "revenue" or "custom" refers to taxes levied

---

15. Murray, *Romans*, 2: 155. The term "devote themselves to" could refer to the immediately preceding "servants of God," understood verbally.

on goods and are similar to our customs or dues paid to support the government (Matthew 17:25). Here we could place sales taxes and import taxes, etc. While the former "taxes" are direct taxes, the latter ("revenue" or "custom") are indirect taxes.

Then Paul identifies the debts of respect and honor. The term "respect" can be rendered "fear" and is the same word as Paul used in Romans 13:3, where it's often translated "terror." In Romans 13:3, Paul meant fear of the punishment to be inflicted, but here he's talking about respectful awe or veneration. In other places in Scripture, the word refers to reverential fear of God (Acts 9:31; Romans 3:18; 1 Peter 2:17) and to the respect due to human authorities because of their office (Ephesians 6:5 and 1 Peter 2:18).

In this context, "fear" probably concerns respect for those of the highest rank of authority, who bear the sword of God. The "honor" mentioned is that paid to those of lower rank, the subordinates of the first group. Both terms emphasize that obligation to government consists not only of subjection to rulers but also of veneration or respect due to them as servants of God.[16]

It's interesting to note that Tacitus (*Annals*, xiii. 50) indicates that, in Paul's day, the extortion of the Publicans had become intolerable. A few months after the penning of this Epistle to the Romans, Nero proposed to the Senate stringent and sweeping reforms.[17]

IMPLICATIONS FROM THIS PASSAGE

In summary, it's possible to make several significant observations from this passage. First, government exists to *punish* evil-doers, to provide for public safety. This is the first function that Paul gives (Romans 13:3). Today, in our permissive Western culture, there is a great need to apply this so that those who break the law are properly punished. Also, citizens must be willing to bear the price of prisons, attorneys, and other costs associated with the criminal justice system.

---

16. Murray, *Romans*, 2: 157. Although "fear" is reserved for God in 1 Peter 2:17, here Paul uses it of men. However, it is possible that even here it refers to God (see discussion in Cranfield, *Romans*, 2: 670–673).

17. Cited in Gifford, *Romans*, 213.

The current age of terrorism poses new challenges to preserving law and order. Discovering, ferreting out, and capturing those who would destroy innocent civilians raises new challenges of how to punish evil or those who plot evil. To what extent those who plot terror should be punished, in comparison to those who carry out terrorism, is a serious concern.

Second, rulers are to punish evil *deeds* or behaviors that violate the order of society (Romans 13:3). They do not concern themselves with beliefs or thoughts *per se*. The application for today is significant in many areas.

For example, in the area of gay rights and society, law and punishment can and should address homosexuality, but punishment can be meted out only when a deed is done, not for thinking "gay." This reflects Paul's terms in the lists of vices (1 Corinthians 6:9–11 and 1 Timothy 1:8–10), for most (if not all) people are characterized there as having committed evil acts. Just which immoral acts should be punished I'll discuss later.

What about those who conspire or plot evil, such as acts of terrorism or anarchy? Should the state arrest and detain those who plot evil as well as those who carry it out? On the basis of this text, it seems that merely thinking terrorism is not punishable, but actually conspiring—making plans—to commit terror or revolution comes under the control of this text.

The third purpose of government is to promote the doing of good. Of course, good and evil need to be defined, but basically they must correspond to revelation—what God has revealed in both general and special revelation as good or evil (to be discussed in chapter 8), and what he has revealed universally to the consciences of all. This is precisely where the Judeo-Christian ethic must be applied. Without a moral standard, government or society cannot survive. Without a Judeo-Christian moral standard or Natural Moral Law, the government will be neither biblical nor good.

Fourth, every form of government has some merit, if nothing other than the ordering of society for good ends. Until they become the purveyors of evil themselves, even totalitarian governments have this justification: They punish evil deeds (stealing, murder, etc.).

In the early church of the second century, Tertullian reflected on Christian submission to Roman emperors. He wrote that the experience of Christians showed that the only persecutors of Christians were bad

The Purpose of Government

emperors (such as Nero and Domitian), whom even the Romans judged as impious, shameful men to be branded with infamy.[18]

Christians served in the Roman army and made a significant impact there. Prayers were made for emperors and the good estate of the interests of the Empire. Tertullian even wrote that Christians viewed Roman rulers in a special way. He said that Christians "in the emperors look up to the judgment of God, who has set them over the nations."[19]

The first edict of toleration for Christians was issued by Galerius from his deathbed in A.D. 311. In it, Christians, he said, were allowed to "exist again," and were "bound to pray their god for our good estate and that of the commonwealth." They were to pray that they might be able to live securely in their own homes.[20]

This attitude of Christians was commonplace, if not universal, in the Roman Empire. Similar references are found in Clement (*1 Clement* 60. 4; 61), Polycarp (*To the Philippians*, 12. 3), Justin Martyr (*Apology* 1. 17), Theophilus (1.11), Athenagoras, and others.

Fifth, it seems to be a legitimate extension of Paul's teaching to insist that government, in seeking to promote the good and punish the evil, has an obligation to protect defenseless classes in a society. In fulfilling its divine design, a government must not allow the oppression of the poor, the widow, and the orphan. Oppression of such deprived classes is a frequent topic of condemnation in the Old Testament prophets.

Sixth, from Romans 13:1–7 it is also pertinent to draw inferences regarding a universal standard of morality and natural law. If government should promote the good and punish the evil, it is fair to conclude that God has revealed truth to provide a standard of morality that is universally applicable. Promoting the good and punishing the evil, as the universal purpose of government, demands an ethical standard and a supernatural religion divinely revealed. These inferences will clearly unfold in the following chapters of this book.

Finally, if government is designed to promote good and punish evil, then it can expect the support of the church. In turn, the church should receive the support of the government, not its animosity or gruff toleration. This is the basis for the support from government that churches enjoy in

18. From Tertullian, *Apology*, 5, in Gwatkin, *Selections*, 111.

19. Ibid., 115.

20. From Lactantius, born c. 260, in his *de Mortibus Persecutorum*, 34, in Gwatkin, *Selections*, 171.

America. These benefits may take various forms, including the exemption from taxation, deductions in taxes allowed to people for contributions to churches and charities, the paying of chaplains for the armed services, housing allowances to pastors, and more.

This passage also supports the idea that government should give support to all churches and religious groups on a non-preferential basis. Government should not be an antagonist to religion, as in promoting a totally secular state and a strict separation of church and state. This support was the original intent of the First Amendment of the U.S. Constitution. The American Civil Liberties Union, Americans United for the Separation of Church and State, and secular humanists have sought to destroy this idea.

In conclusion, it is clear that Romans 13:1–7 establishes two broad principles: (1) Christians should submit to government as ordained by God; and (2) government should promote good and punish evil. The use of force fulfills God's design for government.

Yet how far can government go in using force to punish evil? Government exercises capital punishment to restrain greater evil, continuing the institution of this penalty originally given in the universal Noahic Covenant (Genesis 9) and repeated in the Mosaic Code to Israel. The various forms that a government may use to administer this punishment (beheading, hanging, electric chair, lethal injection, etc.) matter little, so long as the forms are enacted justly and respect human dignity. Government must promote the good by the very forms of punishment it employs. Government should not use abusive, cruel forms of punishment (such as torture, crucifixion, burning at the stake, etc.).

WHAT ABOUT WAR?

The ramifications for participation in war are several. It seems that the just war view, and even the preventive war view, find support in this passage. Such warfare is part of the government's role in punishing evil. It seeks to defend its citizens from aggression, both from within (revolution) and from without.

How do we know that Romans 13:1–7 should not be controlled by the teaching of the Sermon on the Mount, as pacifism teaches? That is, why shouldn't the command, "Resist not evil," also apply collectively to the state, as well as individually?

The Purpose of Government

The answer is quite clear and arises within the context of Romans 13 itself. Romans 12:9-21 is Paul's parallel to the teaching of Christ in the Sermon on the Mount, but not Romans 13:1-7. The other passages concern personal Christian reaction when provoked, whereas Romans 13:1-7 describes civil government's reaction when threatened.

The subjects are quite different. In the Sermon on the Mount, Christ was not dealing with governmental responsibility. It's clear that Paul moves from the personal responsibility of Christians to live out love (Romans 12:9-21) to the government's responsibility to do justice (not love, 13:1-7). Then Paul returns to the personal ethic of love again (13:8-10). While I may not resist someone who strikes and robs me, the ethic of love for my neighbor leads me to call upon the state to keep such a person from harming another.

In summary, governments do not love; individual people do. We may attempt to love through government, but government has another calling as well. Government serves as God's avenger (Romans 12:19; 13:4), while individuals do not. It's an incorrect interpretation of pacifism to apply the personal ethic of love to civil governments.

It's also clear from Scripture that believers in the true God may participate in civil government. During the period of the Old Testament, many godly people participated in pagan governments (for example, Daniel, Esther, and Nehemiah). In the New Testament, we see that those repentant and seeking the kingdom (Luke 3:14) participated in military service without condemnation. One of the earliest Christians is Cornelius, a Roman centurion. Not a word is said that involvement in civil government somehow contradicts the Christian witness (Acts 10-11).

Perhaps the strongest allowance for the use of the sword in personal self-defense occurs just before Jesus was betrayed. In an admittedly obscure passage, which may be metaphorical, Jesus encourages his followers to take up a sword for protection. If they don't possess a sword, he encourages them to sell their cloaks and buy one (Luke 22:35-38). This hardly allows anyone to present Jesus as one who taught pacifism.

It's also incorrect for pacifists to prohibit Christians from taking life in capital punishment or in combat. It is appropriate for government to take life in these cases, and it does so on behalf of all of its citizens. The person who actually takes the life (such as the warden or the soldier) does so as if the collective whole were doing it. No one is exempt. This point is what Genesis 9:6 ("whoever sheds the blood of a person, by *a person*

To Submit or to Rebel against the State

shall his blood be shed") and Romans 13:4 ("he is God's *servant* to do *you* good") are all about. Rather than being an evil-doer, in these instances the taking of life is doing good as God's agent.

Certainly the traditional just war view (and the preventive war view in certain circumstances) is in accord with the biblical teaching on government's role on Earth. When evil rises up, it's appropriate for government to exercise its power to stop it. Yet it must do so under certain restraints, such as those cited previously for just war.

REVISING JUST WAR TRADITION

In recent times, some have sought to revise just war tradition and argue for the "seamless garment" metaphor. Christians must oppose all forms of violence: abortion, euthanasia, war, and capital punishment. This position appears to be consistent, yet it fails to recognize the moral distinctions between quite different kinds of force. The last two forms of force are responses to violence originated by someone else; they are forms of retribution, and they are carried out by governmental authorities to prevent personal acts of reprisal.

Others today seek to make a hybrid of the just war tradition and pacifism, calling it "modern-war pacifism," "just war pacifism," or the "presumption against war" interpretation of the just war tradition.[21] Yet Pavlischek points out that just war tradition starts out with a presumption against injustice, not against war. The order of the criteria is crucial: Just cause, competent authority, and right intention come before reasonable hope of success, last resort, the goal of peace, and overall proportionality of good over harm. The first three are related to the political good of order, of justice, and of peace, and have priority over the last four. The latter developed later and serve as prudential criteria to consider in the waging of war. The concern for "last resort" is the fifth criterion, not the first. The "presumption against war" view inverts the order and renders both traditions "logically, morally, and theologically incoherent."[22] It is with duly constituted authority that Romans 13 begins.

The tradition inherited from Augustine, Aquinas, and Calvin "begins with the belief that in a fallen world, the use of coercion and force,

---

21. Pavlischek, "War," 37:29, discusses these variations.
22. Ibid., 37:32.

including the use of lethal force by legitimate public authority, is not only permitted but also morally required under certain circumstances."[23] Not to use this force to protect the innocent is unjust and dishonors God.

COLLECTIVE RESPONSIBILITY

An important point needs to be made here. In every act that a state takes to punish evil, whether to incarcerate criminals or to wage a just war, it does so in the name of all of the people of the state. The state wages war on behalf of all, and all are equally responsible. It's a betrayal for civilians to distinguish themselves from the military, to consider themselves uninvolved, while enjoying the benefits of relative peace and freedom that soldiers secure and die for. Near the end of WW2, one soldier commented that if we, the United States, should refuse again to get involved and allow such inhumanity as Hitler unleashed on Europe by killing some eight million Jews and millions of others, then we don't deserve freedom and peace. While there are many advantages to a volunteer military, the great disadvantage is that it tends to insulate much of the population from the cost and heartache of war, when all should be paying their part of the cost. During WW2, half of the American people bought bonds, and all restricted their use of special commodities, such as rubber, fuel, and automobiles. This pattern has a lesson to teach succeeding generations.

The corporate responsibility that all share in the struggle for freedom can have a good effect. It helps to ensure better conformity to the principles of just war. At the beginning of WW2, there was general agreement that civilians should not be killed in the conflict. By the end of the war, such concerns were largely forgotten, and 55 million people died, about two-thirds of them civilians. In Europe alone, 650,000 civilians (mostly women and children) were killed by Allied bombing of Germany. There is another sober statistic: In taking Okinawa in the Pacific, U.S. troops killed 70,000 out of 97,000 Japanese soldiers, but 100,000 civilians died, many from suicide. Corporate responsibility gives everyone a stake in preserving the integrity of just war principles.

---

23. Pavlischek, "War," 37:32.

WHAT ABOUT WAR AGAINST TERRORISM?

Some would argue that the just war approach does not concern terrorism. A state may not be directly involved. Instead, terrorists who are spread throughout several states originate the conflict. Therefore, it is concluded, just war criteria do not apply. This is a popular claim.

Actually, the criteria are especially appropriate. Terrorism is no less a cause for exercising just war criteria. Terrorism is evil in its very nature, evil in and of itself. It attacks the foundations of the political community. As Pavlischek writes: "Far from being irrelevant to the war on terrorism, the classic just war tradition developed in large measure precisely to confront and contain the sort of private violence or private war currently practiced by terrorist organizations of all sorts."[24] Warfare is a public issue in order to have civilization. Terrorism is an assault on civilization.

CONCLUDING CONCERNS

How does one define the good and the evil that government should promote and punish respectively? Does it make a difference if the good or the evil as determined by civil government violates the good or the evil as determined by Scripture? What does the Christian do in such a circumstance? Does the Christian submit to government then? Is there any limit to a Christian's allegiance to the state? The next chapter endeavors to answer these questions.

Even Paul's instruction about paying taxes is not clear. We have to consider Jesus' words on this matter. On one occasion, Jesus told Peter that "sons" are free from paying taxes since kings collect taxes from others, not from their own sons. Yet, in order to avoid offense, he instructed Peter to find the means in a miraculous way to pay the taxes anyway (Matthew 17:24–27).

What does it mean to be free from governmental compulsion? How far does this freedom go? What is its restriction? Should Christians pay taxes to fund evil practices? I deal with these questions in the last chapter.

But let's not forget Polycarp as we continue our discussion. After Polycarp's inciting response to the interrogation, the Pro-Consul had his herald proclaim three times: "Polycarp has confessed that he is a

---

24. Pavlischek, "War," 37:27.

Christian." Hearing this, the crowd cried out in anger, "This is the teacher of Asia, the father of the Christians, the destroyer of our gods, who teaches multitudes neither to offer sacrifices nor to worship." Learning that it was legally impossible to deliver Polycarp to the lions, the crowd cried that he should be burned alive. As the flames rose around him, Polycarp prayed:

> O Lord God Almighty, Father of your beloved and blessed Child, Jesus Christ . . . I bless you, that you have granted me this day and hour, that I may share, among the number of the martyrs, in the cup of your Christ, for the resurrection to everlasting life, both of soul and body in the immortality of the Holy Spirit. And may I, today, be received among them before you, as a rich and acceptable sacrifice, as you, the God who does not lie and is truth, have prepared beforehand, and shown forth, and fulfilled. For this reason I also praise you for all things. I bless you, I glorify you through the everlasting and heavenly high Priest, Jesus Christ, your beloved Child, through whom be glory to you with him and the Holy Spirit, both now and for the ages that are to come. Amen.

Some of those present at Polycarp's death later gave witness to the miraculous events that happened next. When the men in charge ignited the flames, they formed an insulating wall around him, so the executioner went forward and stabbed Polycarp with a dagger. Suddenly a dove came out of the dying Polycarp, along with so much blood that the flames were quenched!

The governor refused to hand over Polycarp's body to the Christians—instead, he committed it to the flames. Polycarp, the famous teacher and twelfth martyr of Smyrna, died as a noble example that many desired to imitate. The celebration of his martyrdom is February 22, the earliest recorded history of a martyrdom that Christians have.

6

The Limitation of the Authority of Government

WILLIAM TYNDALE, 1494-1536

"Why can't the King see the desperate need of his people?" William mused. "Why doesn't he deliver the British from the bondage of the Catholic Church?"

William Tyndale leaned back into the shadows on the Belgium wharf as he watched his precious "cargo" loaded onto the ship headed for England. By nightfall, his cohorts on the other side of the Channel would have received his New Testaments hidden in the cargo of hay, straw, and other commodities. The sacred texts would soon be spread throughout the countryside.

The work of smuggling didn't appeal to him, but, if this was the only way he could get his English translations into his homeland, he would do it. No risk was too great to spread God's Word to his beloved English people. If the Catholic Church prohibited his work of translation in England, then he would do it elsewhere, and smuggle his translation of the Bible back across the Channel.

William's thoughts turned to his on-going work of translating the Old Testament from the Hebrew and Aramaic texts. It had been almost ten years since the completion of the New Testament—far too long for people to wait for the Old Testament. But the Old Testament was nearing completion. His collaborator, Miles Coverdale, had been a great help, even if he didn't know Hebrew. When the Old Testament was finally finished, he could smuggle it across the Channel into England.

What a day that would be—a complete Bible in English! His dream that an ordinary plowboy would be able to get and read the Bible in his own language would finally be realized. A plowboy would be able to know more of Scripture than many clergy did!

William reflected on his own youth. His parents had been devout Catholics. Every week they had attended mass in the small chapel. The priest regularly read from the Latin Vulgate, and gave a brief exhortation. But few understood Latin and it meant practically nothing to them. By the time he was 21 years old, Tyndale had earned a Master of Arts degree at Oxford. He then attended Cambridge to study Greek until 1522. That same year, he learned that Martin Luther had given the German people a Bible in their own language. News of the "reformation" spearheaded by Luther and Calvin brought new hope for a reformation in England.

It was time to stop reminiscing. William turned from his post by the dockside and retreated to his lodging for the night to get some much needed sleep. As he walked, he weighed the rumors that Catholic authorities had violated the law and were seeking him in the free territories. For years, his nemesis, Sir Thomas Moore, had bitterly attacked him and his work. If he was captured, what would become of his translation of the Old Testament?

It had been almost twenty years since Erasmus had produced the first printed Greek New Testament. William still recalled the wonder he felt when he first held a copy of this text in his hands. From that moment on, he dreamed that such a text would be the foundation for a printed English Bible. More than one hundred years before, Wycliffe had done a hand-written English translation, and it had impacted the people greatly. Yet his work was too dependent on the Catholic Church's Vulgate. Because Wycliffe's work had come before the invention of the printing press, its reproduction had been hindered. "What a miracle printing is," William thought to himself. Now his dream of smuggling thousands of copies of his New Testament into England could finally be realized. Surely the printing press was a gift from God to his church!

William Tyndale had suffered the consequences of a person in exile: He was hounded by Catholic authorities on the Continent and was deprived of contact with his family. He never knew where he would spend

To Submit or to Rebel against the State

the next night and he was never sure of where his next meal would come from. Such were the discomforts of a smuggler. He was a law-breaker but he felt that the laws banning English translations of the Bible could be violated to serve the kingdom of God. As a Christian, William Tyndale was committed to obeying God when human authority conflicted with God's will.

As he entered his lodging for the evening, he was immediately seized by armed men in league with the Catholic king of Spain, Charles V. Before long, William found himself bound and dragged to a holding cell. The next day he was smuggled out of the free territories and imprisoned in the town of Vilvorde. William wondered what the Catholic Church had in mind for him. Would it be years in prison? Would it involve a lot of suffering, even torture? Would it be worse than even that? Would God intervene to deliver him so that he might finish his translation of the Old Testament?

Principle 3
Allegiance to Government Is Not Absolute

> "Tell us then, what is your opinion? Is it right to pay taxes to Caesar or not?" But Jesus, knowing their evil intent, said, "You hypocrites, why are you trying to trap me? Show me the coin used for paying the tax." They brought him a denarius, and he asked them, "Whose portrait is this? And whose inscription?" "Caesar's," they replied. Then he said to them, "Give to Caesar what is Caesar's, and to God what is God's." —*Matthew 22:17–21*
>
> "We must obey God rather than men!" —*Peter and the Apostles, Acts 5:29*

INTRODUCTION

The previous two chapters have demonstrated two principles from Romans 13:1–7. First, that Christians should submit to government as established by God, and, second, that the purpose of government is to promote good and punish evil. There's a third principle to consider now, one that qualifies allegiance to government: Allegiance to government is neither absolute nor total.

This principle has far reaching application. It will aid us in answering many questions such as:

- Is smuggling Bibles into a closed country justified?
- Should the state be able to impose a state certified curriculum or state certification of teachers on Christian day schools?
- Should Christians pay taxes when such money is used to fund abortion?
- Is prayer or Bible reading in public schools justified?
- Should land-use planning or zoning laws be used to exclude churches, Bible studies, or Christian day schools?
- Should churches pay property taxes?
- Must Christian schools pay unemployment taxes, and should churches pay social security?

To Submit or to Rebel against the State

- Can a church fire its janitor for not believing the same doctrine as the church?
- Should a state provide funding for a tax voucher system that would allow public monies to pay for education in both public and parochial schools?

While virtually all of these questions reflect past or present cases of litigation before the courts in the United States, they are questions of universal significance. They all concern the extent of allegiance to government.

From a larger perspective, many Christians in the third world are struggling against a hostile form of government, whether in Islamic, Hindu, or communist nations. Should Christians submit to the existing form of government and its laws, and perhaps suffer persecution? Or should they work to change the government? To what extent should Christians participate in revolution, if at all? This chapter offers guidance in answering all of these questions.

Government has an important role to play and people should give allegiance to it, including paying the taxes they owe. However, government is only one of several spheres demanding allegiance. Others include the family, the job, and the church, but the most important sphere is the spiritual. People are to give allegiance to God first and foremost. Our Lord's words in Matthew 22:15–22, summarized by the words of verse 21b, are primary: "Give to Caesar what is Caesar's, and to God what is God's."

The Christian is a citizen of two realms. The spheres of accountability often overlap and pose competing demands for allegiance. For example, worship is to be given to God alone, not to an idol, whether it's in the form of the state or anything or anyone else. The Old Testament clearly commands this supreme allegiance (Exodus 20:3): No idols are permitted (20:4–6). In fact, Israel was carried captive into Babylonian exile for her idolatry. Likewise, in the New Testament, idolatry (identified as immorality, uncleanness, and covetousness) is still a sin against God (Romans 1:18–25; Ephesians 5:3–5; Colossians 3:5; 1 John 5:21).

The difficulty comes in the areas where the spheres overlap and both government and God assert a demand on allegiance. For example, in striving to keep the peace and prevent disunion, should the government prevent or restrict the open and free dissemination of the gospel when it provokes opposition or violent response (as in Muslim or Hindu countries)?

PAUL'S RESISTANCE TO CIVIL GOVERNMENT

This situation arose in the history of the early church. The book of Acts shows numerous instances where the two realms conflicted. The ruling authorities of the Jews, called the Council or Sanhedrin (Acts 4:15), attempted to prohibit the apostles from freely proclaiming the gospel and working miraculous healings (4:1–31). The apostles saw this as an unjustified intrusion of the civil and religious authority into God's sphere of allegiance. Thus, they stated their intention to disregard the prohibition (4:19–20). On this occasion, even the Council acknowledged that they had no basis for punishing them (Acts 4:21). However, this did not prevent the Council from threatening the apostles, which also constituted a further abuse of civil authority. The apostles chose to obey God rather than the authorities.

Later in Acts, Paul was threatened with death by an angry Jewish mob (21:27–40), but was delivered by Roman soldiers. Their commander, a soldier in control of 1,000 troops, sought to have Paul "examined by scourging so that he might find out the reason why they were shouting against him that way" (22:24). Evidently, the commander refused to believe Paul's assertion that it was a case of religious persecution involving a supposed infraction of Jewish religious rules (21:28–29).

Paul knew that this civil authority had no right to punish him without the fair trial that was due any Roman citizen. Therefore, he claimed his civil right, as a Roman citizen, to a fair trial (22:25–30). When he could not receive this in Jerusalem, Paul was transferred to Caesarea where, again, a trial was heard. Again Paul stated the fact that neither civil authority nor religious authority had any basis for finding him guilty of any violation. Paul asserted that he had "a blameless conscience both before God and before people" (24:16). In addition, Paul pointed out that the rules for a fair trial were being violated, for his accusers were not present and no deed worthy of punishment could be cited (24:19–20).

However, Felix unjustly kept Paul in custody for two years. Then, when Festus succeeded Felix, Festus placated the Jews by keeping Paul bound rather than releasing him. When Festus gave Paul another trial, Paul again claimed his innocence before the religious (the Jews) and the civil (Caesar) authorities (Acts 25:8). When Festus tried to abort Paul's right to get a fair trial and a just decision by asking Paul to go to Jerusalem for still another trial (25:9), Paul protested. Since he still had not received justice at the hands of Roman rulers, Paul claimed his legal right to be

To Submit or to Rebel against the State

tried before Caesar himself (Acts 25:10–11). The text points out that even the Roman magistrates knew that he was innocent of any crime (26:31).

This account of Paul's conflict with civil and religious authorities demonstrates that Paul and the early apostles had a clear understanding of the role of government and the proper sphere it controlled. They refused to give to Caesar what belonged to God.

On at least twelve occasions in Acts (22:25, 27–28; 23:1–5, 17–21; 24:10–21, 26; 25:8–11, 21, 25–27; 26:1–2, 31–32; 28:18–19), Paul exercised (or appealed to) his rights as either a Jew or a Roman citizen. These rights covered a broad area. They included his right to have a fair trial before Jews or Romans, to have civil protection, to avoid torture, to be able to answer his accusers himself, to be able to face his accusers, to have the charges of culpability specified, to refuse to participate in bribery, and to appeal his case to the highest tribunal of Caesar.

Paul based his refusal to submit to either Jewish or Roman intimidation or coercion on his recognition that civil authorities were intruding into the sphere of allegiance owed to God alone. Even by a death of martyrdom, Paul and the other apostles testified that they rejected the claim of civil authorities to prohibit or unduly restrict the exercise of their allegiance to the one true God.

THE OCCASION FOR CIVIL DISOBEDIENCE

From these examples in Acts, it's clear that civil authority cannot claim absolute allegiance. On occasion, it may be necessary to rebel against civil authority to serve a higher allegiance. These examples make it clear that disobedience anchored in religious conviction often means civil disobedience.

When you first read Romans 13:1–7, it seems that Paul writes in absolutist terms, as he often does when specifically dealing with a topic, but he can't be understood this way here. The instances from the life of Paul as recorded in Acts reveal that Paul believed that government sometimes trespasses upon the authority of God by encouraging evil, or by hindering faith or worship of God—the very One by whom government possesses its authority. Thus Paul would certainly endorse the words of Peter in Acts 5:29 (see also Acts 4:19–20), that on such occasions one must obey God rather than human authorities.

This is confirmed by Paul's later defenses in Acts (about three or four years after he penned the book of Romans), that the crimes of which he

The Limitation of the Authority of Government

was accused concerned religious rather than civil matters. Therefore these matters were not in the jurisdiction of the state. Rather, the state should protect a citizen's liberty to argue these matters (see Acts 23:6; 24:20–21; 25:8–11, 18–21, 25–27; and 26:6–7, 31–32), lest one be put to death at the hands of the state for purely religious differences among people.

In light of these other passages, it isn't surprising that most commentators feel compelled to elaborate on the question of submission to government in their interpretation of Romans 13:1–7. For example, Murray points out the exceptions that arise to Paul's words when allegiance to God and government conflict. He shows that Paul omits at least two large concerns from his discussion: Paul doesn't give qualifications or reservations to one's duty of subjection, and he omits discussion of questions that arise in connection with revolution. With regard to the latter, Murray believes that Paul's words provide some direction when revolution has taken place (13:1 refers to *de facto* or existing government), and that there are principles which bear upon the right or wrong of revolution.[1]

But Paul also omits any indication of a preference for certain forms of government over others. Monarchies, totalitarian regimes, and tribal rule filled his world. He could hardly have anticipated the form of constitutional democratic republics such as the United States, inaugurated over two hundred years ago.

Another writer believes a Christian may teach and agitate for better government but may not lead in resistance or a rebellion (although Cromwell and Washington are cited as those who saw it differently).[2] Another believes that Paul argues only for government and order and doesn't actually oppose "revolution for a change of government"—he simply opposes "all lawlessness and disorder."[3] I'll address these possible options by the end of this chapter.

In Romans 13, Paul writes out of his cultural and historical context. Up to this point in his life, the Roman Empire had never been the persecutor of Christians. Rather, persecution came from the Jews or from unruly mobs. Nero had not yet become a persecutor of Christians, and, in Paul's experience, the Roman rulers had always been associated with order and restraint, as Acts shows.

---

1. Murray, *Romans*, 2: 149–150.
2. Stifler, *Romans*, 215.
3. Robertson, *Word Pictures*, 4: 407.

To Submit or to Rebel against the State

In contrast, the Jews living in Israel were often incited by zealots to oppose the Romans ruling them. This rule began under Herod the Great (39 B.C.) who had secured his kingship over the Jews from Rome. At the time of Jesus' death, Rome had imposed a more direct rule over Jerusalem and Judea by installing governors, such as Pontius Pilate. By the time of Paul's later ministry, Jewish revolts repeatedly broke out in Galilee in the north and in Judea in the south. Many zealots claimed to be messianic saviors who would deliver the Jews from Roman control. By the sixth and seventh decades, Rome was determined to forcibly end the Jewish insurrections. It is against this background of what was happening in Israel that Paul pens his epistle to the mostly Gentile believers in Rome. No doubt Paul did not want the gospel message confused with a hope of political liberation.

Later, when writing to Timothy in Ephesus (1 Timothy 2:1–2) and to Titus in Crete (Titus 3:1), Paul's principles are still the same, or at least unchanged. Paul's instructions also agree with Peter's words written during a time of persecution, as Peter's first epistle reveals (1 Peter 2:13–17; see chapter 10 of this book).

EVIL GOVERNMENT IS UNWORTHY OF ALLEGIANCE

The authority of government cannot be absolute. Paul's words are consistent with the division of authority referred to previously, where the state and church each have their area of accountability and neither is to transgress upon the other. Neither Jesus nor Paul subordinates the church to the state, or the state to the church. Yet at times of conflict between the two realms, allegiance to God is superior to allegiance to government.

Not only is it inconsistent with the total message of Scripture to maintain that Paul teaches an absolute submission to government, but government itself may not deserve allegiance. Sacred history and secular history combine to show that, at times, God has directly and deliberately intervened in particular societies to destroy them (Sodom, Gomorrah, the Philistines, the Midianites, etc.). This included the destruction of their rulers. The cause here was the enormity of the evil practiced by such societies. Indeed, the Flood in Genesis 6–8 was a similar destruction on a much greater scale. One trait of such an evil government is that the very idea of what constitutes government *no longer exists*. The depth of its evil is so great that it lacks credibility and justification to continue.

Scripture also attests to the evil forces behind governments, such as the empires of Persia and Greece, as can be read in Daniel 10. In this account, some unseen, evil forces ("the prince of Persia" and "the prince of Greece"), apparently associated with the governments, sought to hinder the heaven-sent messengers from bringing their message to Daniel.

In the end of this age, the kings of the earth and the government of the antichrist, as supported by Satan, will hold universal power. Then, appearing as the Warrior (Revelation 16–17 and 19), Christ will return, attack them, and destroy them. Psalm 2:1–6 pictures this confederate rebellion of rulers: They will become the objects of God's wrath.

A COMMUNIST STATE VIOLATES GOD'S DESIGN FOR GOVERNMENT

The very fact that communism has, as its stated goal, world domination and the conquest of more lands makes it a political system that comes under the judgment of God. Christians living in communist-dominated countries, as all others, must distinguish between the political system and the government as much as possible. Communism is a great evil on the earth, the very tool of Satan himself to foment war and revolution and to engage in state theft of property. It presents an abuse of the role of the state *vis-à-vis* the church that is unparalleled in the history of nations. Solzhenitsyn's diagnosis that Communism is "something new, unprecedented in world history" is correct. Because it is "destructive of every national entity,"[4] it is contrary to God's plan for the nations of Earth.

One must distinguish between the vast number of dominated people in such lands as China and North Korea who are not communists with those who are communists. It seems that some resistance to communism is certainly valid. Yet, in general, Christians must submit even to such a government when the alternative is total chaos. The difficulty comes when one must try to distinguish the government from the system.

---

4. Solzhenitsyn, "Communism," 48–49.

To Submit or to Rebel against the State

AN ISLAMIC STATE VIOLATES GOD'S DESIGN FOR GOVERNMENT

Today many Islamic nations are oppressive and hostile in their exercise of political power. Prior to 2011, statistics showed that of the forty-one nations that are predominantly Islamic (70%), twenty-six are not free, thirteen are partially free, and only two are free.[5] We can hope that this situation will change in the coming years. It's not uncommon for people who were once Muslim and have converted to Christianity to suffer persecution and even execution by the state under strict Islamic law, called *sharia*. Such states can hardly be regarded as promoting the good and punishing the evil.

It seems apparent, therefore, that the right or authority of a government to rule is not absolute. When a government becomes evil in character, in the sense of promoting the doing of evil and punishing the doing of good, then such a government may have surrendered its right to exist. It has lost its authority as a minister or servant of God.

Note that I didn't say that a government becomes evil by persecuting Christians. The issue is broader than that. It concerns Christians as Christian citizens of Earth and not Christians as Christians *per se*. Of course, attempts by the state to regulate Christians unduly or to prohibit Christian life or witness must be considered in the evaluation of whether a state is promoting good or evil.

OTHER EVIL GOVERNMENTS

Additional examples of governments promoting evil include the reign of Antiochus IV over Israel. This government was totally evil in its designs. The king sought to destroy not only the religion of the Jews, but their culture and way of life as well. In 167 B.C., the Jews, under the leadership of the Maccabees, rebelled against their Greek oppressors. The success of the Jews is still celebrated today as the Feast of Hanukkah. This rebellion seems to be justified.

Again, more recently, the goals of Adolf Hitler were so totally abhorrent, especially with regard to the Jews, that resistance and rebellion were justified. The attempt by Dietrich Bonhoffer and others to assassinate Hitler

---

5. Beverley, "Islam," 40.

The Limitation of the Authority of Government

illustrates how far justified resistance may go. Of course, other factors enter here as well, such as the concept of a just war that gave justification to the neighbors of Germany to defend themselves. The empirical designs of Germany and Japan brought international aspects to the situation, and threatened to destroy nationalism, which acts as a curb on international evil.

Recent history also brings to mind the tyranny in Uganda under Idi Amin, the "killing fields" of Cambodia under the Khmer Rouge (where two million or more were murdered), and the terrible genocide of Bosnia. The massacre of about half the population of Cambodia by the communists illustrates a government void of redeeming value. Libya (until recently), Sudan, Iran, and North Korea could also be listed here.

The Taliban's reign of terror and oppression in Afghanistan is another example of a government's illegitimate use of power. The promotion of Al Qaeda training camps to breed international terrorists makes the Taliban inherently evil in their purpose. It seems just that the United States and other nations brought about a regime change there.

War against the evil in Iraq has been engaged and been basically successful. The international community agreed that the regime of Saddam Hussein was illegitimate because of the treatment of its neighbors (including invasion and conquest, war, genocide, use of WMDs, etc.). A regime change seems justified here also.

There is often no clear line between a government promoting evil and one promoting good. Many factors are involved. There is also no clear line to indicate at what point during a revolution the new government has become the *de facto*, or existing legitimate authority, and the preceding one illegitimate. Here it seems that Christians may be of differing convictions and these must be respected. At the time of the American Revolution, Americans were almost evenly divided among revolutionaries, loyalists, and neutralists. This division probably reflects the Christian community as well.

Whether Christians may ever be among the leadership of a revolution is another, much more personal matter. There are various ways in which someone may be involved in a revolution. Some may actually hold office in the former government, some in the one of transition. It seems a bit naive to say (along with Stifler) that a Christian should always submit and that "God appoints governors for a good purpose, and when they fail to serve it he removes them by his means (Acts 12:23)."[6] This is obviously so, but the means could include personal involvement on the part of Christians. Chapter 10 deals more directly with this matter of involvement in revolution and anarchy.

JESUS AND THE SECULAR STATE

The key to interpreting Paul in Romans 13:1–7 is our Lord's statement in Matthew 22:21 about rendering to both God and Caesar their proper due. One must interpret the general principles of Romans 13 in light of Jesus' words about the state recorded in Matthew. No doubt Paul was aware of this teaching from Jesus. With this understanding, Paul works out the principles of a Christian view of government, including its divine ordination, its beneficial purpose, and its separate function *vis-à-vis* the church.

It's impossible to overstate the importance of Jesus' words for political theory. They are basic to everything regarding government, including ours today. Jesus' teaching lays the foundation for a secular government, a state that institutionally is neutral toward religion. Such a state is infused with religious conviction and gives freedom to religious belief.

This doesn't mean the total separation of church and state. While it appears to be a contradiction, a "religious secularity" in a state is the best assurance for freedom of religion. The state learns from general and special revelation and the history of nations that religion is essential to the state. Both spheres, the religious and the secular, must exist side-by-side and influence the other, but not control it.

Ignatius, the early Christian writer (d. 110), refers to Jesus' words about the images on the coins and interprets them symbolically as depicting two kinds of people in the world. He wrote: "Just as there are two coinages, the one of God, the other of the world, and each has its own stamp impressed on it, so the unbelievers bear the stamp of this world, and the believers in love, the stamp of God the Father through Jesus Christ."[7] The point is that Ignatius validates Jesus' distinction between the two realms, that both realms exist legitimately side-by-side.

---

6. Stifler, *Romans*, 218.

7. *Ignatius to the Magnesians*, 5.2 in Michael W. Holmes, ed., *The Apostolic Fathers* (Grand Rapids: Baker, 2002), 153. Used with slight alterations in the translation by the present author.

JESUS AND SECULAR LAW

Similarly, Jesus' words lie at the foundation of law-making. Until Jesus came, virtually all societies believed that all laws were fashioned by the gods. "Every law was a divine law," Vincent Munoz points out.[8] Philosophers believed that law had to have a divine source in order to bring compliance to the law. To violate law was to disobey the deity. The Old Testament has this same idea—that law comes from God alone. Yet the Jews were willing to improvise where Scripture was silent.

Some Greek philosophers such as Plato (see his *Laws*) questioned this equation of law with divine command. Yet they did not bring an end to this identification. Thus a citizen "was a man who had the religion of the city."[9] For the first time in history there comes an allowance for the existence of "secular" law that could exist side-by-side with divine law, and Jesus brings it about. Jesus' words distinguish piety from citizenship, allowing the state to formulate human law. Virtue is necessary, and both the philosophers and Jesus provided for this.

There are other implications of Jesus' words for the nature of the state.[10] Unlike Islam, Christianity based on the Gospels is nonpolitical. Love, not law, lies at the heart of Christianity. The gospels have no legal code for political governance. The attempts to link Christianity with political form and institution proved disastrous throughout the Middle Ages and in post-Reformation Europe. It has been disastrous to attempt this in more recent times.

THE UNIQUENESS OF THE AMERICAN EXPERIMENT FLOWS FROM JESUS CHRIST

Thus the founders of our Republic, learning from the failures of institutionalizing Christianity in Europe, continued the process begun by Christ. They both separated human law from divine law, and limited law in its purpose and scope of authority. Both of these ideas (separation and limitation) flow from Jesus' words. As the church should not seek to govern the state, so the state cannot legislate peoples' beliefs and opinions

---

8. Munoz, "Religious Liberty," 38:34.
9. Ibid., 42, n. 1.
10. Ibid., 35ff.

so as "to save" their souls. Law can only aim to secure liberty, including "man's natural right to religious liberty."[11] The state cannot curtail this or any other natural right.

Thus the American founders dedicated state craft to liberty, and the first freedom they sought to secure was religious freedom. The decision to limit the state regarding religion assured their decision to limit government in general.

The founders were either libertarian (Madison and Jefferson) or conservative (Washington and Adams), disputing not the ends the government should pursue but the means: whether or not government should endorse and encourage religion.[12] The libertarians felt that the state should be entirely neutral, not taking religion into view (being "religion blind"), yet respecting religion as an "unalienable" right. The conservatives believed that morality and virtue were necessary for political life, and that religion is the basis of morality. While religion is not the aim of public policy, it could be used "as a means to support legitimate public policies" in republican government.[13]

It is the conservative view that is most in line with biblical truth, especially Jesus' words in Matthew 22, and with the history of nations. Yet the founders agreed that the state should not establish religion nor religious truth as a "legitimate goal for American republicanism."[14]

JESUS BETTER THAN MUHAMMAD AND MARX

This is what sharply distinguishes Christianity from Islam. Where Christianity is predominant today, it generally allows total and equal freedom for all religions. It's convinced of the rightness of its view but it seeks to convince, not coerce. It has no fear of the truth.

Where Islam is predominant, it doesn't allow total and equal freedom for all religions. Indeed, Islam believes that Allah is most pleased where Islamic law, or *sharia*, prevails in a state. This law code virtually shackles, if not persecutes, all other religions while promoting Islam alone. A secular authority, such as a state or government, is blasphemous to the

11. Munoz, "Religious Liberty," 36.
12. Ibid., 37.
13. Ibid., 41.
14. Ibid., 42.

sovereign rule of Allah. Church and state are one and the same. When the terrorists of September 11, 2001, visited Western nations, they considered it a sign of the West's spiritual decadence that buildings that stood taller than churches are tolerated. In a Muslim city, the minaret must be the tallest building to symbolize that the city, in submission, is stretching its hands and fingers toward Allah in heaven.[15] I've personally observed this in Afghanistan. However, this is not the case in the more liberal country of the United Arab Emirates (which Islamists hate, no doubt).

Jesus' teaching lies at the heart of the American experiment of government. Seventeen centuries of trial and error, much of it Christian error, led our founding fathers to a form of government that, thus far, is much more in line with Jesus' teaching. The present situation came about through a maturing process that saw the end of state-controlled and state-imposed Christianity. It derives from the nature of Christianity itself, anchored in the character of God. He gave freedom to people to choose or to reject him and the good news of salvation. Coerced Christianity is not Christianity at all.

After fifteen centuries, Islam has learned little regarding just and free government.

Jesus is a better, wiser statesman than Muhammad.

The other extreme form of the state is communism. Marx and his followers sought to obliterate the realm of God. It is only in Jesus and Christianity that both realms find legitimacy, and the basis for freedom is found.

THE AMERICAN EXAMPLE

The American philosophy of government is in basic agreement with biblical principles. The Constitution recognizes and allows both spheres (church and government) to fulfill their respective purposes. It recognizes God as supreme over government. It seeks to promote the good and to punish the evil under law according to a Judeo-Christian law code and ethic. This code and ethic find general acceptance because they

---

15. See the excellent article by Scruton, "Islam," 38:3–15. He notes that where *sharia* prevails, "the emergence of secular politics from the prophetic community is a sign not of civilized progress but of moral decline" (4). Where everything is owed to God, "nothing is owed to Caesar" (5). In the view of Islam, human rights and secular government "display the decadence of Western civilization" (14).

correspond to universal Natural Moral Law (written on the heart) and are revealed in general revelation (to the conscience).

Where the two spheres conflict, where God's claims conflict with those of the state, then God must be followed and the state disobeyed. It is incomprehensible that one would rather choose to obey the state when the state itself exists only because of God's ordination. The difficulty for all Christians is to know when there is a legitimate conflict.

The founding fathers of the United States clearly saw that religion has precedence over the state. For example, James Madison championed the strict separation of Church and State on the basis of fundamental human freedom. Yet he viewed religious liberty to be an inalienable right, which took precedence over the claims of civil government. He wrote that it is " . . . a fundamental and undeniable truth, 'that Religion of the duty which we owe our Creator and the manner of discharging it, can be directed only by reason and conviction, not by force or violence' . . . The right is in its nature an unalienable right."[16]

Madison located the foundation for religious liberty in the nature of human beings and religion. It is an inalienable right because it is a "duty towards the Creator." This duty is, in fact, "precedent . . . to the claims of Civil Society." Thus "no man's right is abridged by the institutions of Civil Society, and that Religion is wholly exempt from its cognizance."[17]

The necessary protection of religious liberty was a central concern of the founding fathers. By putting it in writing, they made sure that the state would never abridge religious expression and that no national church would be established to control government.

Religious liberty is the very first right in the Bill of Rights and has a two-fold aspect. It reads: "Congress shall make no law respecting an establishment of religion, nor prohibiting the free exercise thereof." The original intent of these words is clear. Congress cannot legislate a state church into being, and, on the other hand, must allow any and all religions free expression.

The American system of government should enjoy the support of Christians, in light of the above. It isn't that the system is a "Christian" government, but rather that the system agrees with biblical principles regarding the role of government in general and is based upon, or agrees

---

16. Madison, "Memorial," in Rutland, *James Madison*, 8: 299.
17. Ibid.

with, a Judeo-Christian ethic in seeking to promote good and restrain evil. This ethic defines what the good and the evil are. The precepts agree with Natural Moral Law.

WHAT OF CHRISTIAN RESISTANCE?

It becomes sinful conduct for Christians to compromise their faith by submitting to government when it "usurps the duties of ministers of religion," or "when it prescribes idolatry or religious error."[18] According to Tertullian, the passage of Romans 13 was misused in the early church by those shrinking from martyrdom and wanting a good reason to submit to government when it commanded idolatry. Taking this passage to mean absolute allegiance is a violation of the total teaching of Scripture.

The example of Daniel and his three companions offers us some guidance. They were fully obedient to the government until the law of God was threatened. At that point, their refusal to obey to the point of death became the proper response (Daniel 3). This was also the case for Mordecai and Esther in the book of Esther. They sought to oppose a king's evil plans, and were willing to lose their positions and their lives, if necessary, to do so.

Public education illustrates the abuse of government just referred to. When state education prescribes and inculcates a materialistic, humanistic origin for all things (evolution) to the exclusion of a biblical, creationist viewpoint, it seems that the government has come very close to usurping the place of religion and religious belief. The state has begun to assert an atheistic and naturalistic pseudo religion. Christians have a sacred obligation to insist upon equal time for the biblical account or refuse to submit to the state at this point. Their actions may take the form of voting down all funding for state education, voting for candidates supportive of the Christian view, and even the refusal to pay that portion of taxes designated for state education. Christians may also remove their children from state schools and educate them at home or in a Christian school. This action may involve opposition, ostracism, judicial punishment, and great expense, but to compromise one's faith on this crucial issue should not be tolerated.

18. Liddon, *Romans*, 250.

In addition, it seems to be an inappropriate intrusion by government to insist that teachers and curricula in Christian schools should be state approved, except in the broadest way. Payment of taxes by churches for basic services (sewer, police protection, etc.) seems consistent with the biblical principles we've discussed so far in this chapter, although a tax on property may violate them. However, the power to tax cannot be allowed to control the existence, beliefs, practices, and hired personnel of the church (which unemployment taxes, for example, might do).

Forbidding the possession and reading of Scripture seems to be an unwarranted intrusion of the government into the realm of allegiance to God. Thus smuggling Bibles has both biblical and modern precedents. In Israel, Jeremiah had to make and then secret away a copy of his prophecy against the king's command (Jeremiah 36). During the time of the Maccabean revolt (168–165 B.C.), the Jews had to hide their Scriptures because Antiochus IV had commanded that they be destroyed. During the Reformation, William Tyndale smuggled his New Testaments into England against the king's command. In more recent times, Brother Andrew and others have smuggled Bibles into "closed" countries.

Just as Paul appealed to his legal rights under Roman law, it's appropriate for Christians today to do so. Just as everyone else, they have the right to free religious speech on campuses, street corners, in airports, and elsewhere. The Christian should appeal to the courts when and where such rights are violated. Of course, where the state has allowed a civil right that is forbidden as immoral by biblical standards (pornography, abortion, sodomy, adultery, etc.), the Christian must submit to Scriptural authority and not engage in what the state allows. The Christian should work to overturn such immoral behavior.

PLEDGING ALLEGIANCE TO GOVERNMENT

An important issue needs to be discussed: Is it appropriate for Christians to swear an oath of allegiance to their country? In the United States, the Pledge of Allegiance is not technically an oath. It doesn't go back as far as the founding fathers but was instituted in the 1930's. Recently, the government's approval of policies such as the protection of abortion, gay rights, and euthanasia, which are clearly not Christian, raises the question more starkly. While the terrorist attacks on the World Trade Center and the Pentagon have brought a heightened sense of patriotism, the question remains: Has the time arrived for Christians to refuse to make the Pledge as a statement of opposition to certain governmental policies? The Pledge should not compromise the focus of a Christian's ultimate allegiance to the kingdom of God.

The Pledge should not be confused with the oath sworn to Caesar in the time of Polycarp. Christians believed that to swear an oath to the "genius" (or fortune) of Caesar was really swearing an oath to a demon possessing him and involved his claim to be a god. This is clearly not Christian. The American Pledge of Allegiance does not have this significance.

UNANSWERED QUESTIONS

The passages cited at the outset of this chapter make it clear that Christians have a higher obligation to obey God rather than human authorities when they are in conflict. Christians owe ultimate allegiance to God, not to the government that owes its existence to God. Allegiance to God may require Christians today, as it always has, to be willing to endure persecution and even death for their Lord who is above all lords. For Christians to compromise their allegiance to God means that they have become slaves of an inferior master and invites the slander of the unbeliever.

Yet questions still remain. For one thing, Jesus did not clarify what belongs to God and what belongs to a civil authority. Also, the matter of how Christians resist the government is a major concern. What should Christians do when they wish to engage in a religiously-justified act, which has been (wrongly) forbidden by the state? Obviously, Christians should not retaliate for personal offenses. Yet should they join with others in rebelling—in fomenting a revolution—when all other recourse has failed? How far may the Christian go in opposition to the state? If Paul's words in Romans 13:1-7 deal only with governments that already exist, what is the Christian's role when government is in transition, as during a revolution? These are questions that concern methods and means.

Finally, what does Christian freedom mean in regard to submission to government? If they, as members of a heavenly community, are essentially free from all earthly governments, are Christians free from governmental authority altogether? And are they free to choose what means they will follow in resisting government?

To Submit or to Rebel against the State

I seek to answer these questions in chapter 10. In the meantime, let's not forget the conclusion of William Tyndale's story.

THE LEGACY OF WILLIAM TYNDALE

For fifteen months, William Tyndale suffered in a damp, dark dungeon. Requests for his personal affects and for his Hebrew manuscripts were denied. In August 1536, he was found guilty of heresy and condemned to be strangled and burned at the stake.

The morning of October 6, 1536, finally arrived. The night before he was to be executed, William had prayed and reflected on his life's work. Just a few days before, he had received word that his translation of the Old Testament had been rescued and completed by his assistant, Miles Coverdale. The Old Testament was now available to the people of England. William was able to take great satisfaction in God's special intervention. His suffering and death would be a small price to pay if the English Bible would bring the reformation of the church to England as it had done on the Continent.

The king was the key. Already King Henry VIII had become disenchanted with the Catholic Church's refusal to give him both a divorce and a blessing on his new marriage. Perhaps this estrangement from Rome would be the catalyst to awaken the king.

It was time for the execution. The straw and wood were piled high around Tyndale. The flames began to rise. The executioner came forward to strangle him. At that moment, William Tyndale was overwhelmed with both peace and a tremendous burden for the state of his homeland far away. He cried out: "Lord, open the king of England's eyes!"

William Tyndale did not know that at that very moment God was working to bring the Reformation to England. King Henry VIII had separated his country and the church from Roman Catholicism. Coverdale's Bible was circulating with the king's permission. The events that would make England a Protestant country were underway.

The reverberations of such events would stretch far afield and long into the future. Future British colonies in the recently discovered New World would lay the foundation for a great Protestant nation whose power and freedom would be unparalleled in world history. Part of this greatness would be traced to the Protestant faith and ethic that Tyndale had helped bring to England.

7

The Relationship of Law to Morality

ISAAC BACKUS: CHAMPION OF RELIGIOUS LIBERTY IN EARLY AMERICA (1724–1806)

ISAAC BACKUS SAT AT his writing desk with pen at hand. It was a sober moment for him as he contemplated how to defend civil disobedience. He reflected on what had led up to this moment, in this the year of 1773. Revolution was in the air, not only politically but also spiritually.

For years, Isaac Backus had worked hard to change the laws of Connecticut and Massachusetts that forced Separatist and Baptist churches to pay taxes to the colonies to support the established, Congregational churches. He had written many tracts and articles on behalf of religious freedom, and they had been influential, but the churches had found no relief. Now he was at a turning point. He was about to write in defense of civil disobedience: All the Baptist churches should band together and refuse to obey the law demanding taxes. He could not be sure of the outcome. It could lead to significant trouble for his congregation and the other Baptist churches in Massachusetts.

As he contemplated what he should write, Isaac reflected on how far the movement of New Lights and Separate-Baptists had come. His thoughts took him all the way back to his own humble beginnings. He was born on January 9, 1724, in the village of Yantic, near Norwich, Connecticut, into a family of farmers. His parents were staunchly Puritan. He recalled the impact that the death of his father (from measles) had had on his family when Isaac was just 16-years-old, and his mother's resultant depression.

But the event that changed his entire life occurred the year after his father's death. He and his mother, who had been converted about twenty years before, had attended meetings during the Great Awakening, which had been spearheaded by Jonathan Edwards and George Whitefield. The revivalist James Davenport had done the preaching that led to Isaac's severe soul-searching and the renewal of the faith of his mother. A few days later, on August 24, 1741, while mowing hay in a field, Isaac had been overcome by a sense of personal sin, and had "trusted Christ for salvation." The following year, he joined the local Congregational church, hoping that he could reform it from within. When his church came to oppose the Awakening and refused to turn from its practice of baptizing infants and unbelievers, he and his family (along with some other new converts) left to form a Separate or New Light Church (1746). A few months later, at the age of twenty-two, Isaac received his "internal call" to the ministry and preached his first sermon. Two years later (1748) he helped to start a Separate church in Middleboro, Massachusetts, and was ordained.

Isaac recalled the special events of February 6, 1749. He and his congregation had refused to pay the taxes to support the established state church, called the Standing Order. It was not an easy decision, for imprisonment or confiscation of property was the usual penalty. On that fateful day, the constable came to his home to arrest him and to take him to jail. Isaac later wrote how, just then, the Lord had given him a great calmness that enabled him to neither fear the future nor treat the officer with bitterness. And then the Lord intervened: Just as Isaac was about to be dragged to jail, a former parishioner stepped forward and paid his fine. And yet others he knew, among them his mother and brothers, had indeed gone to prison and paid fines. One woman of his church served as a special example: She spent a whole year in jail for refusing to pay a tax of nine pence that was meant to support the established minister of her parish, and she refused to let anyone pay it for her. It was these events that ignited the struggle that was to become central to Backus' entire life—the relationship of church and state.

Near the end of 1749, Isaac had married Susanna Mason of Rehoboth and bought a home and a farm. (It was there they reared nine children and lived out the rest of their lives.) Then theological controversies in his church had erupted. As New Lights, Backus and his church had embraced

The Relationship of Law to Morality

the idea that church membership should be limited to those who were regenerate believers. But what about infant baptism as practiced by both the Congregational and Separate churches? After a two-year struggle, Isaac became convinced that only adult baptism was Scriptural. In 1751, he and his wife were re-baptized. After further struggles, Isaac led a group out of his church to begin the First Baptist church in Middleborough, Massachusetts (1756), and was ordained as its life-long pastor.

Now, after some years had passed, Isaac found himself considering the growth of his ministry. He had led the transition from New Light to Baptist churches. In 1767, he had helped found the Warren Association, the leading coalition of Baptists in New England. He served on its special Committee on Grievances to hear complaints from Baptists about the civil authorities. Baptists petitioned the legislature to be exempt from paying taxes since they were no longer Separate churches but Baptist ones, which were normally exempt. But the state legislature responded by passing the "Ashfield Act" (1768), requiring Baptists to pay the tax after all.

Two years later (1770), Backus had written a tract, "A Seasonable Plea for Liberty of Conscience," in which he advocated that liberty of conscience should be added to the other natural rights of life, liberty, and private property in the struggle for independence. Backus had quoted both John Locke and the Apostle Paul. He had pled with the other Baptists to join together in refusing to pay any religious taxes so that the authorities would take note of their plight.

Still the forced collection of taxes and other reprisals continued. Out of a sense of having exhausted all the lawful means of redressing their grievances, the Warren Association of Baptists instructed Backus to write a tract to defend civil disobedience. The Baptists wanted to secure religious liberty as a general principle rather than a denominational privilege. So Isaac was determined to write his most controversial tract yet on the separation of church and state. Backus was aware of the fact that some would slander him and the Baptists as enemies of the Revolution, since the Baptists had previously appealed to England to secure religious freedom. If this tract brought reprisals, including imprisonment, he was willing to accept them for the greater cause of religious liberty. He was convinced that the Great Awakening brought "new light" on the matter of church-state relationships, and that Christians should support this "new reformation" with their "lives, liberty, and property."[1] Backus asserted that "America was and ought to be a Christian nation, and he looked forward to the day when it would be a Baptist nation."[2] He believed that independence was just.

BACKUS' APPEAL FOR RELIGIOUS LIBERTY

Isaac turned his attention back to what he should write. The words seemed to flow from the tip of his quill. He began with the basic premise that all connections between the state and institutionalized religion had to be severed in order that America might become "a truly Christian nation."[3] Backus assumed that God had instituted two different kinds of government in the world—the secular state and the church—and that these were different in their nature and not to be comingled. He rehearsed the history of this comingling that began with Constantine the Emperor in the fourth century and was brought to America by the Puritans. The Puritan model worked for a while, but now, with the coming of "new light" to the colonies, a new model was needed; spiritual independence was needed.

Backus identified three areas where Massachusetts had comingled or confounded church and state: it required the churches to practice infant baptism; it required ministers to have an approved academic degree; and it required taxes to support the established church rather than use voluntary gifts. Consequently, questions of theology and orthodoxy took second place to civil matters, so much so that Unitarian heresy and universalism were appearing both among the clergy and at Harvard College.

Isaac argued further that natural rights were not superceded by civil obligations, that safety and good order did not justify the limitation of religious liberty, and that the right of private property (belonging to Baptists) could not be taken away by the civil authorities without the people's consent. Indeed, Baptists were being taxed without representation, just as the American colonists had claimed against the British Parliament.

Citing many examples, Backus showed that the laws exempting Baptists from taxation had been "ignored, perverted, or narrowly construed."[4]

1. McLoughlin, *Isaac Backus*, x.
2. Ibid., xii.
3. Ibid., 123.
4. Ibid., 126.

He rejected the argument that the majority should rule in religious matters, since most citizens in Massachusetts were not truly converted and had little knowledge of religious truth. Such a practice established a secular state where Satan triumphed over true saints.[5]

Backus concluded his tract with a list of five reasons for civil disobedience that arose from his pietism. In contrast to the political appeals of Jefferson and Madison, which were based in deism, rationalism, and natural law, Backus appealed to biblical concepts. The established churches and their laws were wrong because they used civil power to set one religious sect over another; their taxing power was a claim to govern in Christ's kingdom; they led people to judge the liberty of other peoples' consciences; they placed in prominence an earthly power between Christ and his people, leading to abominations; and they violated the law of Christ by which every person is required to judge for himself regarding the essentials of his faith.[6]

After sixty-two pages, Backus was done. He captured the essence of his tract with the title "An Appeal to the Public for Religious Liberty Against the Oppression of the Present Day" (1773). What would be its impact? Would it lead the Baptists to united civil disobedience? Would the civil powers react with even more stringent laws?

---

5. McLoughlin, *Isaac Backus*, 126.
6. Ibid., 126–127.

To Submit or to Rebel against the State

Principle 4
Morality Is Legislated

> We know that the law is good, if one uses it properly [lawfully]. We also know that law is made not for the righteous but for lawbreakers and rebels, for the ungodly and sinful, for the unholy and irreligious; for those who kill their fathers or mothers, for murderers, for adulterers and homosexuals, for slave traders and liars and perjurers—and for whatever else is contrary to sound doctrine that conforms to the glorious gospel of the blessed God, which he entrusted to me. —*1 Timothy 1:8–11*

INTRODUCTION

At the founding of the American Republic, slavery was an institution that had been in place for many years. Yet the rights outlined in both the Declaration of Independence and the Constitution were implicitly at odds with a practice such as slavery. How could someone enslaved enjoy "life, liberty, and the pursuit of happiness"?

Many recognized this inherent conflict, including Washington and Jefferson who released their slaves. Yet economics and other cultural considerations prohibited the immediate destruction of the institution. But the seeds of its destruction were planted. Indeed, the Constitution of the United States avoided the term "slaves" when referring to the manner in which the number of U.S. Representatives was to be calculated: Slaves in the southern states were to be counted as three-fifths of the free population, yet the Constitution uses the term "persons," never "slaves."

LINCOLN AND SLAVERY

Later, when running for the U.S. Senate in 1858 against Stephen Douglas, Abraham Lincoln argued against slavery in the new states. He stated his opposition to the Dred Scott decision of 1856—the decision in which the Supreme Court decided that slaves were not to be reckoned as free persons but as property. The Court stated that this was the understanding of the framers of the Constitution. If this was no longer acceptable, the

Constitution was to be amended, not reinterpreted. The genius of Lincoln was that he saw beyond the Constitution to the Natural Moral Law upon which it was based, and, in this instance, the Constitution failed to agree with Natural Moral Law.

It was not possible that the institution of slavery could survive in our Republic, with its implicit recognition of Natural Moral Law. The Civil War (known in the South as the "War Between the States") broke out over the issues of slavery and states' rights. Lincoln's Emancipation Proclamation (1863) and the North's victory assured the end of the institution of slavery in the United States. The Thirteenth Amendment finally abolished slavery by constitutional amendment.

ABORTION AND HOMOSEXUAL BEHAVIOR

One of the most important legal and moral issues today is that of abortion. In 1973, the Supreme Court decided that the unborn have no rights. In *Roe v. Wade*, the Court overturned laws prohibiting or limiting abortion in all fifty states. This decision reversed a tradition that had endured in Western civilization since the Christianization of Rome, beginning in the third and fourth centuries A.D.

Abortion is one of the most important moral issues today because the consequences are so grave. Each year approximately one million abortions are performed in America. This means that almost every fourth baby conceived is killed by abortion. Of all abortions, 99 percent are done for socioeconomic reasons (not in order to save the life of the mother), or in cases of rape or incest. Some 90.5 percent of abortions are done within the first three months of gestation.

Additional decisions by the Court have expanded *Roe v. Wade* so that (1) abortions are permissible for minors without parental consent; (2) a wife may obtain an abortion without her husband's knowledge or permission; (3) states may *not* require humane disposal of fetal remains; and (4) states may *not* enforce laws to assure informed consent.[7] Abortions of full term babies are now legal—even during the birthing process. Thankfully, in recent years legislation signed by President Bush limits this practice to some extent. But President Obama has gone in the opposite direction, reinforcing the practice of abortion.

7. "Roe," 1: 1–2.

There is hardly anyone who would deny that abortion, like slavery, is a moral issue. Yet many oppose the idea that abortion, as other moral issues, is a matter of legislation. "You cannot legislate morality," people say. "You can't force people to be good. The courts shouldn't invade people's privacy in matters of personal morality." Abortion, it's claimed, is a "right of privacy." This view holds that law should only regulate public offices and civil disorders where another's life, property, or well-being may be involved. So-called victimless crimes should not be the concern of governmental restraint.

The legislating of homosexuality is a similar issue. While the Bible and other sources may judge this behavior as immoral, others insist that this is a private matter. Even though the Supreme Court (*Bower v. Hardwick*, 1986) upheld the rights of states to restrict this behavior, the "gay rights" movement continued to push forward to advance its agenda in every aspect of life. The result of such pressure led the Supreme Court (in 2003) to reverse its earlier decision.

However plausible these statements about legislating morality and private behavior may first appear, it's necessary to look again to Scripture and Natural Moral Law as our guide. What do special and general revelation have to say to the following questions: Should morality be legislated? Should the law reach into one's private life in order to restrict behavior? Who or what should determine what is moral and immoral, good or evil?

The answers to these questions are found in this and the next chapter. This and the next principle are drawn from the same passage of Scripture: 1 Timothy 1:8–11.

MORALITY IS LEGISLATED

The principle of this chapter is this: Morality is legislated. That is, it's appropriate that government should create laws for society that concern morality. Morality is a legitimate concern of those who make legislation.

Paul wrote his first epistle to Timothy from Macedonia, sometime around A.D. 65. Timothy, a pastor in Ephesus, was Paul's son in the Christian faith. At the outset of his epistle, Paul reminds Timothy of the reason why Paul left him in Ephesus: Timothy was to instruct certain people not to teach strange doctrines or to follow fruitless discussion (1 Timothy 1:3, 6). These people wanted to be teachers of the Law of Moses even though

The Relationship of Law to Morality

they didn't understand the Law. Paul refers to Jewish myths and genealogies and disputes about the Law of Moses, with Hellenistic or Greek tendencies (perhaps even a syncretism of the law and Gnosticism—an early heresy that taught that a secret knowledge is salvation, that the God who created all is evil, and that Jesus Christ did not physically rise from the dead). Ideas expressed elsewhere in Scripture (1 Timothy 4:7; 2 Timothy 4:4; Titus 1:14, 3:9) confirm the Jewish character of this false teaching or distortion.

Then, to remind Timothy of the proper place and significance of law, Paul writes that the Law is good if it's used "lawfully" or properly (1 Timothy 1:8). Here the noun for "law" is articular (with the article "the") and refers specifically to the Old Testament Law, namely the Law of Moses. Many translations bring this out by capitalizing "law." Even though the Law of Moses is in view, what Paul says of it may be said of any law or legislation. The Law is to be used as law is used, not as the gospel is used. That is, law may restrain sin, excite sin, or help to define sin, but it can't be the basis or means of salvation or sanctification, as Paul makes clear elsewhere (Romans 3:21-31; Galatians 2:16—3:6, 21-25; see also the introduction to this book).

In 1 Timothy 1:9, Paul deliberately changes his form of writing: "We also know that law is made . . . " The term "law" is now anarthrous (without the article), and refers to the general nature of any law or legislation. The Mosaic Law is just one manifestation or example of such law. Thus, Paul has progressed in his thinking to describe law in general, as a universal principle.[8]

The translation "is made" is the most crucial verb in the passage. Used with the negative "not," it represents the verb *keitai*. This word can have the physical, general idea of "to be laid," "to lie, set, or stand," and is used of persons and things, such as laying a foundation. Here, however, it has a metaphorical idea (consider 1 John 5:19) and means "to be laid down, appointed." The idea of "appoint" fits best here: "Law is appointed" for various persons. Since legislative bodies bring about such law, the idea of "enact" is a good translation.[9]

---

8. Lock, *Pastoral Epistles*, 11.

9. The only other similar uses of "appoint" are Luke 2:34 ("this child is *destined* to cause the falling and rising of many"), Phil. 1:16 ("I am *put* here for the defense of the gospel"), and 1 Thess. 3:3 ("you know that we were *destined* for [trials]"). All of these contexts argue for a strong meaning for the word in 1 Tim. 1:9 as well.

Law or legislation is not enacted for a righteous person but for the unrighteous, Paul says. Paul's point is that law has the proper function of alerting, warning, and restricting people in their expression of certain kinds of unacceptable behavior. It's binding on all people.

The "righteous" person does not describe the justified one or the Christian; it's not used in a forensic sense but a moral one. It refers to any person who is obedient to law in general. It means a "good" person.

FOR WHOM LAW IS ENACTED: THREE CATEGORIES

Paul delineates three categories of people whose behavior law restricts. First, law is made or enacted for the lawless and rebellious. These are those who refuse to obey the law, not those who are without law or are ignorant of it. The first group, the lawless, live as if there were no law, while the second group, the rebellious, refuse to submit to the law which has been laid down. This category, the lawless and rebellious, reflects civil accountability. This role of law views it as an ordinance coming from people.

The second category suggests religious accountability. It views law as the ordinance of God. These, the "ungodly and sinners," refuse to obey the law of God. The former term defines those who are without inward reverence, the latter term points to those who defy God by outward acts.

The third category of dual terms, the "unholy and irreligious," indicates more detailed opposition to the law of God. The terms reflect the moral realm. The first term states in a negative way an opposition to anything that is holy, anything having to do with God. The second term expresses this positively. It means something profane, which may be walked on, and consequently must remain outside of the holy shrine.[10] It conveys the idea of secularity.

Here then are three realms upon which the law or legislation is binding: the civil, the religious, and the moral. All three realms are a proper concern not only of the Law of Moses but all legislation. From another perspective, all three categories comprise multiple characteristics of people who must be bound by law in society. Without this role of law, this rule of law, a society is lawless, irreligious, and immoral. In 1 Timothy 2, Paul exhorts prayer for rulers that they would promote such godliness and morality in a society (see principle 6).

---

10. Bernard, *Epistles*, 27.

EIGHT SPECIFIC VICES

The subsequent terms of 1 Timothy 1:9–10 specify examples of the foregoing classifications, without any intention to distinguish them as civil, religious, or moral offenses. They are all grouped together and may take on the traits of two or more of the categories. Basically, Paul has the order of the Decalogue (the Ten Commandments) in view.

Paul gives eight specific examples of lawless people. The most extreme violation of the commandment is specified in every case.

There is a deliberate, overall pattern for the eight terms. It develops as 2-1-2-1-2. Beginning with the first group, Paul gives two specifications of the fifth commandment, then he gives one specific example for the next commandment, then two, then one, and so forth. Those commandments for which two examples are given are naturally emphasized.

First, "strikers of fathers" and "strikers of mothers" are in view. This includes the idea of smiting, and emphasizes the sin of dishonoring parents. This marks an extreme violation of the fifth commandment, to honor parents, which was punishable by death in Israel (Exodus 21:15).

The next term is "murderers," a term occurring elsewhere only in the Greek Old Testament (the Septuagint) in the Apocrypha at 2 Maccabees 9:28.[11] Here the sixth commandment is in view. It refers to intentional slaughter, what we today call premeditated murder.

The words "immoral men" and "homosexuals" refer to those transgressing the seventh commandment. The former terms probably include illicit intercourse between married persons as well as unmarried persons. The latter term, referring to the sin of sodomy, or same-sex behavior, is more flagrant, narrow, and repulsive than the former term. The issue of homosexuality is discussed more fully in the next chapter of this book.

In "slave traders," the basic idea of slave trading is in view. The word refers to those who steal people, hence kidnappers. This is the worst form of thievery, which violates the eighth commandment. It was also punishable by death under the Mosaic code (Exodus 21:16; Deuteronomy 24:7), as was homosexuality (Leviticus 20:13) and murder.

"Liars" and "perjurers" refer to those who violate the ninth commandment. Lying is a form of false witness where the truth is suppressed.

---

11. The verse reads: "Thus the murderer and blasphemer having suffered most grievously, as he entreated other men, so he died a miserable death in a strange country in the mountains."

To Submit or to Rebel against the State

The extreme form of false witness, perjury, is a false charge made under oath.[12]

These eight vices represent behavior in the form of actions or speech, not thoughts. They represent the second half of the Ten Commandments. The first half of the Decalogue is not explicitly represented. The preceding discussion suggests the following conclusions:

1. Laws or legislation should not coerce or restrict worship of God (idolatry, blasphemy, Sabbath-keeping). The words concern law in general; in other words, that which would agree with Natural Moral Law, not the Mosaic Law.

2. Law should not restrict thoughts but only actions, including certain kinds of speech. This last point supports the idea of censoring filthy or other abusive speech (consider Colossians 3:8), and the idea of punishing the breaking of contracts.

This brief exposition makes it clear that practices deemed lawless and that constitute crimes can also be immoral and antireligious. That is, such deeds not only affect society and humanity, but they also concern God.

While most of the vices represent crimes or sins against other persons, they are also sins against God and sins against collective society. No neat separation of crimes and sins seems warranted. In addition, while most of the vices constitute aggression, the "immoral men" and "homosexuals" include crimes of consent or behavior between consenting parties. Thus, the law can reach into the bedroom for the sake of preserving marriage, the family, and society. These vices constitute transgression, immorality, and rebellion against God (the three categories of 1 Timothy 1:9, as I mentioned above).

One fact is clear: All these vices are worthy of legislation or lawful restriction. At least in these cases, government does legislate morality. By extension, it would seem that similar vices listed elsewhere (Romans 1:28–32, 1 Corinthians 6:9–10, etc.), which destroy the property of others (stealing), which destroy other people inside or outside the home, or which destroy self, should fall under similar legislative restraint.

---

12. Bernard, *Epistles*, 28.

PLATO ON THE LEGISLATING OF MORALITY

At the outset of this chapter, I stated that there is both special and general revelation that supports the legislating of morality. Not only the Bible but also the common morality of people supports the role of law to define what is moral or good. As an example of the latter, I cite Plato of the fourth century B.C.

Early in his life, Plato composed the *Symposium*, a collection of the views of those, including Socrates, who attended a banquet. Common to all the guests is the view that homosexual love, especially in the form of pederasty, is a better love than heterosexual love. The discussion includes praise of adult, life-long mutuality and affirmation that homosexuals are born that way. They embrace what we call sexual orientation. If two men should go into combat together, the one would be willing to die for the other, so great is their "love." Consequently, the participants affirm that laws should protect homosexual love. They find justification for homosexuality in the story that the Greek gods Zeus and Ganymede engaged in same-sex behavior. Thus, the appeal to religion determined the morality of the Greeks.

But in the last work of his life, *Laws*, Plato expresses a different view. His concern is how to bring about a virtuous society. Homosexual love, like two other vices (adultery and incest), needs to be restrained. Public opinion should bring about laws curbing it, and religion should be invoked to call it "utterly unholy." It should also be identified as contrary to nature. Plato also asserts that the story about Zeus and Ganymede is not true, but was concocted by the Cretans to give religious support to the practice of homosexuality.

The implicit appeal to Natural Moral Law could hardly be more clear. Plato asserts that homosexual love is "against nature." For an extended discussion of Plato's and other ancient writers' opposition to homosexuality, coupled with early law codes, read my separate volume on homosexuality.[13]

---

13. De Young, *Homosexuality*, 252–61.

LUTHER SHARES THE BIBLE'S VIEW

Martin Luther, one of the leaders of the Reformation, advocated the idea of legislating morality. He believed that the law is necessary in order "to instruct, constrain, and compel" the unrighteous to do what is good. People need to be "externally restrained from evil deeds" by the law "so that they must needs keep the peace outwardly, even against their will."[14]

Luther's view of law is like that of Plato, but it is diametrically opposite to that of modern legal positivism, which advocates a sociological jurisprudence. The most prominent spokesman of this position, Hans Kelson, asserts:

> The Pure theory of Law retains its anti-ideological tendency by its attempt to insulate the positive law from every kind of natural law—justice ideology. The possibility of a valid order superior to positive law it considers outside its sphere of discussion . . . Legal theory thus becomes a structural analysis, as exact as possible, of the positive law, an analysis free of all ethical or political judgments of value.[15]

Luther's view of the natural juxtaposition of ethics and law cannot tolerate such a view. As F. S. Cohen writes: "There is no way of avoiding this ultimate responsibility of law to ethics. Every final determination of the general end of law, the standard of legal criticism, must reduce to the general form, 'The law ought to bring about as much good as it can.'"

This role of legislation reinforces the concept of the triangle illustration as discussed in the introduction of this book. To say that morality is legislated is to say that law enacts specific standards of morality, the violation of which is crime. Law seeks to uphold and maintain certain moral standards as long as most people comply with the standards so enforced. However, if the morality of most people changes, the law will change.

This brings us back to the issues of slavery and abortion discussed at the beginning of this chapter. Few realize that it was early Christianity that historically brought about the end of both of these socially-condoned practices.

---

14. Luther, "Secular Authority," 369–370.
15. Kelson, "Law," 39.

LAW OPPOSES SLAVERY

The seeds for the destruction of the institution of slavery are planted in the New Testament itself. It was impossible for slavery to survive where Christianity became significant. Paul wrote to early Christians that slaves and masters must show mutual respect to each other. Whether they were fellow believers in Christ or not, respect, sincerity, and impartiality were to characterize the slave-master relationship (Ephesians 6:5–9; Colossians 3:22—4:1; 1 Timothy 6:1–2; Titus 2:9–10; Philemon 1–25).

The result of spiritual equality in Christ ("neither slave nor free," as found in Galatians 3:28 and Colossians 3:11) had its practical expression in daily living. Christianity did not support the revolutions of thousands of slaves in Sicily and Italy, yet a quiet revolution occurred. Spiritual equality in Christ brought admission of slaves to baptism, worship, and clerical positions. Early on, a slave named Callistus became Bishop of Rome (A.D. 217–222). There were marriages among slaves. Finally, church councils and Christian emperors put an end to the practice of slavery entirely.[16]

Later, when governments institutionalized slavery of a different kind, it was tolerated only as long as the morals and religion of the people would support it. Finally, in England, under the inspiration of the Christian legislator Granville Sharp, William Wilberforce led the fight in Parliament to abolish slavery. In 1860, in the United States the judicial decision that once permitted slavery could not restrain the people's opposition, and armed conflict resolved the issue.

LAW OPPOSES ABORTION

What about the issue of abortion? Is there a biblical position on it? The Bible says nothing explicitly regarding it, but the Bible implicitly opposes it. In Exodus 21:22–25, punishment or compensation is mandated for the apparently accidental striking of a pregnant woman that forces her to give premature birth. The degree of punishment or compensation depends on the severity of the injury to the mother or to the child. The law of *lex talionis* ("an eye for an eye") is cited as providing the standard for such a situation.

---

16. Liddon, *Epistle*, 71–72.

It's also noteworthy that abortion was contrary to the common morality within the surrounding cultures at the time of the Old Testament. Ancient Assyria, the empire that captured the ten northern tribes of Israel in 722 B.C., considered abortion such an evil that a woman guilty of an abortion was impaled on a stake and publicly displayed as a warning to others.

In early Christian literature, abortion and infanticide are considered part of the way of darkness and not part of the Christian way of light. Writings such as the *Didache* (chapter 2), the *Epistle of Barnabas* (19.5), the *Apostolic Constitutions* (7.3), the *Apocalypse of Peter* (which describes mothers who have had abortions undergoing the torments of hell), and the church father Tertullian (*Apology* 9) all explicitly condemn abortion.

This ethic of Christianity was contrary to the ethics of the Greeks and Romans, yet the Christian ethic soon became so pervasive that the standard of the Roman government was reversed. Religion influenced morality and it in turn influenced law. This became the ethic of Western society for the next fifteen hundred years. Then, in 1973, this ethic was institutionally rejected in the United States in the *Roe v. Wade* decision.

LINCOLN ON SLAVERY

The parallels between the past debate over slavery and the present debate over abortion are many. The chief one is that both are moral issues ultimately, not just political or legal ones. It is the greatness of Lincoln that he saw this concerning slavery and constantly pointed it out. Lincoln believed that when enough people saw slavery as a moral evil, implicitly recognized by the framers of the Declaration and the Constitution, slavery could endure no more.[17]

Lincoln's words concerning slavery as a moral issue are certainly appropriate regarding the issue of abortion. Implicit is a recognition of a standard of morality derived from religion that will influence law. On the occasion of his seventh and final debate with Stephen Douglas in Alton, Illinois (October 15, 1858), Lincoln said the following:

---

17. Lincoln's stature has not diminished over the years. On Jan. 11, 1982, the *Chicago Tribune* reported that its poll of historians gave first place to Lincoln as the greatest president America has ever had.

The Relationship of Law to Morality

> The real issue in this controversy—the one pressing upon every mind—is the sentiment on the part of one class that looks upon the institution of slavery *as a wrong,* and of another class that *does not* look upon it as a wrong . . . [Those who look upon it as a wrong] look upon it as being a moral, social, and political wrong.[18] (Italics his.)

Lincoln castigated those who wanted silence on the issue, who did not want anything said "about it in the pulpit, because that is religion and has nothing to do with it."[19] He castigated those who would "not say anything about it in politics."[20] He saw the Dred Scott decision as wrong and was for reversing it. He argued on the implicit understanding of the Constitution as opposing the decision.

Lincoln also saw the struggle over slavery as part of a greater conflict and this gave his position its universal appeal. Concerning the immorality of slavery, he stated:

> That is the real issue. That is the issue that will continue in this country when these poor tongues of Judge Douglas and myself shall be silent. It is the eternal struggle between these two principles—right and wrong—throughout the world. They are the two principles that have stood face to face from the beginning of time; and will ever continue to struggle. The one is the common right of humanity and the other the divine right of kings. It is the same principle in whatever shape it develops itself . . . it is the same tyrannical principle.[21]

Finally, Lincoln believed that there could be no middle ground between the right and the wrong, just as a man could not be both living and dead. He also condemned such "sophistical contrivances" as "a policy of 'don't care' on a question about which all true men do care."[22] And he called for commitment in spite of opposition, because of the rightness of his position.

> Neither let us be slandered from our duty by false accusations against us, nor frightened from it by menaces of destruction to

---

18. Basler, *Lincoln*, 3: 312-313.
19. Ibid., 314.
20. Ibid.
21. Ibid., 315.
22. Ibid., 550. This is from his address at Cooper Institute, New York City, Feb. 27, 1860.

To Submit or to Rebel against the State

the Government, nor of dungeons to ourselves. LET US HAVE FAITH THAT RIGHT MAKES MIGHT, AND IN THAT FAITH, LET US, TO THE END, DARE TO DO OUR DUTY AS WE UNDERSTAND IT.[23] (Capitals his.)

The parallels between slavery and the issue of abortion are clear:

1. They are moral issues first and foremost.
2. Silence on either issue is inexcusable, including that from the pulpit.
3. The Constitution must be amended to make explicit what is already implicit—that all life from conception onward is created equal and endowed with the inalienable right of life.
4. Abortion is part of the eternal struggle between right and wrong.
5. There is no middle ground.
6. Commitment to change the situation in spite of obstacles is our duty.

The slavery issue not only parallels that of abortion, but indeed the latter may well surpass the former. For eighteen hundred years, Christianity has opposed abortion. The Supreme Court has decided for a position completely at odds with Natural Moral Law and past precedent. The Court based its decision on sociological or cultural expediency and not on law. It usurped the authority of the legislative branch in Congress and in all fifty states. The decision violates the right to life guaranteed to all by the Fifth, Ninth, Tenth, and Fourteenth Amendments to the Constitution. The decision rejected the Judeo-Christian ethic as a basis for jurisprudence in Western society. Lastly, it rejected the divine design for government in the earth.

Christians should pursue the reversal of this decision with determined commitment. Court decisions must be fought and appealed. Legislation, preferably in the form of a Constitutional Amendment, must be drafted. Protests and sit-ins are needed. Candidates for public office who compromise on this issue should be rejected. In the meantime, a rider should be attached to general legislation to stop the wholesale slaughter of the innocent.

If legitimate procedures to rectify this great evil are exhausted or are not pursued, then the day will come in which another violent course will

---

23. Basler, *Lincoln*, 550.

The Relationship of Law to Morality

arrive. "A house divided against itself cannot stand." While abortion is not our only sin, it carries significant weight. God himself cannot tolerate an apostate church or society. He will allow judgment to overwhelm such a nation. It may come in the form of internal dissolution, terrorism, war, or greater sin. It may well be that a giving over to sin (for example, homosexual behavior) is already in progress and indicates the revelation of divine wrath (Romans 1:18ff; note verse 26).

A KEY QUESTION

One major question remains, which I raised in the beginning. If morality is legislated, who or what determines what is moral and immoral? If government is to promote good and punish evil, how does one define the good and the evil? The next chapter provides the answers to these questions.

We return to the outcome that resulted from the stand that Isaac Backus took to refuse to pay taxes to support the state church of Massachusetts.

THE IMPACT OF ISAAC BACKUS' PLEA FOR RELIGIOUS LIBERTY

The initial response to Isaac Backus' "Appeal to the Public for Religious Liberty" was disappointing. The Warren Commission allowed each Baptist church to decide for itself whether or not to join in concerted civil disobedience and refuse to pay taxes. The Massachusetts legislature voted to extend the limitation on the Baptists. Even Backus' fellow citizens from Massachusetts, John and Samuel Adams, would later refuse to support his appeal for religious freedom from the state church when they met at the First Continental Congress in 1774.

While Backus and the Baptists were trying to decide what to do, including an appeal to the King, revolutionary events overtook the colonies. The Boston Tea Party erupted (December 1773) and the British Parliament closed down Boston harbor. With the call of the First Continental Congress, the Baptist cause for religious independence became one with the political Revolution. Both were struggles against taxation without representation. Once the battles of Lexington and Concord had occurred,

Backus did not hesitate to justify the Revolution. The Revolution was a "providential act to clear the way for the overthrow of the established system."[24] Backus' own family would contribute to the Revolution: Part of his father's estate included an iron foundry that became a source of munitions for the arming of patriots of the Revolution.

Historians point to Backus' "Appeal to the Public" as more significant than he realized. It became "pietistic America's declaration of spiritual independence." Its structure was like Jefferson's Declaration three years later: It laid out a legal defense against a long train of abuses, a theoretical defense of the principle of separation of church and state, and "a moral argument for civil disobedience."[25]

Isaac Backus' pamphlet became the most important writing of his lifetime. It was central to the whole movement for the separation of Church and State in America. More than any other writing, it best expresses the "eighteenth century pietistic concept of separation."[26] This pietistic version of separation was more like Roger Williams' rather than that of Jefferson and Madison. The latter wanted to protect the rights of man; Backus and the Baptists wanted to protect the rights of Christians— "the essential rights of Christianity."[27] Jefferson and Madison appealed to rationalism and deism to create a secular state with a high wall of separation from religion. They explicitly denied that America was or should be a Christian nation.[28] They believed that America would become Unitarian by 1830 with the triumph of reason over superstition. Backus believed that the whole nation would be immersed, evangelical Baptists by that date.[29] He believed that the Revolution was as much spiritual as political so that the country could move toward the gospel. He saw the new nation as the hope of the world, that the Revolution was an important step in bringing in the glory of the latter day, the completion of Christ's kingdom.[30]

24. McLoughlin, *Isaac Backus*, 137.
25. Ibid., 127.
26. Ibid., 123.
27. Ibid., xii.
28. Ibid., xi. Jefferson and Madison opposed chaplains for Congress and the armed forces, and authorization by the state of days of fasting, prayer, and thanksgiving (149).
29. Ibid., 186.
30. Ibid.

More than any other person, Backus formulated and publicized the evangelical view on church and state, which was "ultimately to prevail throughout America."[31] This view came to be represented in Supreme Court decisions.[32] Representing Massachusetts, he participated in and supported the ratification of the Constitution of the United States (while most Baptists opposed it), having particular interest in the First Amendment, which forbids the national government from having a national church (1788). It was his influence that, after his death, in 1818 led to the disestablishment of the church in Connecticut, and, in 1833, to Massachusetts doing the same. It was Backus' influence among evangelicals that helped to temper the cause of freedom in America in contrast to the excesses of the French Revolution.[33]

Backus' views have become standard in America. He held to the "inalienable right of every person to act in all religious affairs according to the full persuasion of his or her own mind," that there should be "unrestrained exercise of religious principles" without governmental interference.[34] As an evangelical, Backus held "that piety, religion, and morality were essential for maintaining the civil order."[35]

Isaac Backus wrote thirty-seven tracts and pamphlets, as well as many newspaper articles and a personal diary (inspired by David Brainerd, who had been expelled from Yale for his piety). He addressed various topics, including freedom of conscience, instructions for the Massachusetts General Assembly on writing a state constitution, the Shaker movement (which he strongly opposed), Universalism, the Freewill Baptists, Arminianism, covenant theology, the nature of the church, baptism, and hyper-Calvinism (which he believed to be fatalistic).[36] Isaac Backus died

---

31. McLoughlin, *Isaac Backus*, 109.

32. Ibid., xii. Throughout the nineteenth century, the U.S. Supreme Court followed the position of Backus and maintained that America was a Christian nation. In the twentieth century, the Court turned toward the secular position of Jefferson and Madison.

33. Ibid., 196.

34. Brackney, "Backus," 28.

35. Ibid. By religion, he meant Protestantism. He argued for a "sweet harmony" between church and state in 1784 (see McLoughlin, *Isaac Backus*, 150).

36. Backus was a moderate Calvinist, opposing, on the one hand, Freewill Baptists and Universalists for their emphasis on human accomplishment, and, on the other hand, extreme predestination among the hyper-Calvinists, "consistent Calvinists," and the New Divinity. He believed that these misrepresented Jonathan Edwards, whom he greatly admired. See Brackney, "Backus," 29.

on November 20, 1806. He had remained pastor of the same church for fifty-eight years. He summed up his own ministry as involving 918 journeys that covered 67,600 miles, and preaching over 9,800 sermons (an average of four per week for almost fifty years)—most of this on horseback. On his longest tour, which was of the South in 1788, he participated in the Second Great Awakening and spoke of his hope that slavery would come to an end.

While having little formal education, he had a keen intellect and writing ability. When the Baptists founded the College of Rhode Island in 1764, Backus was appointed to its board of trustees. In 1796, he completed his three-volume work, *A History of New England, with Particular Reference to the Denomination of Christians Called Baptists*, which is still considered to this day to be essential reading for understanding the religious history of early America.

All Americans are indebted more to Isaac Backus for religious freedom than to any other American.

8

The Standard for Law in Government

CHRISTIANS AID THE COLLAPSE OF COMMUNIST GOVERNMENTS

May 1989, Tiananmen Square, Beijing, China: Massive student demonstrations for freedom focus on this capital city. The streets are filled with joyous and jeering crowds. Some students daringly defy military tanks sent in to quell the crowds. Thousands are jailed and never heard from again.

Joining in the call for a change in government is a small contingent of Christian university students among the great throngs. Their house church had studied Paul's teaching about submission to government as found in Romans 13. They had concluded that their government, in their words, "was no longer a 'terror to those who do wrong,' but the very opposite of what God designed, namely a 'terror to those who do right.' We no longer owed any allegiance to the present government of China," they asserted.

Indeed, some Christian students vowed to use "any means possible short of physical violence" to bring down the government. Both the head of the official Three-Self Patriotic Movement and the official Catholic Church of China joined in support of the student protest.

October 9, 1989, Leipzig, East Germany: The revolution that overthrew communism in the Russian Empire arrives in Leipzig via the activity of Christians. Four main churches daringly protest against the tyranny.

To Submit or to Rebel against the State

On this day, the army and police refuse to fire on the thousands of people who have gathered for a political rally. Similar huge rallies occur elsewhere also.

November 1989, Dresden: A crowd of 100,00 people gather in the city square. When a young communist woman tries to speak to the crowd, she is shouted down into silence. But then another young woman takes the microphone and identifies herself and her husband as having just been released from prison. They had been locked up because they are committed, she says, to seeing freedom and change come to their land.

With the crowd straining to hear her, she continues speaking: "My husband and I are Christians, and I just have to say that I think it was shameful the way that young communist woman was treated a few moments ago. If we are going to build a new society, we must be willing to give others the right to speak. No one has an absolute corner on the whole truth."

The crowd accepts the rebuke. She has paid her dues, yet has found room in her heart to forgive her "enemy" and the courage to speak out.

December 1989, Romania: Six months previously, President Ceausescu vowed to destroy the evangelical church. As a Stalinist, Ceausescu was a committed communist. The institutions of the school, the family, the work place, and the church were to be abolished. The state would abolish the family and it would train the children rather than the parents. The state would abolish private property and centralize all the instruments of production in its own hands. A pure state of communism would replace all countries and nationalities. Finally, communism would abolish eternal truths, all religion, and all morality. Law, morality, and religion were "so many bourgeois prejudices." All of this effort formed what Marx and Engels called "the battle of democracy." The "union and agreement of the democratic parties of all countries" was the goal.

Ceausescu targeted Christians as enemies of the state. Many were killed and imprisoned. Many pastors, such as Joseph Tson, fled to the United States to have more freedom. He had suffered imprisonment many times.

Yet now, in December 1989, Ceausescu is dead and his Stalinist rule destroyed. His end came when he tried to remove a pastor from his own church. This arrogant act ignited the revolt that brought about the end of his reign of terror. In the streets, in train stations, and in public squares the people proclaim that God is alive. In one large city, a pastor leads the people in the Lord's Prayer as they all kneel down in the city square.

Romanian Christians who were in prison or suffering harassment just a week earlier are offered positions in the new government. Christians establish a Christian Democratic Party, and pastors begin to run for positions in parliament.

The revolt in Romania began as a revolt for religious freedom. Christmas has finally come to Romania.

February 1990, Berlin: Former Communist dictator Erich Honecker has been released from the hospital where he has been treated for cancer. At the pinnacle of power just a few weeks before, he is now, after the revolution, homeless and on the street. Despised and hated more than any other people in East Germany, Honecker and his wife are denied all assistance and help by the new government.

Pastor Uwe Holmer, in charge of a Christian help-center to the north of Berlin, has taken in the former dictator and his wife. But rather than checking them into the center, the pastor has taken them into his own home where he, his wife, and their ten children live. For twenty-six years, Margot Honecker had ruled the educational system that denied Christian young people a university education—eight of Holmer's children have been so treated.

When asked why he opened his door to such detestable people, Pastor Holmer replies that he had placed a statue of Jesus in front of the center to remind his staff that no one should ever be turned away. Holmer has taken in the Honeckers because, he says, "We have no bitterness in our hearts, because, as we follow our Lord, we are able to truly forgive."

The church has been the "midwife of the revolution" across East Germany. Christians are among the few who have credibility in the new era. Having been persecuted and imprisoned under the previous regime, they can be trusted with the new powers.

Principle 5
The Standard for Law Is Divine Revelation

> We know that the law is good if one uses it lawfully. We also know that law is made not for good people but for lawbreakers and rebels, the ungodly and sinful, the unholy and irreligious; for those who kill their fathers or mothers, for murderers, for adulterers and homosexuals, for slave traders and liars and perjurers—and for whatever else is contrary to the sound doctrine that conforms to the glorious gospel of the blessed God, which he entrusted to me.
> —1 Timothy 1:8-11

INTRODUCTION

In these remarkable verses, we find two principles. The first principle was the concern of chapter 7: Morality is legislated. The second is the concern of this chapter: The standard for law is divine revelation.

THE ISSUE OF HOMOSEXUAL RIGHTS

The last three decades have seen a revolution in morality unparalleled in the history of Western civilization since ancient Roman times.[1] I discussed this in general terms in the introduction of this book, but now we consider the one issue which represents an attack upon values and attitudes to a degree never seen before: the matter of homosexuality and civil rights.

---

1. A similar revolution in morality occurred in the second century B.C., when Rome conquered Greece (146 B.C.) and became the unrivaled military power of the Mediterranean. Yet Greek customs and morals, including homosexuality, in turn conquered Rome. Contemporary Roman historians such as Polybius, Piso, and Livy declared that "chastity was overthrown" and that the seeds of the destruction of the Republic were sown then. In contrast, this was the precise time when the Jews were able to throw off the power of the Greek ruler Antiochus IV and reassert their faith and the laws and morality built on it. They refused to be conquered by the immorality of the Greeks. It is not surprising then that the American system of government has prospered. While the form and system of government are based on that of the Greeks and Romans, the religion and morals come from the Jews and Christians.

The Standard for Law in Government

It used to be that homosexuals, male and female (lesbians), kept their practice secret (in the closet). Now homosexuals and their supporters demand that their behavior and identity as homosexuals be given legal recognition with the status of a civil right, along with race, sex, color, national origin, religion, and so on. The laws of this country forbid discrimination on these bases.

Today homosexuals demand nondiscrimination of their "sexual orientation" in areas of housing, purchase of property, all hiring (private, religious, public), the ministry and other professions (teaching, law enforcement, sensitive government jobs), health services, and everywhere else. The state of Wisconsin has gone so far as to ban discrimination in all hiring (religious and public), so that homosexuals qualify as foster parents or boy's home parents. Other states are considering such legislation or already have it in place in regard to government jobs (in Oregon, for example).

The "gay rights" movement is militant homosexuality, which attempts to make homosexuality publicly acceptable as a "civil right." It seeks political power by public office and legislation. Already some city or state government offices are considered to be "homosexual seats," virtually guaranteeing a political office to some "gay" person of the community. Homosexuals in San Francisco, boasting a greater percentage of homosexuals among the population than any other city, have it in their power to determine who will be the mayor or a council member. The national Democratic Party platform began endorsing gay rights in the election of 1984. Today, both Democratic and Republican candidates for president vie for the "gay vote."

There are gay newspapers and choirs, bath houses, sado-masochistic bars, "gay pride" days and parades, gay marriages, and a gay church denomination known as the Metropolitan Community Church. Gay clergy are pounding at the doors for admission to the office of clergy in the major denominations. According to an article in *U.S. News and World Report* (1987), as many as half of the Episcopalian priests in San Francisco are gay. In more recent years, the number of gay priests in the Roman Catholic Church has contributed to the recent scandal of pedophilia among the priesthood.

Homosexual behavior has contributed to major health concerns, such as Kaposi's sarcoma (a form of cancer endemic to homosexuals) and AIDS (Acquired Immune Deficiency Syndrome).

To Submit or to Rebel against the State

In the United States in 2009, almost 80 percent of new AIDS infections among males (also known as HIV) were in men who have sex with men (so the CDC, February 2011). AIDS is a disease spread from one gay person to another because of the distorted nature of homosexual behavior. Incidence of AIDS among others (drug addicts and heterosexuals) is due to bisexual activity or heterosexual sexual activity outside of marriage, blood donations by homosexuals with AIDS, and transmission in the blood by way of contaminated needles. Hemophiliacs are at risk from contaminated blood. The incidence of AIDS in Africa has risen to epidemic proportions. Fully 25 percent of young adults in certain African countries are ill with AIDS, basically resulting from heterosexual prostitution and contaminated blood.

Homosexual "rights" have now become the most pressing and explosive legal battle of our time, rivaling the conflict over abortion. Difficult questions arise: Should the identity of AIDS victims be protected with confidentiality in order to prevent identification of those who are homosexuals or drug addicts? Should AIDS victims be separated from others? Should the government pass legislation forbidding homosexual activity in public and private?

The courts have already entered the legal fray over homosexual rights. In 1977, the U.S. Supreme Court upheld the right of a public school in Washington State to fire an avowed homosexual teacher espousing gay rights. In 1986, this same Court decided that homosexuality is not a right protected by the Constitution (in *Bower v. Hardwick*), thereby the Court upheld a law of the state of Georgia prohibiting homosexual behavior, even in private between consenting adults.

However, during the fall of 2002, the Court once more decided to hear another case regarding homosexual behavior. In a Texas case, a gay couple claimed discrimination for being arrested for practicing homosexual behavior in private, which was prohibited by Texas law. The next year the Court reversed its previous history and declared the Texas law void. This decision has opened the flood gates for the "homosexualizing" of America.

In the state of Oregon, legislation has passed that would ban discrimination of homosexuality in all employment, sale of property, and housing. In 1987, legislation went so far as to call upon the public schools to teach a program of education "calculated to eliminate attitudes" hostile to acceptance of homosexuality as a civil right. It labeled any such

The Standard for Law in Government

discrimination of homosexuality as a "threat" and "menace" to the "public policy" of the state. Thus, this law would effectively prohibit any church or individual the right to identify homosexual activity as sinful.

That the courts would ever ban such speech has already been tested in the Netherlands. In 1987, the courts would have barred the Catholic Church from calling homosexual behavior a sin had Parliament first passed a law banning discrimination of homosexuality.

The expansion of legal recognition goes on. States have banned discrimination based in "sexual orientation" and have passed "hate crime" laws that cover crimes seemingly motivated by bias against homosexuals. Gay parents want the right to serve as adoptive or foster parents. In 2009, Congress passed and President Obama signed into law a federal hate crimes law.

This effort is accompanied by the demand that gay marriages be given the same legal status as heterosexual marriages. "Marriage" would be redefined as an arrangement between two people no matter what their sexual orientation is. Marriage would not have to be a contract between heterosexuals. In several states (e.g., California and Oregon), the people voted to define in their constitutions a marriage as that between a man and a woman. Yet the effort to overturn such constitutional changes has moved to the courts in these states. The gay community, with President Obama's support, has succeeded in overturning the "Don't Ask, Don't Tell" policy in the military; and the President will no longer support before the Supreme Court the Defense of Marriage Act (DOMA) passed under President Clinton. In December 2011, the U.S. State Department enacted a new policy whereby foreign aid to countries would be conditioned on whether they approve homosexual behavior—and many African and Muslim countries do not.

The North American Man/Boy Love Association (NAMBLA) seeks to eliminate all legal boundaries to adult-child same-sex behavior. This would bring legalization of intergenerational (man-boy) homosexuality. The goal is to lower the consent age below sixteen or seventeen.

If principle 4 is valid (morality is legislated, which we discussed in chapter 7), then it is necessary to define what is moral in order that it *be* legislated. Where do we turn to find a standard of morality? As this chapter will show, the standard of legislation is divine revelation.

Chapter 7 pointed out that various forms of immoral behavior, including adultery and homosexuality, are the proper targets for legislation. Society does not tolerate unbridled immoral behavior. To determine whether legislation should control immoral behavior, there are always two questions that need to be answered. As applied to homosexual behavior, these are: Is homosexuality immoral, wrong, or illegal? Is prohibition of homosexual behavior by legislation supportable and valid? In answering these questions, we must practice the ethic of love when adopting legislation so as not to violate the dignity of people.

THE BIBLICAL WITNESS REGARDING HOMOSEXUALITY

Chapter 7 provided the answer to the first question: Homosexuality is found in Paul's list of vices in 1 Timothy 1:8-10. It is grouped with the other six vices, including murder, perjury, and kidnapping. Paul's list of vices parallels the second half of the Ten Commandments.

Homosexuality is also in Paul's catalogue of vices in 1 Corinthians 6:9-11, where the same Greek term for homosexuality (*arsenokoitai*) occurs as in 1 Timothy. In Romans 1:26-27, homosexual behavior and lesbianism are clearly defined and just as clearly viewed as sinful and perverted acts, evidence of God's judgment of an individual who has committed other sins. That is, God's wrath is revealed against idolatry (Romans 1:18-23) in the form of delivering one over to other sins, including homosexuality (1:24, 26, 28).

In recent years, many have sought to reinterpret these passages in such a way that they allow for homosexual behavior in some form. They will not succeed. Paul makes it clear that he is condemning lesbianism (Romans 1:26) and male homosexuality between *consenting adults* (Romans 1:27). He calls it "unnatural" because it violates the order of creation as male and female (Romans 1:19ff.) and the order of marriage given at the very beginning of the human race (Genesis 1-2). These words cannot be limited to aggressive violation of another person, or to prostitution, or to pederasty, as though his words would allow homosexual behavior in "loving arrangements."

Scripture also does not allow for homosexual orientation as an unchangeable condition and thereby justified. Rather, this orientation is part of the fallen nature of human beings, as are all other sinful desires. A person's heart (one's thoughts that affect one's total being) needs to be changed, and can be. It happened to some of the most licentious people of the Roman world—the Corinthians. They were able to find forgiveness and deliverance from same-sex orientation and behavior (1 Corinthians 6:11). Gratifying an evil disposition or orientation is sin. The idea that homosexual orientation is justified by claiming that it is an inherent, inborn predisposition does not find support in Scripture.

Granted that homosexual behavior is immoral (as found in 1 Timothy 1:8–10), should it be illegal (our second question)? The biblical answer is yes, since Paul says that legislation is "appointed" for the "lawless," the "immoral," and the "irreligious," and he includes those who engage in homosexual behavior in his list of specific examples.

Yet by what standard should this and similar laws legislate morality? Why should a Christian viewpoint prevail over others? The answer to such questions constitutes principle 5, that the standard of all legislation is divine revelation. To assert the prior place of Christian truth on this issue runs directly counter to the current fad for pluralism and political correctness. However, contemporary thinking is simply the old immorality in a new cultural setting. And the prior place of Christian truth will carry with it the prior place of Christian love and compassion.

THE MEANING OF THE TEXT

Note how the passage cited at the beginning of this chapter speaks to our present principle: "Whatever else is contrary to the sound doctrine" is the concluding phrase to the list of vices. This phrase is similar to the words, "and if there be any other commandment," found in Romans 13:9, where Paul clearly refers to the Ten Commandments. In this catalogue in 1 Timothy 1, violations of the tenth commandment (dealing with covetousness) are not specified since human law or legislation cannot punish the evil thoughts of men. However, the phrase "whatever else is contrary" emphasizes the impossibility of escape for anyone. No one can escape, including those teaching contrary to the truth in Ephesus where Timothy ministered.

The "sound doctrine" refers to that which is healthy or wholesome doctrine or teaching. Hence, false doctrine is reckoned as "diseased" (consider 2 Timothy 4:3 and Titus 1:9; 2:1). It contrasts the pure gospel, especially its moral teaching. It is significant to note that the gospel is viewed as absorbing the Law of Moses into itself. That is, just as these sins are dealt with in the Law of Moses (1 Timothy 1:8), so they are contained in the gospel itself (the "sound doctrine"). In addition, the natural law written on the hearts of the heathen must be included.[2] This is a certain proof of the ongoing sinful nature of these vices. They were considered sin in the past and are still so regarded, virtually universally.

The standard of the "sound teaching," as well as of the entire discourse regarding the role of law (1 Timothy 1:8–10), is signified by the words, "according to the glorious gospel of the blessed God," with which Paul had been entrusted. The revelation of the gospel substantiates Paul's position about the role of law and its application. The teaching of these verses is not simply Paul's personal opinion but part of the revelation he has received from God.[3]

The words "according to" represent the Greek preposition *kata*. Here it has the idea of "being fit for," "in keeping with," "conformity to," and so on. The phrase means that the vices are not in conformity with the gospel. The preposition presents the idea of a standard; thus the gospel is the standard by which to measure behavior.

It should also be noted that Paul writes in terms that are transcultural and universal. He is not addressing Jews only, nor is he to be limited to a Christian audience. Rather, he is writing about the role of law or legislation in a society, and his words refer to all societies. The gospel of the New Testament, then, provides a standard, a source for determining whether certain legislation for restraining deeds of lawlessness and sin is appropriate. Is there evidence that Greek and Roman cultures would support Paul? I show below that this is indeed the case.

THE SEVERAL SOURCES AND STANDARDS OF TRUTH

The standard of truth and righteousness as found in the gospel is the same as that revealed earlier in history in the Mosaic Law, which is the topic with which Paul began this passage (verse 8). Together, the Mosaic Law and the gospel define, in part, what is the good that government should promote and the evil it should restrain.

It is important to note that I have not claimed that the Bible is the only standard; the standard is broader than special revelation. It encompasses

---

2. Lock, *Pastoral Epistles*, 12.
3. Kelly, *Pastoral Epistles*, 51.

The Standard for Law in Government

general revelation as well. That is, not only does the Bible reveal God's standards for right and wrong but so does Natural Moral Law.

Natural Moral Law is divine revelation because all that we know comes from God directly or indirectly. The creation, the law in the heart and the conscience, and history should be considered part of God's revelation of moral law, along with Scripture, miracles, and Jesus Christ himself.

The creation reveals God and his moral law, according to Romans 1:18-32. Humanity is culpable for recognizing not only God's nature (verses 18-23) but also his moral law. The text reads, "Although they know the ordinance of God, that those who practice such things are worthy of death, they not only do the same, but also give hearty approval to those who practice them." The word for "know" is intensive and forceful; they "fully know" or "understand," not intellectually alone but also experientially. The "wages of sin is spiritual death" (Romans 6:23).

The law written in the hearts of Gentiles who do not have the Law of Moses makes them culpable (Romans 2:15). The conscience bears witness to obedience, and the thoughts of men are involved also.

History also reveals the will of God. Humanity is accountable for properly responding to God's past acts of judgment upon disobedience (Romans 1:32; 2:2-12). This is the basic force of God's destruction of Sodom and the subsequent references to it as a past event. Even Christ said, "Remember Lot's wife" (Luke 17:32 and 2 Peter 3:5-7). Also, the collective experience of man has discovered immutable moral laws such as: "Whatever a person sows, even this shall one reap" (the principle which Paul repeats in Galatians 6:7).

Thus, 1 Timothy 1:8-10 sets forth just one aspect of the revelation of God's will, namely the gospel, which carries on the standards of the Mosaic Law. This is divine revelation that is special and direct. In contrast, the creation, the law in the heart, and history are forms of divine revelation, which are general, perceived by all men. These facts reinforce the premise that all law or legislation everywhere should have as its standard divine revelation, whether general or specific.

To Submit or to Rebel against the State

EXTREMES TO BE AVOIDED

Those who maintain the principle that the standard of law is divine revelation must avoid several different extremes. On the one hand, there is the view that is called "theonomy," meaning "God's law." Representatives of this view include Greg Bahnsen, Rousas J. Rushdoony, Gary North, and various organizations. This position maintains that the kingdom proclaimed by Christ is now present and must be institutionalized in the United States and throughout the world. All Old Testament laws, it is claimed, should be applied to nations today unless the New Testament specifically abrogates or annuls these laws. Such an application of laws means that it is wrong to charge interest or usury; the land of the United States should lie fallow every seventh year; the military draft is wrong; Christians should tithe a tenth or more; and pastors, churches, and offerings belong to God, as did the Old Testament Levites and priests, the temple, and the offerings. This position is the direct descendant of the post-millennialism of early colonial America. Like these people, the Puritans perceived America as the New Jerusalem prophesied about in Scripture.

While this view has some merit, there are several serious concerns:

- There is a wrong hermeneutic involved. The principle of interpreting the Old Testament is incorrect. It is better to say that only those parts of the Mosaic Law that are restated or taught in the New, or transcend the time of the Law and the nation of Israel, are still in effect. These are usually the universals and absolutes of the Moral Law, such as the Ten Commandments and the vices of Leviticus 18–20. These universals existed prior to (and came to be embodied in) the Mosaic Law.

- It confuses the nature of Christ's reign, making it *de facto* (actual) while it is only *de jure* (by right). One day what is *de jure* will become *de facto*. Another way to speak about this is to say that the kingdom is here in essence or essentially, but not in historical form or existentially. Failure to make this distinction is similar to the failure to reconcile passages that teach God's supremacy and sovereignty over all with others that teach us to pray that his will be done on earth.

- This view often rejects natural revelation, yet this is unfortunate in light of passages referring to natural revelation and its value cited

The Standard for Law in Government

previously.

- This view tends to bring all of humanity under the law. Therefore, it is in danger of dissolving the gospel of grace into a law of bondage.
- This view tends to compartmentalize various aspects of the Mosaic Law, pitting moral aspects against ceremonial or social/legal ones. Yet the Law is a whole and cannot be dissected into parts, some binding and some not (Galatians 3:10, 5:3). Theonomy has the effect of either institutionalizing Christianity, or inciting such negative opposition by its opponents that it is relegated to irrelevancy.

The opposite extreme to avoid regarding the principle of this chapter is that of historical Anabaptists, pacifists, and some contemporary dispensationalists. These believe that Christians are citizens of heaven and are to have no dealings or involvement in politics or civil government. Others have hopes for the special removal of the Church that leads them to ignore civic affairs. These views are more widespread than theonomy and directly opposite to it. It is prevalent in third world countries due to early missionary teaching and practice.

In Nigeria, for example, the national Christian church, the Evangelical Church of West Africa (ECWA), has been virtually subjugated by the Islamic minority. The reason for this, according to Christian nationals, is that the Sudan Interior Mission taught converts for a hundred years not to become involved in government and politics.

It is an erroneous view because it fails to recognize that Christians have responsibility in several spheres or realms. It also fails to recognize the relationship of faith or religion to morality and law or legislation. Those aspects of a Christian's calling to be both salt and light in the world (Matthew 5:13–16) are dismissed. It defines differently the proper use of law, its application to various moral/social concerns, and the standard for such laws.

There is one more extreme view regarding the place of law. It is not a group *per se*, but a mindset. It is antinomianism. The word means "against law." Those who practice antinomianism believe that grace alone controls a person's relationship and responsibility to God, not laws or rules. This view exalts grace and salvation by faith at the expense of the total abrogation of law. All standards, particularly those derived from the Old Testament, are rejected.

To Submit or to Rebel against the State

The faults of this view are several. It fails to distinguish legitimate uses of law (restraint, guidance, instruction) from illegitimate ones (justification, sanctification; consider Romans 3:27–31), and it confuses legalism (use of law for improper motives) with proper functions of law. Ultimately antinomianism leads to unbridled license and sin. It is condemned in Scripture (Romans 3:5–8 and Galatians 2:17–21). This error is part of the basis for the recent attempts to remove some or all prohibitions of homosexuality for the Christian.

APPLICATION OF THE PRINCIPLES

Next I want to discuss the imposition of moral standards reflected in law in light of the two principles of chapters 7 and 8. What right does one have to impose one's morality on others? If one does have such a right, how should one do it? These questions concern the justification and manner of such imposition.

The right or justification for imposing a moral standard concerns the recognition that everyone has some kind of moral standard, and every nation has a public moral standard without which a society could not survive (as shown in the introduction). The question is not: What right do you have to impose your morality on the rest? Rather, the question is: Whose standard of morality shall be imposed?

The standard of Judeo-Christian ethics should have preeminent claim to first place in the United States. This claim is based on several things, including historical precedent (it was the ethic at the founding of the United States and assumed in its founding documents), historical validation (it has guided the nation well for two hundred years), divine special revelation (God has set forth certain universal standards of morality), and general revelation (it accords best with common morality and Natural Moral Law among all peoples).

The manner of imposing any standard of morality upon the public is by legislation. In the United States, most laws are in place by consent of the people. Enough people recognize the validity of Judeo-Christian ethics and they desire that this standard should continue. Thus we gain morality through special or general revelation and promote that morality in the state through legislation.

THE PRINCIPLE APPLIED TO HOMOSEXUAL BEHAVIOR

What are the consequences when one applies principle 5 to the topic of homosexual behavior? Because the special revelation of Scripture presents homosexual behavior as both sinful and lawless, homosexual behavior is a proper object of church and state restriction and law because it violates both religious and legal standards.

Yet the case against homosexual behavior need not rest on special revelation alone. Homosexual behavior violates general revelation as well. Paul can say that it is "unnatural" and "contrary to nature," that is, contrary to the order of creation (Romans 1:19-25) and the order of marriage (Romans 1:26-27). It is contrary to nature because it cannot reproduce the race. It violates the order "to be fruitful and multiply" that God gave to the human race after the creation and after the flood. The vast majority of people recognize that homosexual behavior is perverse.

History gives us the lesson of the destruction of Sodom. "Sodomy" is the term most of history has used to describe this behavior. Illness, disease, and short life are associated with it, historically (AIDS) and biblically (Romans 1:32 and Job 36:14). Even the Jewish writer Philo pointed to the disease that accompanies same-sex behavior.[4]

The law in the heart and conscience (Romans 2) recognizes that homosexual behavior is immoral. Even in ancient Greece, where homosexuality flourished more than anywhere else, certain forms (such as pederasty and prostitution) were forbidden by law, and certain regions apparently outlawed all forms.

Even the Greek philosopher Plato could recognize the immorality of homosexual behavior, as I pointed out in chapter 7. While Plato is often cited as glorifying homosexuality in his work the *Symposium*, he takes a directly opposite view in his last work, *Laws*. There he writes that homosexuality and lesbianism, with adultery and incest, are contrary to nature and are enslaving (*Laws*, 636 b-c; 836 a--c; 838; 841 d, e). Earlier Greek apologists for homosexual behavior appealed to the tradition that it was practiced by the Greek gods Zeus and Ganymede, and this gave religious sanction to the practice. But Plato asserts that this tradition was a lie concocted by the Cretans. This recalls Paul's agreement with a Cretan poet's claim that the Cretans are always liars (Titus 1:12-13). Plato actually calls

---

4. Philo, *On the Life of Abraham*, 133-137. See De Young, *Homosexuality*, 246, 265-268, 345.

To Submit or to Rebel against the State

upon the force of religion, public opinion, and law to restrain homosexual behavior and orientation.[5]

Later, Roman writers (Seneca, *Moral Epistles*, 47.7; Plutarch, *Dialogue on Love*, 751 c–e, 752 b–c; Dio Chrysostom, *Discourse*, 7.133–135, 151–152; 21.6–10; 77/78.36) condemned homosexual behavior as exploitative, indecent, contrary to nature, lawless, and lustful.[6]

Thus there is a common standard of morality against homosexual behavior. Not only the Bible but many ancient Greek and Roman writers viewed it as immoral behavior.

This virtually universal opposition means that homosexual behavior should not be given civil rights status nor be protected by law in other ways. It ought to be restricted as evil and unlawful by governing authorities.

The Bible's ethic is no more stringent or harsh on this matter than the common person's ethic expressed throughout history. In fact, the Bible's ethic is more humane because it is based upon belief in the basic dignity of all people as bearing the divine image of God. The Judeo-Christian ethic, while opposed to homosexuality, protects the homosexual from harsh, demeaning, and degrading treatment. Love must always accompany the application of the truth. The state must always recognize the inherent dignity of people as made in the image of God, including those who engage in same-sex behavior. The application of law must be informed by Christian compassion.

HOW CHRISTIANITY HAS SHAPED PUBLIC MORALITY IN THE PAST

There is a persuasive illustration from the past of how Christianity can influence legislation. In the early centuries of the Christian Church, drug-taking was wide spread. Evidently the use of hallucinogenic drugs was an intrinsic part of the mystery religions, the chief rivals to Christianity in the Roman Empire.[7] The worship of Demeter was one such mystery religion; it also involved homosexual behavior (see Philo, *On the Special Laws*, pages 37–42).

---

5. See De Young, *Homosexuality*, 253–254.
6. Ibid. 257ff.
7. Wasson, Hofmann, and Ruck, *Eleusis*, 51ff.

The Standard for Law in Government

These indigenous religions of the Roman Empire practiced many rituals that paralleled Christianity. They held to sacrifice by blood (a form of baptism) and initiatory rites. When Christianity began to influence culture in the fourth century, the mystery religions, and the drugs and homosexuality that went with them, were stamped out by legislation.[8] Several references in Scripture (Galatians 5:20; Revelation 9:21, 18:23, 21:8, 22:15) condemn the use of magic and sorcery (the Greek word is *pharmakeia*). Early Christian writings (*Didache*, 2. 2) support the idea that this word includes a reference to hallucinogens. Hence, Christian faith influenced morality to the extent that laws were enacted to eradicate the practice.

The alternative to having one standard or set of morals is to have many—to embrace moral pluralism. Yet moral or radical pluralism has several flaws. First, moral pluralism is vaporous, for no true pluralism in morality could ever exist in the same entity (nation). Anarchy would result. Second, pluralism is seductive for it really is a smoke screen for replacing one standard with another that, when fully embraced, will be more intolerant and dictatorial than the former one.

CONCLUDING OBSERVATIONS

Let's summarize the foregoing discussion of 1 Timothy 1:8-11. First, all of the persons listed in these verses are culpable for their behavior and subject to the restraint or punishment of law. Even liars are punished when they violate the truth in court under oath or in contracts. Sexual immorality, polygamy, and adultery are circumscribed by certain legal requirements.

Second, one can assume from the list of vices that these forms of behavior are recognized universally as sinful and/or subject to criminal prosecution. This is the case because the law in view is without national restriction. It is universally applicable.

---

8. Wasson, Hofmann, and Ruck, *Eleusis*, 57–58. The triumph of Christianity that ended the use of drugs in society is greatly lamented by the authors of this book. They believe that religion should simply be a "high" (76)! They believe that hallucinogens enable one to experience "religion in its purest essence, without intellectual content" (23). Such a distorted view means that the battle for a moral standard in this area needs to be waged all over again!

Third, those who teach that certain behavior is victimless and private, amoral, and not of civil concern are wrong. In this passage, homosexuality and sexual immorality (fornication) are classed without distinction with murder, kidnapping, and lying. People are not free to do sexually as they please in their own home. They cannot lawfully abuse or torture their spouse or children, engage in incest, polygamy, or bestiality, engage in child pornography and sex, and take drugs. Practicing immorality or homosexuality in one's home will eventually spill over to the community and corrupt community morals. Each act has societal implications, such as for the family.

The institution of marriage is one of the hallmarks of a civilized nation. It is not an albatross around people's necks but rather provides the greatest freedom within limitations so that everyone may experience its benefits. The dissolution of the institution of marriage as defined as that of a man and a woman would lead to the collapse of other institutions and threaten civilization itself.[9]

Fourth, there is a continuity between the moral standards of the Old and New Testaments. The revelation of God's righteousness in the gospel (Romans 1:17–18) is consistent with and flows from the standard revealed in the Old Testament.

Fifth, both the law of the Old Testament and the gospel of the New are sources for lawmaking and jurisprudence then and now. While avoiding theonomy, nations would do well to go to Scripture for their jurisprudence. Since Israel's laws are the most righteous of all the nations (Deuteronomy 4:8), then whatever nation has laws corresponding to Israel's will have righteous laws to define the good and the evil. These laws will have divine support or approval.

Sixth, all such behavior as cited in this passage reflects all three aspects or spheres of accountability given in the passage. They have civil, religious, and moral dimensions. Government, God, and society are all involved. This point is one of the most significant ones to be made.

Seventh, the three divisions or categories of 1 Timothy 1:9 reflect the three parts of the triangle discussed in chapters 3 and 7 above: Law, religion, and morality correspond to the "lawbreakers," "ungodly," and "unholy" or "irreligious." Religion is the basis of morality, and morality is the basis of law.

---

9. Blankenhorn, *The Future of Marriage*. See a defense of the traditional institution of marriage in De Young, *Burning Down the Shack*, 71–82.

The Standard for Law in Government

And eighth, if the triangle discussed in chapters 3 and 7 is a valid way to represent the relationship of religion to morality and to law, then some standard of morality will provide the standard for laws. This chapter defends the view that that standard is and ought to be what God has revealed (whether in general or special revelation).

In light of the foregoing, the Christian should never be reluctant to insist that the standards of right and wrong as found in the Bible should be upheld in society. This is especially true for those living in America where, at the nation's founding, a Judeo-Christian ethic provided the standard of morality. Legislation should reflect the common revelation of the Testaments and general revelation.

This chapter lays the foundation for chapter 9. If biblical revelation is the standard for morality and law, a question naturally arises: How can Christians influence their government to embrace biblical moral standards? The next chapter discusses the vital and unique role that Christians have in society.

9

The Christian's Unique Role in Government

ONLY TRUE CHRISTIANS CAN SAVE THEIR COUNTRY

THREE VOICES FROM THE past remind us of the crucial role that Christians can play in saving society from its demise. From the second century (A.D. 130–150) comes one of the most eloquent statements of who a Christian is. Although Christians were a tiny minority, they still had a powerful witness at that time. For the inquisitive person, the author of the *Epistle of Diognetus* answers this question: "What is a Christian?"

> Christians are not distinguished from the rest of mankind either in locality or in speech or in customs. For they dwell not somewhere in cities of their own, neither do they use some different language, nor practice an extraordinary kind of life . . . They dwell in their own countries, but only as sojourners; they bear their share in all things as citizens, and they endure all hardships as strangers. Every foreign country is a fatherland to them, and every fatherland is foreign. They marry like all other men and they beget children; but they do not cast away their offspring. They have their meals in common, but not their wives. They find themselves in the flesh, and yet they live not after the flesh. Their existence is on earth, but their citizenship is in heaven. They obey the established laws, and they surpass the laws in their own lives. They love all men, and they are persecuted by all. They are ignored, and yet they are condemned. They are put to death, and yet they are endued with life. They are in beggary, and yet they make many rich. They are in lack of all things, and yet they abound in all things. They

are dishonored, and yet they are glorified in their dishonor. They are evil spoken of, and yet they are vindicated. They are reviled, and they bless; they are insulted, and they respect. Doing good, they are punished as evildoers; being punished they rejoice, as if they were thereby quickened by life. War is waged against them as aliens by the Jews, and persecution is carried on against them by the Greeks, and yet those that hate them cannot tell the reason of their hostility. In a word, what the soul is in a body, this the Christians are in the world.

Another eloquent statement of Christian identity comes from the 1700s. In Great Britain, two Christian men led the way for the eradication of slavery in the British colonies: Granville Sharp and William Wilberforce. A Greek grammarian and brilliant biblical scholar and attorney, author of more than seventy books and pamphlets, Sharp led the way for the abolition of slavery. From England, he wrote a widely circulated book on behalf of the American cause for independence. A friend to Benjamin Franklin, Thomas Jefferson, and others, he influenced Jefferson in several of the concepts and the wording of the Declaration of Independence. Sharp was chiefly responsible for the purchase of land for a colony of freed slaves in West Africa, known as Sierra Leone. In 1804, he became the first chairman of the British and Foreign Bible Society. Until his death in 1813, he remained true to his calling of philanthropist, promoter of Christianity, abolitionist, and scholar.

As a member of Parliament, William Wilberforce spoke to the British people about the blight that the slave trade had on society. In *A Practical View of the Prevailing Religious System of Professed Christians, in the Higher and Middle Classes in This Country, Contrasted with Real Christianity*, Wilberforce defines who is a true Christian.

> I have maintained that true Christians are always the most important members of the community. No sound or experienced politician would deny that. But we boldly assert that there never was a period when this was truer than of the present time . . . The progress of irreligion and the decline in morals is enough to alarm every thoughtful person and to fill us with foreboding about the growth of evil. We can only depend upon true Christians to give some remedy against its decline. Zeal is required in the cause of religion and only they can feel it. Singleness of purpose, consistency of behavior, and perseverance in effort are needed. Only true Christians can provide these qualities.

Principle 6
Christians Must Pray for Leaders of Governments

> I urge, then, first of all, that requests, prayers, intercessions and thanksgivings, be made for everyone—for kings and all those in authority, that we may live peaceful and quiet lives in all godliness and holiness. This is good, and pleases God our Savior, who wants all men to be saved and to come to a knowledge of the truth.
> —*1 Timothy 2:1-4*

> Also, seek the peace and prosperity of the city to which I have carried you into exile. Pray to the Lord for it, because if it prospers, you too will prosper. —*Jeremiah 29:7*

INTRODUCTION

It has become fashionable in recent years for various individuals and groups to promote a secular humanism perspective in American society; public schools are the special focus of this movement. Christians and others argue that this promotes secular humanism as a new religion, violating the Establishment Clause of the First Amendment of the Constitution of the United States.

This focus on secular humanism is but one aspect of a larger conflict over the role of religion in the United States. This conflict spills over into many aspects of American life. It occurs in the form of court decisions banning school-sponsored prayer and Bible reading, taxation of churches, banning of church schools lacking state certification of curricula or teachers, pastor-led protests against abortion and homosexuality, eviscerating the definition of obscenity to allow more pornography, removal of the Ten Commandments from public schools and the courtrooms of our land, the evolution versus creation controversy, banning evangelism in public places, debate over public funding of the chaplaincy in the U.S. military and Congress, barring the Boy Scouts from the public schools, the use of school vouchers for education in both public and religious schools, repeal of "Don't Ask, Don't Tell" in the military, opposition to the Defense of Marriage Act, and so on.

More recently, the terrorist attacks on the United States and her allies raise the question of how tolerant our government should be toward

The Christian's Unique Role in Government

Islamic fundamentalism. Should "relief agencies" funded by Muslims be allowed to channel funds to terrorist groups abroad? In a larger perspective, should federal funds go to faith-based programs that aid the poor, the prisoners, and others needing help?

The symbol of the cross that was formed by steel girders from the collapsed World Trade Center (2001) was a picture caught by the media—it symbolized the deep role of faith in American life. But just what this role should be is an ongoing debate (the ACLU opposed the public display of the cross). The debate goes back to the meaning of the Constitution.

UNDERSTANDING THE FIRST AMENDMENT

Much of the debate hinges on an understanding of the freedom of religion clauses of the First Amendment to the Constitution. These provide that "Congress shall make no law respecting an establishment of religion, nor prohibiting the free exercise thereof."

Until recently, these words were understood to mean, in line with their original intent or setting, that Congress should make no law prohibiting a state to have its own separate state church (several state churches continued to exist, the last ending in Massachusetts in 1833), and that Congress would allow free reign nationally to religious expression. Indeed, it was believed that freedom of religion was an "unalienable right" (as President Madison termed it) to be protected by government. It was believed that government could aid or benefit religion equally, on a nonpreferential basis. This view went with a narrow interpretation of the Establishment Clause—that it prohibits only the legal union of a single church or religion with the national government.

Today a view quite different from the preceding has usurped the traditional interpretation of the First Amendment. It derives from Supreme Court decisions enacted over the last fifty years and is the view of secular humanists, liberal jurists and historians, the American Civil Liberties Union (the ACLU), and Americans United for the Separation of Church and State. These assert that government and religion, state and church, should be strictly separated. The Establishment Clause is broadly interpreted as virtually *opposing* all forms of religion and the government's involvement in them. These "preferentialists" oppose any aid to religion, however nondiscriminatory or impartial it may be.

To Submit or to Rebel against the State

THE MEANING OF 1 TIMOTHY 2:1-4

The passage of 1 Timothy 2:1-4 makes a direct contribution to this controversy. It provides insight into the proper relationship between state and church.

The Christian has a crucial role to play in government, which the unbeliever cannot. Perhaps no passage substantiates this more clearly, and shows the consequence of this function for the roles of state and church, than that of 1 Timothy 2:1-4. The crucial function stipulated here is that of prayer and its attendant activities. This passage finds its almost exact equivalent in Jeremiah 29:7.

Prior to this passage, Paul warned about false doctrine (1 Timothy 1:3-7) and addressed the validity of the law with regard to civil, religious, and moral conduct (1:8-11). The gospel provides the standard for right and wrong (1:11). These verses were the focus of the discussion in chapter 8. At this point, Paul expresses thankfulness and praise to God for saving him from sin and entrusting him with the gospel (1:12-17).

In 1 Timothy 1:18, Paul commands his son in the faith to "war a good warfare" by the prophecies previously made about him. Timothy's activity as a soldier (2 Timothy 2:3-4) is to be accompanied by keeping faith and a good conscience, lest he become shipwrecked regarding the faith, as some others have (1 Timothy 1:19-20).

Paul's words in 1 Timothy 2:1-4 then comprise the first way in which Timothy is to "fight a good fight." The exhortation that follows is the *first*, a preeminent pursuit of a good Christian soldier—it is the very mark of a Christian. It is powerful proof of Christian faith.

What is this crucial exhortation, the obedience of which will carry out the first obligation of a soldier of Christ? It is to pray for governmental leaders. The exhortation is not to witness, to preach, to evangelize, or to teach—it is to pray. In the spiritual warfare involving the thrust of God's kingdom into the realm of the world under satanic power, the Christian has, as his first obligation, prayer. It is by prayer that that part of the supernatural realm under demonic control can be penetrated and the rulers, powers, world forces of darkness, and the spiritual forces of wickedness in the heavenly places can be defeated (Ephesians 6:12). It is using spiritual means to defeat spiritual forces.

Prayer for leaders in government will thwart the demonic forces always attempting to exert their will and program through human government. Their aim is to bring about the end of God's purposes for humanity in human government. Its culmination is the rule of the Messiah on earth over all nations (Isaiah 11:1ff.).

This passage is a reminder of Daniel and his prayer for the accomplishment of God's will among governments. His praying had a direct connection with the unseen battle fought between Michael, the archangel-protector of Israel, and the demonic princes of Persia and Greece (see Daniel 10).

FOUR FORMS OF PRAYER

Therefore, it is not surprising that Paul places great emphasis on prayer. He enforces this emphasis by using several terms for prayer.[1] First, prayer is to take the form of petitions, entreaties, or supplications; the term refers to needs keenly felt. This kind of prayer springs from feelings of want or need.

There are certainly many felt needs of American society for which the Christian should pour out entreaties for God to intervene. Not the least need is to have leaders of principle and moral courage. This form of praying is especially pertinent where Christians are being persecuted, as they are in most communist and Islamic lands today.

Next, Paul exhorts that prayer should also be for needs always present. That is, Paul urges Timothy (and us today) to make "prayers" in general. This general term for praying emphasizes one's approach to God with a spirit of devotion—a term never used when addressing someone with a request for something. Christians should always pray for their leaders, whether they are being persecuted by the government or are enjoying a time of tranquility.

The third word defines prayer as formal petition, as to a superior such as a king. It implies the idea of conversing freely, connoting boldness of access or confidence. This word reminds one of the exhortation of Hebrews 4:16: "Let us therefore come boldly to the throne of grace" (KJV). The context here supports the idea of prayer on behalf of others (intercession), not so much the idea of prayer for one's own needs. When believers approach God on behalf of governmental leaders, they do so with confidence. They know that God is pleased with such prayer and has determined it as part of the means for bringing about his will among

---

1. Bernard, *Pastoral Epistles*, 38; Hendriksen, *Pastoral Epistles*, 91-93.

people in the form of government. One brings not so much one's own needs to God but the needs of the leaders themselves. In order to bring about the conditions of 1 Timothy 2:2, rulers need wisdom, guidance, discernment, and more; for such things, the Christian prays to God on behalf of the rulers, whether pagan or Christian.

The fourth term, "thanksgivings," should complement all true prayer (note Paul's example in his epistles). The term connotes the idea of gratitude for the manifestations of grace in the lives of those for whom prayer is made, including kings. Hence Christians give thanks for all people, including saved and unsaved leaders of government, for evidences of both common and special grace.

These forms of prayer, the particular and the general, the petition and the praise, serve to enhance Paul's exhortation to pray. The terms emphasize the variety and the richness of the forms of prayer.

THE UNIVERSAL SCOPE OF PRAYER

Another evidence of the primacy of prayer is the universal scope of it. Paul says that believers should pray on behalf of *all* people, without distinction of race, nationality, or social standing. This may reflect the error of exclusivism at Ephesus that Paul addresses (1 Timothy 1:3–7). Timothy is not to limit his ministry to any particular group.[2] Timothy is to pray even for those unworthy of being praised, for God's sun rises beneficially on both the good and the bad (Matthew 5:45).

THE NARROWING OF THE SCOPE OF PRAYER

The words "all people" are specified in 1 Timothy 2:2 as "kings and all those in authority." The parallelism between these phrases in verses 1 and 2 suggests that Paul is either defining the "all people" by governmental leaders, or cites the latter as the first example or particular of the "all people." It is clear that Paul views prayer for governmental leaders as particularly strategic since he cites no other groups. His reason for citing them, in light of the following context, derives from their responsibility in God's design to bring about favorable conditions for the furtherance of the gospel and God's rule in the hearts and lives of people.

2. Hendriksen, *Pastoral Epistles*, 94; Kelly, *Pastoral Epistles*, 60.

The Christian's Unique Role in Government

Paul wrote to Timothy around A.D. 65, when Nero was the reigning emperor. Because Christians opposed the state religion of idolatry, they were brought under the suspicion of the rulers. Christians needed to demonstrate their loyalty to the state (but not to the state religion) by praying for leaders—because of these circumstances, Christians were prone to despising the magistrates of Rome; yet because the magistrates were God's servants (Romans 13:1–7), believers were commanded by Paul to pray for them.

It is important to note that Paul uses the term "kings" here with obvious reference to the emperor. In the West, the emperor was *princeps* or *imperator*, never *rex*, but in the East he was bluntly termed *basileus* ("king").[3] Yet the injunction is general and includes local rulers as well. A term similar to "authority" ("all who are in authority") occurs both in Romans 13:1 and 1 Peter 2:13. The reference is to those possessing authority or power to rule.

It is clear that the early Christians applied Paul's exhortation to themselves and heeded it. For example, Tertullian, in his *Apology* (5), writes that "the great draught in Germany was removed by a shower of rain obtained by the prayers of Christians who chanced to be serving in the army."[4]

THE PURPOSE FOR PRAYER

In 1 Timothy 2:2, Paul shows the strategic purpose of such prayer when he says that prayer is to be made on behalf of rulers for the purpose of having a "good" (for lack of a better term to summarize Paul's words) society. This is the primary reason for such praying. To pray on behalf of rulers' salvation would be a secondary purpose.

Paul employs four terms to characterize such a life within society: "peaceful," "quiet," "godliness," and "dignity." These terms fall into two groups. The first two terms describe the life to be experienced; the last two terms state the conditions that ought to prevail during such a life.

First, Paul urges prayer for rulers in order that Christians may live a peaceful life—government should provide a peaceful society. This imposes upon rulers the two-fold obligation to punish evil and to reward good, as seen in Romans 13:2–4.

---

3. Liddon, *Romans*, 247.
4. From Gwatkin, *Selections*, 113.

To Submit or to Rebel against the State

Leaders need divine blessing and guidance, which will enable them to discharge their office adequately and wisely according to the divine design for government. Only then will Christians be able to live a peaceable life.

In our contemporary elections, the concern as to whether or not a candidate is a Christian is a misplaced emphasis. While a Christian leader ought to provide better leadership, our primary concern should be upon a leader's promise and ability to perform the functions of government according to divine design.

The peace Paul has in mind, then, is the objective condition of peace, not personal peace. Two terms point out the aspects that are involved in this kind of peace.

First, the word "peace" (or "tranquil") probably refers to freedom from outward disturbances. Decisions should be made that will promote peace between nations. Although the second word, "quiet," may only be meant to enhance the former word, it is better to see it as a reference to deliverance from trouble within.[5] Society should not be in turmoil, distress, or anarchy.

It is quite obvious that Paul's words compel a specific, proper response from Christians living in any society. In order for these conditions to prevail, Christians must live in reverential obedience to the laws and the legislation that are in effect in the society in which they live. It is good to remember Lincoln's words exhorting such obedience to the law. Of course, the exceptions are those laws that are contrary to God's rule.

The specific force of this first purpose for praying for rulers is that *sound* government might prevail. This is government based on law, order, and justice. Christian prayer, work, and influence promote the peace that any society, such as America, enjoys. If these traits are lacking in a society, perhaps Christians are not praying and working as they should.

The second specific purpose for praying for leaders is so that one might live in a moral society, one regulated by God's laws and based upon a Judeo-Christian ethic. The words "godliness" and "dignity" may be meant only to enhance the former words "peaceful" and "quiet," yet they do argue for a connection in society between law, morality, and religion. Without a divine sanction to law and morality, a sound government of peace will not prevail and civilization will fail (in accord with the triangle

---

5. Most commentators support at least some such distinction between the terms. See Kelly, 61; Hendriksen, 95; Bernard, 39; Lock, 26.

of chapter 3). This connection between morality, religion, and peace forge a strong rebuke to those who want peace without religion and morality.

The moral nature of society is characterized by two terms. First, a condition of "godliness" will prevail. This refers to a godliness of the heart and is true reverence directed toward God. It is a religious attitude in the deepest sense. In the New Testament, it is always restricted to God and has no reference to human superiors,[6] hence prayer is made on behalf of rulers in order that they protect and promote religion and reverence for God. They are not to attack religion, nor are they to be worshipped.

This then provides another specific way whereby government is to promote good (Romans 13). The government should enhance the status of religion in society, not ridicule, undermine, or go on the offensive against it. The current push toward a largely secular society in America, as perhaps has already been achieved in Western Europe, is contrary to divine design. It will bring about the downfall of civilization. Our founding fathers understood this clearly, as seen from the quotes linking government and faith in appendix 1.

According to Acts 17:30–31, in the light of its context, all people everywhere should repent and believe the gospel. Good and moral government will establish conditions conducive to this end. If 1 Timothy 2:2 speaks of the obligation of believers to pray and implies a supportive attitude toward government, then verse 2 also reminds rulers of their obligation to regulate society in order to promote peace and religion in general.

The second condition that will prevail in a moral society is that of "dignity." This word may also be rendered "decency" or "gravity."[7] It makes reference to one's conduct or attitude directed toward mankind, in contrast to "godliness" (which is directed toward God). The word points to the intense conviction about the seriousness of life and the difficulty of realizing the Christian ideal. It is moral earnestness reflected in outward conduct and supported by inner intention.[8]

Just as Christians pray for daily bread, they also pray that God's will be done on earth as it is in heaven. A condition of "dignity" is part of realizing that design on earth. It is clear here that rulers have an obligation to regulate morals as a sacred duty. If millions of innocent lives have been

---

6. Kelly, *Pastoral Epistles*, 61; Bernard, *Pastoral Epistles*, 39-40.
7. Calvin, *Epistles to Timothy*, 52.
8. Kelly, *Pastoral Epistles*, 61; Bernard, *Pastoral Epistles*, 40.

terminated by abortion since 1973, this holocaust can hardly characterize a society where dignity for human life prevails. Equally, the enforcement of the death penalty is a recognition of man's dignity (Genesis 9:6).

If the specific force of the first two terms of 1 Timothy 2:2 means that believers should pray for rulers in order that *sound* government prevail, the last two terms have the specific force that *good* government should prevail. Both aspects are crucial to the viability of any society. They remind us of the four essentials of any civilization discussed in chapter 3: a system of economics; education and the arts; a form of political organization or government; and a standard of morality. The latter with its divine source should infuse and affect the other three ingredients to prevent them from becoming devoid of divine design.

The purpose of prayer given in verse 2 reminds us that there is national or collective accountability: If a nation (and its government) pursues sinful aims contrary to divine design, national sin exists and the nation is in need of salvation lest it perish. The national "soul" is in peril. Under Nazism, the people of Germany suffered the consequences of a nation gone bad. Similarly, the people of Afghanistan and Iraq suffer the consequences of a government given to terrorism.

THE APPROPRIATENESS OF SUCH PRAYER

First Timothy 2:3–4 teaches the appropriateness of such strategic prayer as that commanded in verses 1–2. Paul says that prayer for such purposes is "good and pleases God our Savior, who wants all people to be saved and to come to a knowledge of the truth." Such prayer pleases God. This is the second reason for such praying.

First (verse 3), Paul designates this praying for such purposes as both "good" and "pleasing" before God. The basic thrust of these words is that such praying is God's will. It is proper and lawful. The true motivation for praying for leaders is obedience to God—it is his will and he approves it. No other motivation is contemplated. All prayer should be regulated by his will and command.[9]

---

9. Calvin, *Epistles to Timothy*, 53. The "good" may be taken by itself to refer to the intrinsic excellence of such prayers; see Bernard, *Pastoral Epistles*, 40.

Why should Paul designate such praying this way? Precisely because God has ordained prayer as a means to his sovereign control over the nations in bringing about his will on earth.

Second (verse 4), Paul teaches that such praying for the purposes specified is a means to the salvation of all people, and this includes governmental rulers. Such praying will bring about the conditions of verse 2, which will provide a climate conducive to the success of the gospel: Men and women will be saved. This verse explains why such prayer is "good and pleasing." Since God, as part of his general purpose, wills all people to be saved and to come to the knowledge of the truth, He also wills both that governments be sound and good and that prayer be made to bring about this kind of a society.

Note how universal the statement is. The general purpose for praying for such government knows no limitation—all ranks of people and all nations are involved. This again points to God's sovereignty over all nations and reminds us of Acts 17:30–31 (NAS), where Paul emphasizes (in at least four ways) God's universal sovereignty.

> Therefore having overlooked the times of ignorance, God is now declaring to men that all people everywhere should repent, because he has fixed a day in which he will judge the world in righteousness through a Man whom he has appointed, having furnished proof to all men by raising him from the dead.

It makes no difference whether people belong to a government of the West or the East, whether "enlightened" or not. All rulers are to provide conditions conducive to evangelism and to the exclusive claims of the gospel of God revealed in Jesus Christ. There is no room here for a pluralism in religion or ethics.

There is no room for what would qualify or in any way limit or restrict the claims by God in these areas upon any society, American or other.

The "knowledge of the truth" in 1 Timothy 2:4 is joyful recognition, that deep spiritual discernment of the truth of God. It is not merely intellectual knowledge but includes acceptance by faith. This kind of knowledge is the means of obtaining salvation, identified in these verses as the general content of God's desire.

There is no place for a watered-down gospel or liberal theology. One must be faithful to Christ, especially when one proclaims the gospel under governmental permission, and to rulers, where the temptation to compromise the proclamation would be greatest. The herald of salvation demands nothing less than what God demands (as Paul so clearly identifies it in Acts 17:30–31). Again, Daniel comes to mind as one who exemplified the believer's consistent practice without compromise.

The subsequent verses of 1 Timothy 2 carry on the idea of the accountability of governments and the need to pray for all rulers. The truths that God is one and that Christ Jesus as a human being is the only worthy mediator between God and humanity (1 Timothy 2:5) are uniquely Jewish and Christian ideas. They imply a contrast with the whole world of people (verse 1) and their rulers. Believers are viewed with all people as enjoying the same benefits because there is one God over all who has made provision for the salvation of all (verse 6). Paul is a herald and apostle and teacher of this message (verse 7). Because believers will be found in all nations, believers everywhere should pray for their rulers. Then Paul returns to the subject of prayer and the proper decorum for men and women in church (1 Timothy 2:8–15).

As I pointed out previously in the discussion of Romans 13, Paul's designation of government as "God's minister" and "God's servant" is implicit in the Pastoral Epistles. This understanding is even more significant than in Romans. When Paul wrote the Pastorals, Nero had begun to persecute Christians and Paul was in prison in Rome. He would soon die at Nero's hand, yet he does not qualify his earlier exhortation in Romans 13:1, that all should submit themselves to the existing government.

Yet I believe that in this passage, as perhaps also in 1 Timothy 1:8–11, there is a subtle, indirect reminder to the Roman authorities that God, the sovereign Ruler over all nations, has special designs for human government. These pastoral messages provide specifics that Romans 13 does not, namely how a government is to punish evil and of what evil consists (1 Timothy 1:8–11), and how it can promote good and of what good consists (2:1–4).

It should be clear to all that an exhortation to pray for rulers carries with it an attendant obligation to work. Praying while doing nothing is the surest sign of hypocrisy, yet this situation prevails today far too often among Christians in various countries, especially our own.

THE SPECIAL MESSAGE OF JEREMIAH

The Old Testament parallel to 1 Timothy 2:1-2 is Jeremiah 29:7. This significant verse provides a principle universally applicable, even to Christians today. In the setting of Jeremiah, God tells Israel through Jeremiah that they should become fully immersed in their land of captivity, Babylon. Until deliverance comes, Israel should seek and work toward the prosperity of Babylon, for in its success Israel would prosper.

In parallel with Old Testament Israel, believers today find themselves as sojourners in a strange land awaiting their arrival in that better land where they even now have citizenship (Hebrews 12:22-24; Ephesians 2:19; Philippians 3:20). As citizens of an earthly kingdom, however, they are to heed Jeremiah's words: "Also, seek the peace (or welfare) and prosperity of the city to which I have carried you into exile. Pray to the LORD for it, because if it prospers, you too will prosper." (Parenthesis mine.)

As this verse shows, believers are both to pray for and to seek the peace and prosperity of the country in which they dwell. Their obligations do not end with adequate praying.

Another parallel passage is Ezra 6:10. Cyrus the king promoted the cause of religion in Israel by decreeing that public treasuries be used to help pay for the cost of rebuilding the temple in Israel (Ezra 6:4). Taxes levied on the general public were the source of these funds (Ezra 6:8-9). The only thing that Cyrus (also called Darius, Ezra 6:12) asked in return was that the Jews "offer acceptable sacrifices to the God of heaven and pray for the life of the king and his sons." Later, King Artaxerxes issued a decree having similar benevolences for Israel at the expense of the empire. Here the king was motivated, and rightly so, by fear of divine disapproval if he failed to please the God of Israel. Ezra 7:23 reads: "Whatever is commanded by the God of heaven, let it be done with zeal for the house of the God of heaven, so that there will not be wrath against the kingdom of the king and his sons" (NAS).

BELIEVERS IN A PAGAN KING'S COURT

These examples from Jeremiah and Ezra are instructive regarding the relationship of the state and the church. If distributed evenly, public monies can be used to assist religion, especially in carrying out benevolent services to society. Yet the state should make no attempt to control the church or determine its beliefs or message.

A similar link between the intercession of believers and the peace or success of a pagan government occurs in Daniel 4:27. At the end of his interpretation of Nebuchadnezzar's vision of a great tree, Daniel applies the meaning to the king directly. He says: "Therefore, O king, may my advice be pleasing to you: Break away now from your sins by doing righteousness and from your iniquities by showing mercy to the poor, in case there may be a prolonging of your prosperity" (NAS).

Here we see a direct connection between obedience to God's design for government according to his standards and a pagan nation's prosperity or success. It is clear that Paul has these several Old Testament passages in mind as he writes 1 Timothy 2:1–2.

CONTEXTUALIZING 2 CHRONICLES 7:14

This brings forth the question of whether Christians should utilize 2 Chronicles 7:14 as a pattern and principle for their behavior in seeking renewal in America. It is true that "my people" and "heal their land" refer directly to the Jews and Palestine and her prosperity, and one must keep in mind Israel's special ordination as a nation in God's divine plan. Daniel, in his great prayer in Daniel 9, was following the principle and procedure of 2 Chronicles 7:14. This is the surface interpretation.

Yet surely there is a universal sense to the interpretation in light of such passages as we've discussed so far. As long as one is clear in distinguishing the meaning then from the meaning now, the passage is appropriate for Americans, and equally for Gentile Christians in any other nation. But it does not have special meaning for America alone.

THE RAMIFICATIONS OF 1 TIMOTHY 2:1–4

The ramifications of 1 Timothy 2:1–4 are not hard to see. It is clear that revolution and anarchy are conditions contrary to God's purpose for humanity and his pattern for government. The Christian living in such unstable situations has a clear biblical mandate: He is to pray and work to the end that revolution and anarchy cease.

The Christian's Unique Role in Government

During the American Revolution, Christians had a clear command based on 1 Timothy 2: Only when peace prevails can Christianity benefit the most and government function most appropriately as divinely ordained.

MARTYRDOM: THE SEED OF THE CHURCH?

It is often said that martyrdom is the seed of the church. This may be so, but when martyrdom arises in a time of persecution from government, the situation is not conducive to the progress of Christianity. Rather (as seen before from other passages), Christianity will flourish most productively during a time of peace when the government promotes good and is benevolent to Christianity. Such a government will recognize Christianity's contribution in providing a religious sanction to public morality and law.

CHRISTIANITY: A BENEFIT TO THE STATE

The early Church clearly saw their obligations toward government on the basis of 1 Timothy 2:1–4. Tertullian wrote in his *Apology* (32):

> We are under another and a greater need of praying for the emperors, and further for the good estate of the Empire and the interests of Rome, knowing as we do that a mighty shock impending over the entire world and the end of the age itself with the fearful calamities it threatens are delayed by the respite which the Roman Empire gives. Thus when we pray for those things to be put off which we do not wish for ourselves to experience, we are in favor of the long endurance of Rome. Furthermore, even as we do not swear by the genii [demons promoting idolatry] of the Caesars, so we do swear by their health, which is more august than all the genii. Do you not know that the genii are called *daemones*, and thence by the diminutive word *daemonia*? We in the emperors look up to the judgment of God, who has set them over the nations.[10]

There is a striking parallel between the conditions of Tertullian's day and that of the present. The great evil of communism and the totalitarianism of Islam and the "fearful calamities they threaten" are impending over the whole world. Christians living in unstable places might well follow Tertullian's example in seeking the status quo, rather

---

10. Gwatkin, *Selections*, 115.

than a change, which might bring about the greater evil of a communist or Islamic government. Yet there is an end to evil promoted by government.

As derived from 1 Timothy 1 and 2, communism is a greater evil than a dictatorship on two counts. First, it promotes revolution and anarchy within and without, seeking to destroy all existing institutions (church, government, labor, home, and family) on a world-wide scale. Second, it prevents and seeks to destroy reverence for God and dignity toward man. Its system of jurisprudence rejects *any* religious sanction and *any* moral base. Communism, it seems, is a political philosophy unmatched in its evil in the history of mankind.

Similarly, Islamic fundamentalism poses no less a threat to peace and freedom. While communism disavows all religion, Islam avows only Islam and pursues it in a totalitarian way. The only difference between the two is that one is atheistic, the other theistic. Yet the god of the latter operates no differently from the humans of the former.

Another quote from the period of the early church will show that even pagan rulers had a proper concept and expectation of a Christian's role in society. In A.D. 311, Galerius decreed from his deathbed what is called the first Edict of Toleration. Lactantius recorded this edict, part of which said:

> We therefore in consideration of our most mild clemency, and of the unbroken custom whereby we are used to grant pardon to all men, have thought it right in this case also to offer our speediest indulgence, that Christians may exist again, and may establish their meetings, yet so that they do nothing contrary to good order. By another letter we shall signify to magistrates how they should proceed. Wherefore, in accordance with this indulgence of ours, they will be bound to pray their god for our good estate, and that of the commonwealth, and their own, that the commonwealth may endure on every side unharmed, and they may be able to live securely in their own homes.[11]

Once again, it's easy to see the superiority of a government ruling on the basis of divinely revealed law. Such a government will provide a society that is both peaceable and stable, on the one hand, as well as dignified, just, and good on the other hand. But, in light of the record of Islamic states, one can scarcely imagine a ruler making such a declaration regarding Islam and its establishment of the law of *sharia*.

11. Gwatkin, *Selections*, 171.

AN APPLICATION TO SLAVERY

An application of Paul's words can be made with regard to slavery. If Abraham Lincoln's Emancipation Proclamation, which set free the slaves in America in 1863, needed a biblical mandate, it may be found here in Paul's words that Christians should pray on behalf of rulers, in order that they might live a life of dignity. The black slave trade violated the concept of dignity to a degree that the slavery of Paul's day never did.

It is clear that Paul does not elsewhere decry the institution of slavery. In the light of the teaching of this passage (that peace should prevail in a society), Paul's teaching is consistent. Yet here there might also be the veiled suggestion by Paul that slavery when it violates the dignity of human beings is contrary to God's design for government and its institutions. On one occasion, Paul even encourages slaves to seek their freedom if they can have it (1 Corinthians 7:21-24).

OTHER RAMIFICATIONS FOR SOCIETY

Paul's words regarding dignity have application for the institutional improvement of life in many ways. The basic underlying premise of the dignity of man is that he is a creation of God, made in his image.

This basis for dignity has ramifications in many areas today, including the justification for the death penalty, the atrocity of abortion and euthanasia, the dangers of genetic engineering, cloning, etc. Gene-splitting is for biology what atom-splitting is for physics. Both are revolutionary in their implications for the life of mankind.[12] Concern for dignity means that the Judeo-Christian ethic must prevail or a nation's life is imperiled.

It is clear then that the Christian's role in society is more crucial and significant than the unbeliever's. The Christian has a unique contribution that the unbeliever cannot make. Only the Christian can be salt and light (Matthew 5:13-16). It reminds us again of the role that such believers as Daniel, Esther, and Nehemiah fulfilled in their governments. If the number of Christians in a land be few, or if their maturity and spirituality be

---

12. On Sep. 11, 1981, ABC televised their close-up series, "The Gene Merchants." The most repeated concern voiced throughout the program was that regarding ethics. Universities, business, the medical profession, agriculturists, stock analysts, the Supreme Court, and government are all involved in decision-making that directly confronts the Judeo-Christian ethic. The recent experiments in cloning cells and animals, and the idea of cloning humans, raise similar ethical issues.

compromised and apostasy reigns, it is more likely then that poor government will prevail than if the opposite conditions prevail.

Without Christian values, corruption, bribery, lying, cheating, theft, and all such vices take over. If these characterize the authorities in government, they will trickle down to the populace. The people will find justification for living by such perverted values. The effect on the whole society is apparent.

Does this not seem to be substantiated, at least in general? After two thousand years of Christianity, Western Europe and North America are generally recognized as the leaders among the nations of the world. They have had unparalleled success in advancing civilization—in government, the arts and education, business and economics, political theory, ethics, etc. Only in recent generations, coinciding with the compromise of their Christian heritage in religion and ethics, have these same nations begun to lose their distinctive greatness and come to be part of what is termed the "demise of the West." Likewise, in Africa the stability of newly arising nations can in large measure be attributed to Christians and the influence of Christianity. Nigeria and Kenya seem to be examples.

As Christians pray and seek the peace and success of a government, the benefits reach far beyond them. Not only do unbelievers participate in the benefit, but even the ungodly and lawbreakers. The latter enjoy a stable government in spite of their own criminality. Even with regard to the latter they can expect fair and equal justice, tempered with mercy. Today, it is a better thing to be a thief in America than in Iran, Saudi Arabia, or North Korea!

NO COMPLETE SEPARATION BETWEEN CHURCH AND STATE

In applying the principle of this chapter to the relationship between church and state, it is clear that there can be no strict separation between these spheres. That is, government is to promote the good (Romans 13:1–7), legislate a standard of morality which conforms to divine revelation (1 Timothy 1:8–11), and promote godliness and human dignity (1 Timothy 2:1–2)—again as revelation would define godliness and dignity. This means that a narrow, non-preferential interpretation of the Establishment Clause is biblical. The state may, indeed should, aid religion, promoting godliness on a broad scale.

But is this interpretation also historical? Is it the meaning intended by the original framers of the Constitution? Indeed it is. Historians, legal scholars, and virtually all Americans held this view until recent years. Even Jefferson, who first used the phrase, "wall of separation," did not believe the wall was insurmountable. During the Revolutionary War, he called for days of prayer and fasting, and authored the Bill for Punishing Disturbers of Religious Worship and Sabbath Breakers. As President, he signed an Indian treaty that used monies to assist missionaries to the Indians! As a congressman, Madison helped to create the military chaplaincy (unique among the world's armies), and, as President, he proclaimed days of prayer and fasting. The First Congress and others also supported such treaties, days of prayer, and the chaplaincy.[13]

The change that has taken place in the interpretation of the First Amendment is due to a hidden agenda on the part of activist judges who wish to impose new, sociologically determined meaning and new laws. They wish to *make* law rather than *interpret* law, as shown in chapter 3.

SUMMARY AND CONCLUDING OBSERVATIONS

In summary, these observations are derived from 1 Timothy 2:1–4:

1. Christians have the practice of prayer as their primary mark of being diligent.
2. Christians should give a primary place in their prayers to rulers and all in authority.
3. This prayer is for the purpose of living a life in conditions of peace and goodness.
4. The government itself must be sound and good.
5. Peace refers to the absence of war without and to tranquility within.
6. Goodness refers to godliness (reverence for God) and to dignity or morality among people.
7. It is incumbent upon government not only to *provide* but to *promote* peace and religion and to *regulate* morality.
8. God has willed such praying as part of his plan for the salvation of

---

13. See Price, "Establishment Clause," 49–58, 82–84.

people everywhere.

9. The results of such praying provide an atmosphere conducive to the gospel and its receptivity.

Other observations are pertinent, though less obvious than the preceding:

1. Christians are to respect their leaders, whether or not they command respect. One can hardly pray for "all in authority" if one harbors personal hatred or animosity for any one of them.
2. Peace among nations must be pursued for the gospel's sake, and war must be engaged only as a last resort. The same holds true for stability within nations.
3. Peace and goodness go together. A nation will hardly promote reverence for God and dignity for humanity if it is engaged in strife without or within.

Similarly, a nation can hardly expect to enjoy any peace if reverence and dignity are not upheld and promoted. If strife does not arise within, then it may come from without. And God himself will surely intervene directly or indirectly (as at Sodom and Gomorrah, as seen in Genesis 18–19; and at Babylon, as seen in Jeremiah 49–51, Habakkuk 2:6–20, and Daniel 2, 4, 5, 7–12; and in Israel), wherever his law is violated. This is why the promotion of gay rights by governmental authorities has such serious consequences.

There is another special contribution that Christians can make to their society that the unbeliever cannot. It is the enablement to perform the good. Unbelieving society may have high motivation, great anticipations, and significant ideals, but, without the power to perform, all these things will remain unfulfilled and unrealized. Personal and national salvation and growth can come only from above, as the Holy Spirit indwells each believer. Philippians 2:12–16 says (in part):

> Therefore, my dear friends, as you have always obeyed—not only in my presence, but now much more in my absence—continue to work out your salvation with fear and trembling, for it is God who works in you to will and to act according to his good purpose . . . so that you may become blameless and pure, children of God without fault in a crooked and depraved generation, in

The Christian's Unique Role in Government

which you shine like stars in the universe, as you hold out (on to) the word of life. (Parenthesis mine.)

This passage once again vindicates the relationships expressed in the triangle illustration in chapter 3. A believer should pray that peace would prevail. What happens if tumult, war, and revolution do occur? What part does a Christian take in these? If Christians are free and belong to a heavenly realm, why should they have any involvement in an earthly realm?

Christian freedom, its lengths and its limits, is the concern of the seventh and last principle, and we'll take a look at it in the next chapter. But let's not leave William Wilberforce's quote hanging. He continued his thought on who Christians are by writing the following in *A Practical View of the Prevailing Religious System of Professed Christians, in the Higher and Middle Classes in This Country, Contrasted with Real Christianity*:

> Let true Christians . . . boldly assert the cause of Christ in an age when so many who bear the name of Christian are ashamed of him. Let them accept the duty to serve, if not actually to save, their country. Let them serve not by political interference, but by that sure and radical benefit of restoring the influence of true religion and of raising the standard of morality.
>
> Let them be active, useful, and generous toward others. Let them show moderation and self-denial in themselves. Let them be ashamed of idleness. When blessed with wealth, let them withdraw from the competition of vanity and be modest, retiring from ostentation, and not be the slaves of fashion. Let them be moderate in all things. Let them cultivate a catholic spirit of general good will and of kindness toward others. Let them encourage men of real piety—wherever they may be found—and others to repress vice and revive and spread the influence of real Christianity. Let them pray earnestly for the renewal of its vitality.
>
> Let them pray continually for their country at this time of national difficulty. Who can say how intercession before the Governor of the universe may avert for a while our ruin.

Wilberforce's words are remarkably relevant. "The decline in morals is enough to alarm every thoughtful person and to fill us with foreboding about the growth of evil." Let Christians "accept the duty to serve, if not actually to save, their country." He was convinced that only true Christians could restore "the influence of true religion and of raising the standard of morality." His concern was to move "true Christians," for only they—not politicians, teachers, attorneys, entertainers, or sportspeople, and not even religious leaders and false Christians—could save their country.

Sharp and Wilberforce helped to save their society. To them belongs the chief credit for the abolition of the slave trade from England decades before the Civil War abolished it in the United States.

10

The Limitation to Liberty: Is it Right to Rebel?

AN AFGHAN WOMAN FINDS JESUS

WHEN HER DAUGHTER FELL ill with a fever, Tamana grew concerned. The fever could develop into something far worse. With eight children and a sick husband, Tamana had no resources to attend to her daughter. She decided to go to the Masons and see what they could do for her.

A young mother in her early thirties, Tamana had suffered for some time from chronic pain in her leg. She was basically uneducated. Although Tamana had a widow card from an aid agency, she would often visit the Masons' home seeking food and work. The Masons were aid workers with Shelter Now International. She had also come to know a new arrival living with the Masons, Dayna Curry.

"Do you mind if I pray for your daughter to be healed in the name of Jesus?" Katherine Mason asked when Tamana arrived. And Tamana accepted. By the time she got home, her daughter's fever was gone.

Afterward, Tamana told Katherine, "My daughter got better. Who is this Jesus you prayed to?"

Sometime later, Dayna gave Tamana a cheap radio. She told her that she could learn more about Jesus by listening to radio programs beamed into Afghanistan.

To Submit or to Rebel against the State

After about a year, Tamana had two dreams. First, she dreamed that Jesus came to her, touched her leg, and healed her. Another night she went to bed very worried for her eight children—how she would feed them, what kind of future they would have. In her second dream, Jesus came into the room and put his hand on each child's head. He said, "Don't worry. I will be their father. I will take care of them."

To Muslims, dreams have special significance. Tamana was certain that her dreams were meant to be a sign to her. She brought all of her children to the Masons' gate and asked how they could get closer to this Jesus. Dayna Curry and the Masons invited them in and explained that becoming a follower of Jesus would be very dangerous. The government under the Taliban persecuted those who converted to Christianity. In was not unusual that Afghan Christians would suffer beatings, imprisonment, even death.

The Masons had to be extremely careful in speaking about Jesus Christ since foreigners in Afghanistan are forbidden from proselytizing. Christians cannot witness openly concerning their faith. While private home meetings are allowed, these are limited to those who are Christians.

The government under the Taliban was extremely harsh, especially toward women. Not only were women and girls forbidden to have employment and schooling, but they had to be totally covered when in public by a *burkha*, which allowed sight only through a small slit in the smallest panel over their eyes. Women were often beaten in public by men wielding whips; foreign women were not exceptions. Dayna Curry and other aid workers had experienced these beatings themselves.

"Do you understand what this means?" Chris Mason asked Tamana. "Do you understand the risks? You could lose everything, even your children. You could die."

Tamana was afraid. She asked: "Would you be able to help me if something bad happens?" The Masons told her that they couldn't give her assurances of material help, but that they would pray for her and support her in friendship. God's presence would never leave her.

Tamana and her oldest children decided to take the risk. Later, Dayna Curry and the Masons showed Tamana and her children the Jesus film in order to give them some understanding about the faith they had chosen. Tamana and her children were deeply moved by Jesus' life. They all wept during the scene when Jesus was beaten and crucified.

A few weeks later, the Taliban appeared at Tamana's gate. Tamana's neighbor had reported the family to authorities for failing to fast during the Muslim holy month of Ramadan, a common complaint used by Afghans to settle rivalries. When the police ransacked Tamana's house, they discovered a book about Jesus. The oldest son was beaten severely, and the Taliban imposed an enormous fine on the family. Dayna Curry and the Masons were devastated.

After the beatings, Tamana came to the Masons' gate in hysterics. She pounded frantically on the gate. When Dayna let her in, she pulled down the neck of her dress to expose long, thin, red welts on her back. Dayna prayed for her and tried to comfort her. "I wish I had been beaten instead of you," Dayna said.

To Submit or to Rebel against the State

Principle 7
Liberty Is Not License

> Submit yourselves for the Lord's sake to every authority instituted among men: whether to the king, as the supreme authority; or to governors, who are sent by him to punish those who do wrong and to commend those who do right. For it is God's will that by doing good you should silence the ignorant talk of foolish men. Live as free men, but do not use your freedom as a cover-up for evil; live as servants (or bondslaves) of God. Show proper respect to everyone: Love the brotherhood of believers, fear God, honor the king. —*1 Peter 2:13-17* (Parentheses mine.)

INTRODUCTION: THE CHALLENGE OF LIBERATION THEOLOGY

One of the most pressing conflicts raging in Latin America and elsewhere is the debate over liberation theology.[1] As its name indicates, liberation theology defines the gospel as a proclamation of economic freedom for the poor and the oppressed classes. These classes are encouraged to revolt against their oppressors, whether businessmen, land owners, or government officials.

In 1971, the Peruvian priest Gustavo Gutierrez published his work, *A Theology of Liberation*. This "bible" of liberation theology wedded Marxist sociology and economics with a hermeneutic (or system) of interpreting the Bible. Adherents believe that the Bible proclaims salvation as liberation of oppressed classes: God is on the side of the poor and is using the Marxist revolutionary movement to establish his kingdom now.

Many Catholics and Protestants in Latin America, especially in Cuba and in Nicaragua, have proclaimed this gospel of new concepts. The root cause of peoples' ills is not sin but capitalism. The solution is a communist revolution. Man, not Christ, is the redeemer of humanity. Redemption is by way of revolutionary class struggle. Theology is not a study of God but a study of a person's reflection on oneself. In proclaiming liberation for

---

1. See such articles as Henry, "Liberation Theology," 4–6; and other articles in the same issue. Also see "Curious Contradiction," 54–55; Webster, "Liberation Theology," 635–638.

the poor, this new gospel embraces violence as the means of social change, at least as a last resort. The primary interest is sociology and economics, not theology. In effect, the old theological liberalism has given theological sanction to revolution.

Other forms of liberation theology have arisen. A significant one is women's liberation. Women should be set free from the shackles of a male-dominated society. Patriarchy must be eliminated and replaced with equality or even matriarchy. Women should be able to assume leadership in all institutions, including the pastoring of churches. Women's liberation would interpret the Bible to remove all barriers to a woman's equal role in the home, church, and society.

Gay liberation is another form. As I mentioned before, homosexuals increasingly stretch their demands for equality with heterosexuals. They would redefine marriage and change existing cultural norms, criminal laws, and rights to place homosexuality on an entirely equal footing with heterosexuality.

All forms of liberation theology have common faults. Liberation theology is bound together with moral or radical pluralism. Liberation has pushed out theology. Liberationists forget the unique claims of Christ because the emphasis is not on Christ but on culture.

Liberation theology promises a contemporary utopia, not a future heaven. Political revolution will bring in the new world consisting of material abundance for all through an equalization of wealth or status. Heaven is not by-and-by but here-and-now.

The conflict over liberation theology threatens to split several denominations. Evangelicals within these larger bodies refuse to fund projects and missionaries promoting liberation theology. Liberationists themselves threaten to bring their struggle to all the institutions of the United States and to export it abroad wherever it is needed.

It is the revolutionary aspect of liberation theology, with its call for confrontation and even violent revolution, that is the concern of this chapter. For while liberation theology may have wrong doctrines regarding the nature of man, the person of Christ, the substance of the gospel, and the meaning of heaven, it remains a potent force of social change by its methodology of confrontation and revolution. While many Christians would not endorse the doctrines of liberation theology, there is widespread sympathy with the idea of "violence as a last resort," or at least with the idea of breaking the law in order to alleviate human suffering and to obey a higher law.

This chapter specifically addresses the restraint placed on the Christian's freedom and seeks to answer the questions: Is it ever right to rebel against a government and its laws? If so, when and how should one do so?

These questions have been an issue from the beginning of this book. The search for answers will consider briefly the views of the leaders of the Reformation, in addition to the teaching of Scripture.

THE MEANING OF 1 PETER 2:13-17

First Peter 2:13-17 touches upon and substantiates many of the propositions dealt with already in this book. In this passage, Peter writes that the Christian must submit to government as God's will, and that the design for government is to punish evil-doers and to praise those who do good, yet the passage has an additional message.

The emphasis of this passage falls upon the Christian's role in society. The believer's conduct should be above reproach; there should be no occasion for punishment by the state for wrong-doing. The believer has freedom in Christ, but he is not above the rule of the government. He should honor the king. He does not have license to do evil. As a slave or servant of God, he must fear his Master. Just as a government's authority is not absolute, personal freedom is not absolute.

THE CONTEXT

In this Epistle, Peter deals with several topics, including the destiny of the believer (1:1—2:10), his duty of subjection (2:11—3:12), and his discipline through suffering (3:13—5:14). In the first section, Peter discuses the believer's relationship with God (1:13-21) and with brothers and sisters in Christ (1:22—2:10).

The passage at hand comes under the section where Peter discusses the believer's relationship to the world (2:11—3:7). The first two verses are more general, being an exhortation to abstain from "sinful desires that war against the soul" (verse 11). A pattern of life that leaves the opponents of Christians having no valid accusation against them makes submission to government easier and more necessary (2:12). In verses 13-14, Peter

The Limitation to Liberty: Is it Right to Rebel?

gives the requirement and extent of submission to government, then the reason or ground for it (1 Peter 2:15–17).

"SUBMIT YOURSELVES"

In 1 Peter 2:13, Peter commands his beloved readers to "be subject to every human institution because of the Lord." The word for "be subject" may be understood as middle ("submit yourselves") or passive ("be subject"). Six of the thirteen times that the word occurs in the New Testament are found in 1 Peter. How it is rendered here is significant.

The context uses the term several times. Similar compliance or obedience is exhorted of servants to masters (2:18), wives to husbands (3:1, 5), young men to elders (5:5), and citizens to rulers (2:13); heavenly beings are subject to Christ (3:22). Since later Greek had a tendency to use the passive aorist form (the tense used in 1 Peter 2:13, 3:22, and 5:5; the present tense used in 3:1, 5) with the force of the middle voice, such exhortations naturally take a reflexive form (the middle sense, rather than the passive), as seen best in verse 13.[2] Hence, the translation adopted at the beginning of this chapter is "submit yourselves." This way of reading the command calls for the willing compliance of the reader, a more demanding command than simply the idea of "be subject."

The use of the aorist, in contrast to the present tense, points to a decision needed by which to start the life of submission. It finds its parallel in the first command in verse 17, which is followed by three present tense commands. Peter's use of the aorist inculcates "an act of faith rather than a rule of conduct."[3] Life begins with a proper decision, then the subsequent commands describe the pattern of living.

---

2. Johnstone, *Peter*, 152. In 1 Peter, the verb may be either middle or passive in form (2:18; 3:1, 5); three times it is clearly passive in form (2:13; 3:22; 5:5). Whether the middle-passive form should be rendered middle ("subject" or "submit yourselves" or "be subject") or passive ("be subjected") must be determined from context and usage. The same problem exists in Romans 13:1, where the middle sense is more probable. It makes the command more demanding, since it calls upon the willing compliance of the person so commanded. This seems best for 1 Peter 2:13 as well. Three times (2:18; 3:1, 5) the word is present; three times (2:13; 3:22; 5:5) it is aorist. Four are participles (2:18; 3:1, 5, 22), two are imperative verbs (commands) (2:13; 5:5).

3. Selwyn, *St. Peter*, 172.

To Submit or to Rebel against the State

"EVERY AUTHORITY INSTITUTED"

The word "instituted" comes from a term which elsewhere in the New Testament refers to God's creation. The terms used here could literally be rendered "every human creature." Yet this is too wide a meaning (implying subjection to any others) in light of the context of 1 Peter 2:13–17, and is a strange way of saying "all people." The reference is not to social relations either, but to government as organized by people. It is that "creation" of a person's thought, an "institution."[4] This finds support from secular Greek where the term was used for the founding of a city or for instituting, creating, and inventing.[5]

Civil government in general is a divine institution, which is the point Paul stresses in Romans 13. In 1 Peter 2, Peter points to the fact that the special form which government may take in any particular nation (such as monarchy, democracy, republic, etc.) is determined by the people, hence it is a "human institution," the established legal order. The translation, "every authority instituted among people," captures the idea well.

These are mere means of carrying out God's design for government. The authority of the king comes from the state, not immediately from God. The authority to rule rests upon the needs of human society and exists by the will or sufferance of those over whom it is exercised. The words "human institution" also suggest that the government's jurisdiction is limited to the secular affairs of its people.

We see how Peter, like Paul, agrees with Jesus' words in Matthew 22. There is a proper sphere and allegiance belonging to the government ("Ceasar's") and a proper one belonging to God.

In Romans, Paul describes the king as a servant of God; in 1 Peter 2, Peter assumes God to be King, but he rules through law and men (hence "human institution").[6] Peter and Paul need not be set at odds to one another; rather they are complementary and both must be consulted to get the complete teaching of Scripture. As Paul stresses the divine origin of government, Peter stresses its divine functions.

---

4. Johnstone, *Peter*, 153.
5. Liddell and Scott, *Greek-English Lexicon*, 1003.
6. Johnstone, *Peter*, 154; Bigg, *St. Peter*, 139–140; Selwyn, *St. Peter*, 172.

"BECAUSE OF THE LORD"

Submission to human government is to be done for the motive of obeying Christ ("because of the Lord"). It is obedience to the teaching of Christ (Matthew 22:17-21) and his apostles and for the sake of his church (1 Peter 2:15-16). "For the Lord's sake" is the chief reason for submission. It points to inward as well as outward loyalty. Obedience, Peter is saying, will be defective in principle unless it recognizes in human government a higher, more sacred authority than that of a human being (Psalm 82:1).

THE LEADERS OF EARTHLY GOVERNMENT

Peter then identifies the leaders of government or "human institutions" under which his readers lived. A definite article ("the") is not used with "king" and "governors"—the terms are general; yet certainly, as seen at 1 Timothy 2:2, the Emperor of Rome (probably Nero at the time) and his subordinates are meant. Governors were appointed heads of provinces or similar divisions. Again, as pointed out at 1 Timothy 2:2, "king" (*rex*) was the designation employed in the East whereas the Romans used the term *imperator*.[7]

In the phrase, "as the one in authority or to governors as sent by him," the "as" has its subjective force, meaning "remembering him to be." It introduces the reason why one should give submission.[8] The "one in authority" translates a word denoting comparison with the lesser rulers, or the governors. In Romans 13:1, the word is rendered "governing" and implies a contrast with the people in general.[9]

We should understand the governors as sent by the king, commissioned from time to time (hence the present participle). The words "by him" do not mean that they are sent by the Lord. In that case, a stronger preposition of direct agency (*hupo*) would have been used instead of that implying intermediate agency (*dia*). Also, the preposition limits only the governors, not the king, which is strange if "by him" refers to the Lord. One may infer that the indirect words "by him" suggest the more

---

7. See 1 Timothy 2:2 and Johnstone, *Peter*, 155; Bigg, *St. Peter*, 139-140; Selwyn, *St. Peter*, 172; Lillie, *Lectures*, 137.
8. Johnstone, *Peter*, 156.
9. Ibid.

direct form (*hupo*), there being a greater Sovereign behind all leaders of government.

PURPOSE OF GOVERNMENT

The purpose for the appointing of governors is "to punish those who do wrong and to commend those who do good." The claims of justice are asserted—are vindicated—by punishing those who do evil. The commending of those who do good (or right) is a reference to "practical commendatory recognition," not to actual words of praise.[10]

Basically 1 Peter 2:14 means that government will secure peace and liberty for a doer of good, but only in exceptional cases will actual reward be given. Through his subordinates, the king carries out this goal of government as designed by God. Although the individual believer is forbidden to take the law into his own hands and avenge himself (Matthew 5:39), the state must. It fails to do so only at the risk of its own destruction, for citizens cannot long tolerate great injustices, and lawlessness and anarchy will soon prevail. The overthrow of communism in Russia and Europe starkly illustrates this.

According to one commentator, Roman law did not make a sharp distinction between what is "immoral" and what is "criminal." The governor was father as well as magistrate.[11] This paternal jurisdiction meant that a Christian's conduct might not be considered "good" by the rulers just because he kept the law and obeyed. Yet it does argue for the principle that rulers ought not only to punish evil but also promote good. It also argues that the moral element in every law is intrinsic and necessary; even non-Christians recognize it.

This moral purpose for government is very similar to Paul's teaching in Romans 13:3–4. In fact, the same two words ("punish" and "commend," or "praise") are employed by both 1 Peter 2 and Romans 13. This and other connections suggest that Peter may have read Romans. He does know of several of Paul's epistles according to his own words (2 Peter 3:15–16).

---

10. Johnstone, *Peter*, 157.
11. Bigg, *St. Peter*, 140–141.

THE REASON FOR SUBMISSION

In 1 Peter 2:15, Peter writes: "For it is God's will that by doing right you should silence the ignorant talk of foolish people." The first terms may be rendered as "because that is in accordance with God's will . . . " God's will is the reason either for the preceding exhortation to be submissive, or perhaps for the function of government to regulate morality.[12] It seems more likely that the former construction is to be preferred: It is God's will that believers submit themselves.

However, it is also God's design that government carry out its moral function, as taught elsewhere (Romans 13:1ff.). Also, in 1 Timothy 2:1-4, praying for rulers in order to have a sound and good society is said to be "good and pleasing before God who desires all people to be saved." On this subject, the teachings of Peter and Paul are practically equivalent.

This will of God is restated to be that which is the doing of right ("doing good" according to the NIV), and then the implication of this principle is drawn out. The "doing of good" is one of the key words of this Epistle, being used more often here than in all the rest of the New Testament. It occurs twice in 1 Peter 2:14-15.

SILENCING IGNORANT TALK

By means of doing good, "the ignorant talk of foolish people" will be muzzled or silenced. The foolish people are those of verse 12 (the article is used in verse 15 to point back to those already mentioned) who slander believers as evil-doers but are put to silence when they observe the good deeds. The deeds are "good" because they are profitable and beneficial to society. Johnstone calls this obedience to rulers "the great *apologia* of Christianity."[13] Obedience commends Christianity to unbelievers.

The word "ignorant" refers to that which is willful or obstinate. Therefore moral blameworthiness is involved. The people are "foolish" because of the great folly involved in denouncing a way of life they did

---

12. It seems to be more probable that the "thus" ("such," NASV) from *houtos* refers to what has gone before—the submission to government as a doing of good—not to what follows (defining the participle "doing good" or the infinitive "to silence," as the will of God). See also Bigg, *St. Peter*, 141; Selwyn, *St. Peter*, 173; Johnstone, *Peter*, 158.

13. Johnstone, *Peter*, 158. See also Leighton, *First Peter*, 195.

not care to understand (consider Romans 1:22). Peter's words remind us of the ways of fools as described in Proverbs 17:28 and 26:1–12.

THE PROPER SPIRIT OR MOTIVE AS FREE

1 Peter 2:16 literally reads, "as free people, and not as having freedom as a cover-up for evil, but as servants of God." In the original text, there is a missing verb at the beginning. Thus the words must either go with a verb afterward (verse 17: "honor") or before (verse 13: "submit yourselves"; or verse 15: "by doing good"). Since verse 16 does not go well with each of the commands in verse 17 (such as, "love the brotherhood"), it is preferable to take it with the preceding. Of the options here, it seems best to take it with the main verb of verse 13 rather than the participle "by doing good" of 1 Peter 2:15. This allows verse 16 to specify the spirit in which submission is to be done (verse 13) rather than expanding the idea of "doing good" (verse 15). Thus, verse 16 means that believers are to "submit themselves," not as slaves but as free people. How ennobling this is to Christians in whatever nations they are citizens!

First Peter 2:15 should not be relegated to a parenthesis. Verse 16 "enunciates the principles which, as motives," will lead to the doing of good in verse 15.[14] This verse illustrates the whole passage of verses 13–15. The NIV renders verse 16, "Live as free people." This captures the broader idea of the passage well.

The idea is to submit oneself to human institutions of government, and thereby to do good as God's will (verse 15), in the proper spirit and with proper motives (verse 16). All three clauses introduced by "as" in verse 16 ("as free . . . not having freedom as a cover-up . . . as servants . . .") must be considered in the definition of the proper spirit or motives, with the last two clauses modifying the first.[15] All three clauses are needed, for the first ("as free") might be thought to be inconsistent with the command, "submit yourself." The clauses "as a cover-up" and "as servants" help to clarify what "as free" means.

The idea of the participle "having" is that of possessing and having the right to employ freedom, hence "using freedom." Believers are to

---

14. Johnstone, *Peter*, 159–160; Bigg, *St. Peter*, 141, also takes the verse with the verb of verse 13.

15. Johnstone, *Peter*, 161.

The Limitation to Liberty: Is it Right to Rebel?

submit and do good as free men, yet not as using freedom as a covering for evil, but as being servants of God. The thought is that being "servants of God" is inconsistent with the doing of evil.

The word "covering" occurs only here in the New Testament but occurs in the Greek Old Testament for the covering of the tabernacle (Exodus 26:14) and of a cistern (2 Samuel 17:19). This seems preferable to the translation "cloak" or "veil." The "freedom" here is spiritual, not political. Hence Christians are not to use their freedom in Christ as a covering for doing evil in society.

A BIBLICAL WORLDVIEW OF FREEDOM

What 1 Peter 2:16 is affirming reflects a biblical worldview of reality. In Christ, Christians, as sons of the kingdom, are absolutely free from all allegiance to any earthly authority or power. In their essential reality or identity, they owe allegiance to no one but God, yet Christians give up their absolute freedom to live within earthly governments, possessing divine authority for the course of this age.

It is not that Christians do not have absolute freedom; in Christ they do—yet they give up the exercise of this freedom for the present era and become the best or greatest servants of all. The very fact that Peter says that Christians do not have or possess their freedom as a cover-up for evil implicitly acknowledges that it is theirs to choose not to exercise.

Moreover, there is a divine compulsion to give up the exercise of this freedom. They do it as servants *of God*. Thus, Christians are the freest of all people on the face of this earth. On the other hand, none can exceed them in sacrificing this freedom in becoming servants of all. Again, Jesus is the model for servant hood. For example, he washed his disciples' feet (John 13); and, at his arrest, he could have called on myriads of angels to deliver him, but he chose not to.

ULTIMATE FREEDOM IS FREEDOM TO CHOOSE TO SUBMIT

Christians, through grace, have escaped the bondage of sin and the bondage of law (Galatians 4:8–9) and are to stand firm in the freedom for which Christ set them free (Galatians 5:1). Yet this freedom is not antinomianism (freedom from all law and restraint). Indeed there is a paradox here, for Christian liberty means a freedom to do good ("through love, serve one another," Galatians 5:13), to serve God and to obey his ordinances (such as obedience to government). Christian freedom is bondage to God, a service which is true, ultimate freedom (consider John 8:31–36 and Romans 6:14–23). The Christian is the servant of God by right of purchase or redemption (1 Corinthians 7:22–23). From both the standpoint of conscience and divine justice, Christians cannot use their freedom as a covering to hide wickedness. Again Paul and Peter are one on this point.

All men are enslaved to someone or something; all serve some master. The apostles of liberty gloried in the title "Servant of Jesus Christ." As Johnstone says, " . . . the only possible moral condition for man is that of bondage to the one or the other of two masters."[16] This is clearly taught in 2 Peter 2:18–22: The lawless promise freedom, but they are themselves slaves of corruption, since they have been overcome by their master, lawlessness. Christian freedom involves a change of master, not escape from obligation.[17]

FOUR COMMANDS

In 1 Peter 2:17, Peter summarizes his teaching on the subject by giving four commands: "Honor all people; love the brotherhood of believers; fear God; honor the king." This short series of injunctions is closely connected with the preceding context. Christians enjoy freedom and are citizens of a heavenly country. Yet they have obligations, not only to rulers as citizens of a nation but to unbelievers as well. Their obligations extend beyond their fear of God and love for other Christians.

The arrangement of the four commands is the subject of much discussion. In light of the context, it seems best to view them all on the same level, not in such a way that the last three expand the first one (which apparently is the way the NIV reads the text).[18] The arrangement then

16. Johnstone, *Peter*, 160.
17. Selwyn, *St. Peter*, 174.
18. This seems best, even though the first is in the aorist tense, and the last three are present. "All people," if defined by the following words (brotherhood, God, king), fails then to include all the lost. It also seems irreverent to include "God" under "all" alongside the brotherhood and the king. The aorist can be explained as having no distinction here

consists of two pairs, each of which contains an injunction some Christians might doubt and one which was universally recognized ("honor all people, love the brotherhood of believers; fear God, honor the king"). The first pair refers to duties toward equals of the readers; the second pair refers to duties toward superiors. The order of the second pair is reversed from the first, allowing special emphasis to go to the duties in the beginning and end of the series, which were doubted by the readers and needed special attention: "honor all people . . . honor the king." Believers would readily comply with the second ("love the brotherhood of believers") and the third command ("fear God").

Honor All

To "honor all" is to have respect for people as people. Different honor is due to the king, the master, the husband, the wife, the church elder; and all people are owed some measure of esteem.[19] The verb form (an aorist tense) suggests that the command has a cryptic or succinct nature to it (in contrast to the present tenses used in the last three clauses).

Love Other Christians

"Love the brotherhood" reminds readers that there is an ongoing, special obligation to Christians that goes beyond honor. The present tense used here and in the last two commands stresses the continuous need to exercise these duties. Love is the badge of Christians. The Christian has freedom but he is to exercise his freedom to serve others through love (Galatians 5:13).

To love other Christians is to esteem them on the basis of their truest or essential reality. They are one in the body of Christ where all earthly distinctions (ethnic, social, cultural, gender) melt away in light of their heavenly oneness (Galatians 3:28 and Colossians 3:11).

---

from the present, or, preferably, as being more pointed than the rest because of the need expressed in the context to carry out obligations toward others who are not believers. It would have the thrust of *beginning* the duty toward all people; the commands in the present tense emphasize the continuous nature of the last three duties. The aorist points to the moment of decision-making. See Johnstone, *Peter*, 162ff.; Selwyn, *St. Peter*, 174.

19. Leighton, *First Peter*, 198–199.

To Submit or to Rebel against the State

Fear God

"Fear God" shifts the duties to the class of those possessing authority over the Christian. The supreme duty is to fear God, implying holy and loving reverence (consider 1 Peter 1:17 and 5:6). Under this fear, all religion is comprehended.[20] Kings in particular need to be mindful of this duty to fear God (consider Psalm 2:10–12). They need to observe this passage.

Honor the King

"Honor the king" is the second duty next to fearing God. Coming last in the series, it is probably emphasized and brings the whole discussion from 1 Peter 2:13 forward to conclusion. This duty is not inconsistent with fearing God, but parallel to it. Here Peter reflects the Lord's teaching of rendering to Caesar and to God each his proper due (Matthew 22:21). He may also have in mind Proverbs 24:21: "Fear God, my son, and the king." It is God's will that one should submit to the king (verses 14 and 15); therefore, because one fears God, he honors the king.

These four commands are brief but they encompass great meaning.[21] Duty to God must regulate all else.

The passage regarding one's civic responsibilities (verses 13–17) follows a doctrinal section (verses 1–10), which deals with the nature and purpose of the church and its relation to Christ. First Timothy 1:8–11 and 2:1–4 make it clear that society is to bear the character of the divine design. The Christian is not to seek escape from the world but, by obeying rulers and by doing good, to change society into that which conforms with God's will. As Jesus said, only the Christian can keep society functioning and surviving. Christians are the light and salt of the earth (Matthew 5:13–16).

SUMMARY

The following are some observations which can be derived from 1 Peter 2:13–17. These will summarize the contribution of the passage to the subject of the Christian's responsibility to government. They also touch upon

---

20. Leighton, *First Peter*, 202ff.
21. Ibid. Leighton devotes about ten pages to their explication (196–206).

The Limitation to Liberty: Is it Right to Rebel?

the question of a Christian's involvement in a changing society, especially one changed by revolution.

- The forms of government are immaterial as far as the command to be submissive is concerned. Peter uses words that point to various options: "*whether* to the king *or* to governors." However, that form of government that does not punish evil and praise the doing of good (as the Bible or conscience define the evil and the good) opposes the divine design for government. Such a government will hardly inspire obedience and respect. There must be equity and justice both in the formation and in the administration of government. A socialist or communist government violates divine laws regarding private property, and, like a tyrannical or totalitarian state (which destroys the dignity of man), is contrary to divine design. Yet a worse form is ongoing anarchy.

- Still, certain forms of government are preferable to others. That form which allows the citizenry to enjoy and pursue peace, godliness, and dignity is most in accord with divine design (as discussed on 1 Timothy 2:1–4). This agrees with Proverbs 14:34: "Righteousness exalts a nation, but sin is a disgrace to any people." Consider also Proverbs 24:15–22, 25:5, 26 as well as chapters 28 and 29.

- Peter agrees with Paul in stipulating that the number one responsibility of leaders in government is to enforce the law—to punish those who do evil and to praise those who do good. This is especially appropriate for America with its soaring crime rate. This is also instructive for those who view government as having its chief responsibility in the material welfare of its citizenry rather than law and order. All four passages covered in this book (Romans 13:1–7; 1 Timothy 1:8–11 and 2:1–4; 1 Peter 2:13–17) give unanimous witness to this foremost responsibility of government.

- Why should the enforcement of law be supreme? It is because law and justice, coupled with love, are supreme with God in his rule over all (consider Genesis 18:25 and Acts 17:31)—this is consistent with his person and work. Redemption reveals this best. Instead of resorting to brute force (the way of the materialist-humanist worldview), God used justice.[22] Christ the righteous one (1 John 2:1–2) satisfied

22. Henry DeBracton of the thirteenth century, quoted by Schaeffer, *Manifesto*, 27–28.

To Submit or to Rebel against the State

- the demands of the law in order to redeem man (Galatians 3:10–14 and 4:4–5). God brings this to the believer by way of a covenant, a legal transaction.

- In the introduction, I showed that law is intrinsic to the divine ordination of government. Law is God's way. Inalienable rights mean that law is supreme, not people; and law is supreme because there is a Law-Giver.[23]

- The authority of government comes from God. It is by divine providence that people are raised to places of authority. Such leaders or rulers should live in fear of God and seek to promote his kingdom. Rulers strengthen their own office when they promote God's place, for they can count on Christians to obey and give allegiance. Government and leaders, as all people, are to fear God. This has been a refreshing trait of those presidents of the United States who advocated a strong place for the role of religion and religious people in American life.

- It is well to remember those significant passages from the Old Testament that remind everyone, leader and follower alike, that God is ultimately in charge in human government. God is sovereign over all rulers; he does as he pleases in heaven and on earth. The pagan king of the great Babylonian Empire had to learn this lesson (Daniel 4:34ff.).

- Just government and an obedient citizenry are the gift of God and evidence of his blessing. The lack of these is God's judgment by which he punishes the sins of both rulers and people (consider Judges 9:20 and Romans 1:18). The breakdown of law and order is one of God's judgments.

- Implicit to Peter's description of government as a "human institution" is a rebuke to theonomy in its extreme form, as discussed in chapter 5. During the present era, the forms of government are left to people to decide. God purposes no special, direct, divine rule at present as he builds the Church and his invisible kingdom.

- The special contribution of this passage to the subject of the Christian's responsibility to government is to remind Christians that their liberty in Christ is not license to live as they please in the nation in

---

23. Schaeffer, *Manifesto*, 32–33.

The Limitation to Liberty: Is it Right to Rebel?

which they reside. Christians should be model citizens, obeying the laws and the rulers who make them, as long as this obedience does not violate their obedience to God. Submission to rulers is not only commanded by an apostle, but it is necessary "because of the Lord."

- As model citizens, Christians should participate in civic affairs. They cannot avoid their duties here, as in any other station of life, as Luther pointed out in his "Secular Authority" (as discussed in an earlier chapter). Their example of living by restraint in a land of freedom is desperately needed today and will silence the slander of the enemies of the cross. A good Christian cannot be a bad citizen.

- The command to be submissive to every human institution makes it clear that Christians should not engage in sedition, promoting anarchy, or the inciting of riot or revolution. This would place Christians in the category of the "lawless and rebellious" (1 Timothy 1:9) and put them at odds to the divine design for government, namely that it provide a society of peace where godliness and dignity prevail (1 Timothy 2:2). Christians should rather "aspire to the crowns of martyrs, not of tyrannicides."[24] The very freedom the believer may plead to justify rebellion to government is actually defined here as freedom to serve God and his laws (represented by governments).

- First Peter 2:13 gives support to the idea of a "politics of structure," in the words of Niemeyer.[25] Christians should not seek the wholesale destruction of a society, but rather follow the principle of piece-meal reform. The founding fathers recognized this when, in the Declaration of Independence, they affirmed: "Prudence, indeed, will dictate that Governments long established should not be changed for light and transient causes . . . " Yet there was a place for revolution.

- Peter's instruction refers to government in place and does not apply, it seems, to government (i.e., the lack of it) in transition or revolution. This is obvious, for during revolution no government exists, or at least the various human institutions are changing and several are claiming the allegiance of the people. At such a time, loyalties among Christians may be divided. However, the informed obedience to constituted authority in peaceful times will mature the Christian

---

24. Lillie, *Lectures*, 144.
25. Niemeyer, "Democratic Disorder," 16: 73.

to know how to resolve the questions facing him during a political revolution. If Christians are called upon in helping to form a government, they should be guided by their understanding of what is most in accord with sound and good government (1 Timothy 2:1–2).

- Legal protest or judicial procedures are not ruled out, however, to test cases by appeal in those nations that allow such. Paul's actions in Acts demonstrate this aspect of citizenship. Christians, using every legal means available, should work to have bad laws abrogated and good laws enacted. As other forms of government are ordained by God, so our republican form of government is ordained by God. Submission to such involves the routes of appeal, civil protest, lawsuit, and so on.

GOVERNMENT BEING TRUE TO ITSELF

Basically Peter's words, in light of the teaching of the rest of Scripture, mean that a government and/or its leaders and rulers must be true to itself, and to the idea of government taught by Scripture or general revelation. If any government violates its own creed, laws, constitution, or whatever form of charter it has (if any), then the citizens of that country have "a solemn duty" to suppress the usurpation.[26]

For example, before the time of the American Revolution, England began redrawing the form of the colonial government, including its own right to a legislature that had the right to fashion legislation. England was violating its own contract with the colonies.

Today the government in the United States of America is derived from the Constitution, and it is the supreme authority. If officials, defeated in an election, refuse to vacate their post, violating the Constitution, they should be removed by force.

Similarly, if legislation is passed which violates basic rights granted by the Constitution, even if the Supreme Court should uphold such legislation, the Christian has the duty to join with others in seeking to overturn such legislation and to hold accountable those officials responsible for such legislation. Also, disobedience to law that clearly violates God's law is necessary.

---

26. See Lillie, *Lectures*, 143–144.

THE CIVIL WAR

John Lillie wrote his comments on 1 Peter during the Civil War. He used the words, "Honor all men" (2:17), as the basis for attacking the institution of slavery in the South and discrimination in the North. He condemned the silence of people opposed to this evil. He rebuked the popularity of denouncing "the madness of the abolitionists, and the heresy of the higher law." He believed the latter at least showed that "the national conscience was not dead." Milder remedies had failed to right the great wrong of slavery, and therefore Lillie wrote: "I can yet at times rejoice with trembling that the great explosion has come." Without war, he believed that the nation would have been soon corrupted and destroyed without remedy. Liberty and slavery were "hostile twins," locked in a "deadly grapple." For that, "let every patriot praise God," Lillie wrote. Only with the end of slavery could the great and noble principles of the Declaration of Independence receive "their nobler embodiment."[27]

Now if Lillie could believe and write this about slavery under the application of the words "honor all people," should not Christians today be similarly concerned about abortion, euthanasia, and gay rights? The pertinent words of 1 Peter 2:17 may be those chosen by Lillie, or the next phrase, which is even more compelling—they are the words, "fear God." As Lillie prayed for the day when all slavery would be gone, so Christians should beseech God for the day to dawn when there will be new respect for human life and dignity.

In light of the above, it is clear that liberation theology is a great perversion of the meaning of the gospel and its application, especially in its promotion of violence and revolution as an essential element in the gospel itself. Christ himself never so defined the gospel, and he explicitly condemned a recourse to arms and violence.

Yet should Christians ever join a revolution? If so, just when should they do so? These are questions that the Reformers also faced and discussed, and their insights are still helpful. I've summarized their views in appendix 2.

---

27. Lillie, *Lectures*, 158–159.

To Submit or to Rebel against the State

CONCLUSION: A CHRISTIAN MAY PARTICIPATE IN REVOLUTION

In conclusion, I believe that the question raised at the beginning of the chapter regarding Christian participation in revolution has a positive answer with several qualifications. Christians may go so far as to participate in revolution (that is, in the transition from one government to another); however, they should not incite nor provoke revolution or anarchy unless they themselves are already duly constituted civil servants. Rather, they should follow the lead of a duly constituted member of the government. They must also evaluate the merits of a revolution by considering the limiting factors cited in chapter 5 as the standards for a just war.

This appears to be the extent to which one may go in participating in revolution and have biblical justification. Yet many may decide not to go nearly this far. Christians must respect the differing convictions of personal conscience now, just as during the American Revolution.

Appendix 2, giving the views of the leaders of the Protestant Reformation (Luther, Calvin, Knox), shows general agreement with my own conclusions regarding Christian participation in revolution. The information there also bears witness to the variety of views on this issue.

THE UNKNOWN END OF TAMANA'S STORY

Several days after Tamana's beating, she visited Dayna Curry again. As they conversed, they heard an Afghan woman in the house next door let out a piercing scream. The woman continued to scream for some time, and it soon became apparent that her husband was beating her. Tamana told Dayna that they could do nothing to stop the man, as there were no laws to protect wives from such abuse. Tamana remarked gravely: "Those screams are nothing compared to the screams that came from my house when the Taliban were there."

Later that same week, Tamana's oldest daughter, a teenager with her mother's round face, visited Dayna at the women's health clinic. She, too, recounted the beating story and cried when describing how badly the Taliban police had beaten her brother. Then she said something that startled Dayna: "It's okay," she said, "because Jesus was beaten for us." In Dari, her native tongue, she said "*lat khord*," meaning Jesus "ate lashes" for us. Dayna was amazed that none of the family had been killed.

The Limitation to Liberty: Is it Right to Rebel?

After Heather Mercer joined Dayna Curry in Afghanistan in March 2001, Tamana confessed to the women that she was not really a widow after all. She had been hiding this in order to keep her widow card, but she had been having nightmares that the Christians would discover her lie. She was willing to give up the food guaranteed to her. Amazingly, the staff of the agency allowed Tamana to keep her card. Providing for eight children and a sick husband was close enough to a widow's plight to qualify her.

Just prior to the arrest of Heather Mercer and Dayna Curry in August 2001, they and the Masons were planning to set Tamana's husband up in a small shop. Space was rented and supplies ordered. But the whole process came to an end when Heather and Dayna were arrested by the Taliban. What subsequently happened to this needy family is unknown.[28]

---

28. Curry and Mercer, *Prisoners of Hope*, 76–78, used with slight alterations. Shortly after Sept. 11, 2001, Dayna and Heather were rescued by U.S. Marines who flew helicopters over 500 miles to reach them.

Conclusion

In an Age of Terrorism, What Does the Future Hold? Facing the Coming Unrest and Revolution

THE UNIQUE PLACE OF CHRISTIANITY

IN PART 1, THIS book attempted to show the origin and interrelationship of religion, morality and law in government or nationhood. It has shown that government, morality, and law have a deeply religious nature. The winds of revolution would change the traditional and biblical understanding of all three of these essentials to civilization. Indeed, we are currently experiencing government terrorism, moral terrorism, and legal terrorism.

Yet some would charge that it is biblical Christianity that is at fault. Christians seeking to impose their moral beliefs are the cause of the storm threatening the West; Christians are to blame for the internal strife because they are not willing to compromise, "to live and let live," in a pluralistic world.

Such a charge is not the first time that Christians have been blamed for social unrest and anarchy. The Apostles were charged by the Jewish religious leaders of their day with turning their world upside down by teaching that Jesus is the Christ, the Son of God, and Lord of all (Acts 2:36; 4:10, 16; 5:28–42).

At the time of Polycarp, in the mid-second century, Romans accused Christians of being atheists and threats to the state because they would not swear allegiance to Caesar who claimed to be a god. Subsequently, in the fourth century, when the mighty Roman Empire was deteriorating and

Conclusion

losing political control, the people blamed the Christians. They claimed that the secular gods of the state were angered because their adherents had forsaken them for Christianity. At that time, Augustine stepped forward and convincingly argued to the contrary in his *The City of God*.

In part 2, I unfolded several biblical passages to show the contribution they make to understanding the nature and role of government on Earth. They show the relationship of law to morality. These passages also reveal the duties that Christians have as citizens of whatever nation they indwell. These passages are Matthew 22:21; Romans 13:1-7; 1 Timothy 1:8-11; 2:1-4; and 1 Peter 2:13-17. I have focused on seven principles, taken from these passages, that I think are the most relevant today.

1. Human government is ordained, established by God. (Romans 13:1-2, 4-6; cf. 1 Peter 2:13)

2. Government is to promote good and punish evil. (Romans 13:3-4; 1 Timothy 1:9-10; 2:2; 1 Peter 2:14-15)

3. Allegiance to government is not absolute. Indeed God's kingdom has the ultimate, supreme claim upon the allegiance of Christians. (Matthew 22:21; Acts 4:19-20; 1 Peter 2:17)

4. Legislation should properly regulate morality and religious values in society, not only civil or legal matters. Indeed such a distinction between moral and legal is unjustified, for all law is enacted morality and reflects a divine standard (God's laws). (1 Timothy 1:8-11)

5. The standard for law and morality is divine revelation, both general and special revelation. (1 Timothy 1:11; Romans 13:5)

6. The Christian has a crucial and unique role to play in society, which the unbeliever does not have. This is prayer for leaders (1 Timothy 2:1-4) and the freedom to submit to leaders (Romans 13:1ff.; 1 Peter 2:13ff.) in the doing of good. In answer to their prayers, God is moved to prosper nations, or to withhold his blessing.

7. Liberty is not license to do as one pleases. (Romans 13:1, 5; 1 Peter 2:13-17)

I have exposed several additional truths in the course of making observations on each passage or when summarizing each one. Yet the seven main principles form the fountain from which all the rest flow.

Conclusion

IMPLICATIONS BASED ON THE PRINCIPLES

I devote the final pages of this section to the implications that flow from the seven main principles of this book. If I have shown with some degree of plausibility that the foregoing principles are true and authoritative for the Christian today, what is their significance? I believe that they provide the underpinnings for the reshaping of American society, and of civilization as a whole. They provide the blueprint for a plan of renewal, which will once again secure sound and good government. In our terrorist age, America especially needs a Second Revolution.

WE STAND ON THE BRINK

I believe that the demise of the West is a stark probability. Unless it, and America in particular, return to their spiritual moorings, a day of darkness unprecedented in the annals of history will fall upon the earth.

The vehicle by which this could occur is readily at hand. One catalyst is the terrorism affirmed by radical Islam. Terrorists have (or will have) at their disposal WMDs that could destroy significant portions of America's infrastructure and economy. And with such a blow, the ramifications would be global. Another catalyst is economic terrorism—the growing unrest calling for the end of capitalism and for a new (undefined) order.

It is in this sober light that I seek to impress the reader with three things: the true nature of the problems in America and in the West; the urgency of the hour; and the solution to these problems, especially regarding the role that Christians must play.

THE TRUE NATURE OF THE WORLD'S PROBLEMS

The problems of America in particular, and of countries around the world in general, are, in the end, spiritual. Civilization has turned her back upon the God of the Bible and upon the Judeo-Christian ethic as revealed in the Bible. All other areas usually identified as problems facing the world (such as global warming, resources of energy, pollution, food distribution, lawlessness, the economy, military preparedness, and others) pale into insignificance when placed next to the religious apostasy that has afflicted the West in particular.

Conclusion

Because people are first and foremost spiritual beings, all problems of materialism are secondary in importance. The spiritual and moral sickness has brought about or intensified the other problems. Economic stress is, at heart, a problem of greed. Only with the healing of the spiritual illness can there be any hope of relieving or solving the other problems.

EDUCATION DEVOID OF THE SPIRITUAL

Many forces have contributed to this spiritual sickness. Perhaps none is so great as the demise of significant spiritual values in public and private education. Eventually such education weakens the moral fiber of the citizenry and its leaders. It has stopped teaching the fear of God and obedience to him.

The greatest force in education contributing to the downfall of spiritual values in general, and, therefore, of the American tradition in particular, is the teaching of the theory of evolution. This has brought about a false and incomplete education, for it denies the reality of the spiritual.

The teaching of evolution in the schools has had a far greater impact on other disciplines than on science itself. It strikes at the very soul of the person and the nation. It denies the spiritual nature of man and henceforth destroys any real basis for his dignity. Theology, jurisprudence, economics, sociology, social ethics, psychology, etc., have all been fatally wounded by this dagger of deceit. With the admission of evolution into the classroom, and the expulsion of God, prayer, Bible reading, and the Ten Commandments, the United States has begun its pell-mell plunge into distress, and, ultimately, into obscurity and oblivion.

SPIRITUAL RENEWAL IS THE ANSWER

In education, there needs to be the inculcation of moral and spiritual values, and of gratitude and appreciation for past generations. Christians should compel their society to return to a government not hostile to, but conducive to, the spread of Christianity.

Several years ago, Russell Kirk cited ten principles that would reinvigorate higher education. The very first one is that "the college should reaffirm that the objectives of higher learning are wisdom and virtue, and that it seeks to attain an ethical purpose through an intellectual means."[1]

His second principle elaborated on how to attain this ethical end. His third principle recognized the relationship between morality and religion: "The college should return to a concise curriculum emphasizing humane letters, history, the theoretical sciences, languages, moral philosophy, and religious knowledge."[2]

Charles Malik has also grasped the most central issues of the day and the urgency needed to address them. At the dedication ceremony of the Billy Graham Center at Wheaton College, September 13, 1980, he said:

> Nothing is as important in the world today as for the Christians of America to grasp their historic opportunities and prove themselves equal to them. I say "the Christians," but I must add also "the Jews," because what is fatefully at stake today is the highest spiritual values of the Judeo-Christian tradition. If the highest Christian values be overturned, so will the highest Jewish values.[3]

What he said then is still true some thirty years later. Spiritual renewal must occur in education in America. Without apology or embarrassment, Christians should insist upon a reinstatement of the Judeo-Christian ethic to the classroom and society as a whole.

HISTORICAL PRECEDENCE FOR CHRISTIAN VALUES IN PUBLIC EDUCATION

Such an insistence has historical precedence. It is deeply rooted in significant laws of the past. In 1787, the U.S. Congress passed the Northwest Ordinance, which provided for the government of that territory, later known as the states of Illinois, Wisconsin, Michigan, Indiana, and Ohio. It forbade slavery and guaranteed trial by jury and freedom of religious worship.[4] With regard to the latter, it specifically stipulated: "Religion, morality, and knowledge being necessary to good government and the happiness of mankind, schools and the means of learning shall forever

---

1. Kirk, "Reactionary Radicalism," 232.
2. Ibid.
3. Malik, "Two Tasks," 289.
4. Billington, "Northwest Ordinance," 14: 408.

Conclusion

be encouraged."⁵ Today Christians should warn that we cannot survive as a nation by receiving an education that is devoid of all religion and morality.

TRUE PLURALISM

To those who decry this and insist upon a pluralistic education, and will not reform, then I say: Let pluralism in education truly reign! Let government desist from promoting and providing secular humanism alone and allow the teaching of the biblical alternative upon which the nation was founded! Let it desist from compelling Christians to support by their taxes only one system or approach in education! Let it at least allow citizens to support the schools of their choice with their taxes! Let Christian schools multiply up and down the land!

The recent decision by the U.S. Supreme Court, which found that the use of vouchers to fund education in religious schools is constitutional, should promote Christian schools. Similarly, the policies of President Bush encouraged the growth of Christian schools. It is the teachers' unions that operate as major obstacles to the renewal of public education.

WARNINGS FROM SEVERAL QUARTERS

Others have written with similar alarm regarding broader aspects of the spiritual apostasy of our society. Gerhart Niemeyer of Notre Dame wrote:

> Let me suggest that we are observing an advanced state of dissolution of our cultural patrimony, which is Christian. We are a Christian society, a fact that has little to do with the number of faithful and active Christians in our midst, but rather with the foundation of our culture. Western civilization came into existence through the unifying impulse of Latin Christianity. No other religion has ever wielded a similarly powerful influence in the centuries of our existence.⁶

Niemeyer goes on to divide Western humanity into three distinct groups: (1) The nihilistic ideologists who, under the sway of History deified, believe *in* nothing; (2) the urbanized and educated middle class of

---

5. Quoted from Schaeffer, *Manifesto*, 37.
6. Niemeyer, "Democratic Disorder," 16: 67.

cultural leaders who know not in what to believe; and (3) those who believe in the God of Christianity.[7]

Niemeyer insightfully shows how the second group, providing the leaders of education, the media, and government, are spiritually, intellectually, and morally adrift. Motives (compassion, freedom, perfection, equality) still abound but now without principles. Recent surveys confirm that those in media invariably are more antagonistic to traditional values than the average person. Indeed, recent studies show that agnostics and those hostile to Christianity have taken over the Democratic Party. Hopefully, the rise of the Tea Party will reinvigorate our spiritual values.

The hearts and minds of those who have discarded the regenerating faith of Christianity have thrown away our Christian heritage. They have no firm grasp on reality.[8] Since the "democratic disorder" of our society stems from spiritual roots, no political remedy will do. Solzhenitsyn, quoted by Niemeyer, said in the conclusion of his *Letter to the Soviet Leaders*, "Christianity is the sole alternative."[9] The fall of communism underscores his claim.

TWO PATHS BEFORE THE WEST

There are two paths that lie before America and she can take only one or the other. Both necessitate a new revolution. One path leads to a secular society with the attendant loss of inalienable natural rights, reminding one of the French Revolution, which was based on the rights of people. This would be a violent, anarchical revolution leading to totalitarianism.

The other leads to a virtuous society based on revealed law and natural rights, a second revolution to return to former moorings. The former is a broad, easy way, which will come by itself quite naturally. It is apostasy. The latter is a narrow, hard course that requires vigilance and sacrifice. It is spiritual renewal. The former leads to national death, the latter will lead to new life for the nation.

The status quo—to keep our present standard of living and our personal pleasure—is not an option. The seeds of change have been sown

---

7. Niemeyer, "Democratic Disorder," 16:69.
8. Ibid., 70.
9. Ibid., 71.

Conclusion

and well-watered. History does not stand still. Christians must mold the changes toward a renewal of society or they will be swept along by a tide of secular humanism and spiritual rebellion. The events of September 11, 2001, give us a bold reminder that things have changed, that danger lurks on the horizon, that we need to change.

SPIRITUAL RENEWAL AT AMERICA'S FOUNDING

The solution to the problems besetting the West cannot come by way of education or dedication alone. A spiritual awakening, a revolution of the spirit, as profound as the first, is needed. Such a renewal occurred prior to the Declaration of Independence in the form of the Great Awakening. As Bellah (not an evangelical) points out, this national movement was not only a religious one but such that "provided many of the conceptions and symbols of a good social order which it was later hoped that the Revolution would bring about."[10]

The importance of a Christian world-view at America's founding cannot be denied, even by those hostile to it. As Singer writes:

> A Christian world and life view furnished the basis of this early political thought which guided the American people for nearly two centuries and whose crowning lay in the writing of the Constitution of 1787. This Christian theism had so permeated the colonial mind that it continued to guide even those who had come to regard the Gospel with indifference or even hostility. The currents of this orthodoxy were too strong to be easily set aside by those who in their own thinking had come to a different conception of religion and hence of government also.[11]

Perry Miller, a convinced atheist, was, in his day, the best historian of the colonial era, according to Schaeffer. He recognized the spiritual nature of the American Revolution. In his *Nature's Nation* (1961), he concluded, according to Schaeffer:

> Actually, European deism was an exotic plant in America, which never struck roots in the soil. "Rationalism" was never so wide-spread as liberal historians, or those fascinated by Jefferson, have imagined. The basic fact is that the Revolution had been

---

10. Bellah, "Religion and Polity," 15: 111.
11. Singer, "American History," 284–285, quoted by Rowe, "Christians," 7.

preached to the masses as a religious revival, and had the astounding fortune to succeed . . . [We] still do not realize how effective were generations of Protestant preaching in evoking patriotic enthusiasm.[12]

SPIRITUAL REVIVAL

The present crisis in America cannot be solved by rededication or reeducation alone. Rather, our traditional religious and moral values must be revived. We need a religious renewal. Again Bellah writes:

> The crisis of our society is so profound and our grasp on our tradition is so uncertain that a mere "rededication" to past values does not seem adequate . . . Perhaps only a new eruption of the sacred out of the unconscious depths can show us in immediate experience the source of our ethical vision. Certainly many times before in our history an experience of spiritual awakening has preceded a renewed effort to build a good society. Indeed, there are at the moment in America many groups, some with a long history, others much more recent, that claim to be the bearers of religious renewal . . . Certainly the increasingly evident failure of modern secular culture to solve the problems it has created suggest that traditional wisdom may have a future potency that only recently few would have imagined.[13]

The historian, Arnold Toynbee, saw the issues in a similar way, except that he viewed America's problem in the light of all of Western civilization. At the height of communism he wrote:

> The West has erred because it has chosen to fight Communism with Communism's own material weapons. As long as the battle is fought on these terms, the Communists will keep on winning. The West must base its appeal on religion. Only in this way can democracy turn the tables on Communist assailants. The grace of God might bring about this miracle.[14]

12. Schaeffer, *Manifesto*, 128.
13. Ibid., 121–122.
14. Quoted in Lipscomb and Dunn, *War*, 11. Elsewhere Toynbee has written in a similar vein (*America*, 149, 153):

> The American Revolution was a truly glorious revolution. It was glorious for two reasons. The basic issues that it raised were spiritual, not material; and,

Conclusion

Communism has fallen, and religious people had a significant role to play, especially in Poland and Czechoslovakia. It will be Christian people who will be at the forefront of the collapse of communism in China and the bridling of Islamic terrorism.

It is important to point out that the contemporary appeal for human rights or civil rights is not adequate either. It places the needed emphasis in the wrong place. We need to appeal to inalienable rights as divinely-sourced, which is a spiritual appeal. "Human" rights avoid accountability to a Supreme Being and salves the conscience of its moral and spiritual failure.

The renewal must recognize the potential for evil in people and society. We must humbly admit the ultimate impossibility of realizing a truly just society, i.e., "transcendent justice," by means of science or reason. The transcendent must be applied in the present. Bellah writes:

> even if this may not have been the intention of some of the Founding Fathers, it was in effect, as Jefferson perceived and Emerson proclaimed, a revolution for the whole human race, not just for the people of the Thirteen Colonies. The shot fired beside the bridge at Concord was not only heard round the world; it was taken as a signal, given to the world by the embattled American farmers, that the World Revolution had begun . . . The American Revolution was glorious because it staked out human rights, and staked them out for all men. What is this mighty force that has sent that sound rolling round and round the circumference of the planet? The impetus behind the American Revolution is the spirit of Christianity.

These remarks are made in a chapter titled, "Can America Re-join Her Own Revolution?" Toynbee's point is that America abandoned her own revolution about the First World War because of her materialism and affluence, becoming a defender of vested interests. He believes this handicap can be overcome. Presidents Ronald Reagan and George W. Bush have done more than other presidents in calling for a renewal of the spiritual values that have made America great. By globalization, the opportunity to export these values around the world has never been greater. The parallel with Rome at her zenith of military power in the second century B.C. is clear. Materialism, wealth, and power destroyed traditional Roman values so that Greek values and customs conquered Rome. Significantly, this did not enhance democracy, but within one hundred years the republic was replaced by a dictatorship. America has no basis for believing that she will escape the same political consequence should she continue adopting Greek ways *(Cont. footnote 14)* today. Matthew Arnold saw the distinctive differences between the worldviews of Hebraism and Hellenism when he wrote his essay, "Hebraism and Hellenism," in 1867. While our structure of government is heavily indebted to the Greeks, it is the Jews (and subsequent Christians) that have bequeathed to us our morality and faith. Arnold's assessment is even more pertinent now almost a hundred and fifty years later.

> It seems reasonably clear to me that science and reason are unlikely to bring about the motivational transformation that alone can make the next decades of our history something other than a complete nightmare. Only, and it is, I think, an outside chance at best, an experience of transcendent order could provide the basis of such a transformation.[15]

The events of September 11, 2001, and the present war on terrorism give special poignancy to Bellah's warning about a coming "nightmare." The great earthquake and tsunami that struck Japan on March 11, 2011, are reminders of other devastations that are meant to turn people to God. Jesus said that all such disasters are reminders that we all are sinners who need to turn to God to avoid judgment (see Luke 13:1–5).

THE PARALLEL WITH ESTHER OF THE BIBLE

The role of evangelicals in this hour of crisis could hardly be clearer. The Christian finds himself in the very position that Queen Esther had in the court of King Ahasuerus of Persia. When perplexed over her responsibility toward the Jews who were on the brink of extinction, it was her cousin Mordecai that challenged her concerning her individual responsibility. The Jews were in God's sovereign care but human accountability was also involved. Mordecai said to Esther (4:13–14):

> Do not think that because you are in the king's palace you alone of all the Jews will escape. For if you remain silent at this time, relief and deliverance for the Jews will arise from another place, but you and your father's family will perish. And who knows but that you have come to royal position for such a time as this?

THE ROLE OF CLERGY

Not only do Christians in general have a unique role to serve in this spiritual renewal, but the clergy in particular have special responsibility. Just like the Old Testament prophets, they need to call this nation, and the West, and the East, back to God and to spiritual moorings. They need to identify sin for what it is and make clear the path to renewal. While the government may make a practice legal (such as homosexual behavior) it

---

15. Bellah, "Religion and Polity," 122–123.

cannot make it moral. The clergy needs to perform this moral assessment. Again there is historical precedent for such involvement of the clergy. Baldwin writes:

> The New England preacher drew his beliefs largely from the Bible, which was to him a sacred book, infallible, God's will for man. Of necessity, it colored his political thinking. His conception of God, of God's law, and of God's relation to man determined to a large extent his conception of human law and of man's relation to his fellows. If his ideas of government and the rights of man were in part derived from other sources, they were strengthened and sanctioned by Holy Writ.

This was of course especially true of the clergy. They stood before the people as interpreters of God's will. Their political speeches were sermons, their political slogans were often Bible texts. What they taught of government had about it the authority of the divine.[16]

JOHN WITHERSPOON

The role of the clergy in preserving liberty was clearly perceived and exemplified by Rev. John Witherspoon. He understood the connection between religion and liberty. He said: "He is the best friend of American liberty who is most sincere and active in promoting pure and undefiled religion."[17] The clergy seek to preserve virtue, without which there can be no liberty. Witherspoon warned: "A republic once equally poised must either preserve its virtue or lose its liberty."[18]

Witherspoon put his beliefs into practice. At one point in the early part of July 1776, it was he who encouraged the delegates not to despair but to pursue the signing of the Declaration of Independence. His was the only clergyman's signature on the document.

God raised up the Baptist preacher, Isaac Backus (whom we discussed in chapter 7), to help promote spiritual renewal during the years leading up to and following the American Revolution. Because of him, we enjoy the freedom to worship without being forced to support with our taxes a particular state church.

16. Baldwin, *Clergy*, 12; quoted by Rowe, "Christians," 6.
17. Schaeffer, *Manifesto*, 33–34.
18. Ibid., 33.

THE URGENCY OF THE HOUR

The crisis is so great and the hour so late that it seems nothing will prevent our calamitous destruction. Only a supernatural intervention will spare the nation. Since this has happened in the past, such as at the Great Awakening in the 1740s and in the mid-nineteenth century under D.L. Moody and others, there is hope. But the hour is late and Christians alone, and especially the clergy, possess the key to unlock the entrance to divine blessing. To fail to act will only ensure destruction. As Edmund Burke said so famously: "All that is necessary for the triumph of evil is for good men to do nothing." America can be either a blessing or a curse among the nations.

It is a thin line between the two destinies.

A POINTED REBUKE

I want to conclude with a sober but pointed reproof of Christian indifference from the pen of a well-known Christian educator, Dr. V. Raymond Edman, once the President of Wheaton College. Perhaps his comments on the passage Judges 8:33—9:57 (especially 9:7–20) will stir God's people to action.

> The olive tree, the fig tree, and the vine are representatives of the best elements in society. They are typical of men whose "fruits" or "works" are a blessing to mankind, honest men of stature in the community and pillars in the economy, men endowed with ability, experienced, educated, and trained. However, in the parable each one was unwilling to assume the responsibilities and burdens of leadership. They were materialists and not idealists, self-centered and not sacrificial of spirit, cowardly and not courageous. They were able to fulfill the proffered assignment but were unwilling to sacrifice their own interests for the welfare of all. In that sad day, when Israel needed a true leader under God, there were men of piety and platitudes but not of patriotism. They enjoyed the blessings of free government but would not risk their personal interests to bear its burdens. There were good and godly men, but they were sadly lacking in civic responsibilities and in a sense of the times in which they lived. For the heroic dead and the heritage of freedom they held no gratitude.[19]

19. Quoted by Rowe, "Christians," 6.

Conclusion

It is not a call for great men and women but for committed ordinary people. After the prolonged battle for Guadalcanal during 1942–1943, the successful Admiral William Halsey in reply to a comment about his being a great commander said something to the effect: "There are no great men, only great challenges that ordinary men must arise to meet." So it is yet today.

Epilogue

The Great Hymns of America

INDEPENDENCE DAY: JULY 4

THERE ARE NO BETTER words to form a final note to this book than to quote the great American hymns that celebrate the birth and struggle of our nation. They articulate both the hope and the reality of the American Revolution. The role of faith and character are explicit. There is no place for pluralism in religion and ethics here. It is unfortunate that most of us are only familiar with the first stanza.

O Beautiful for Spacious Skies

> O beautiful for spacious skies, for amber waves of grain,
> For purple mountain majesties above the fruited plain!
> America! America! God shed his grace on thee,
> And crown thy good with brotherhood from sea to shining sea!
> O beautiful for pilgrim feet, whose stern, impassioned stress
> A thoroughfare for freedom beat across the wilderness!
> America! America! God mend thine every flaw,
> Confirm thy soul in self-control, thy liberty in law!
> O beautiful for heroes proved in liberating strife,
> Who more than self their country loved, and mercy more than life!
> America! America! May God thy gold refine,
> Till all success be nobleness and ev'ry gain divine!
> O beautiful for patriot dream that sees beyond the years
> Thine alabaster cities gleam, undimmed by human tears!

Epilogue

America! America! God shed his grace on thee,
And crown thy good with brotherhood from sea to shining sea.

[Note: Our American cities, since 9-11,
are no longer "undimmed by human tears"!]

My Country 'Tis of Thee

My country, 'tis of thee, sweet land of liberty,
Of thee I sing:
Land where my fathers died, land of the pilgrim's pride,
From ev'ry mountain side, let freedom ring!
My native country, thee, land of the noble free,
Thy name I love:
I love thy rocks and rills, thy woods and templed hills;
My heart with rapture thrills like that above.
Let music swell the breeze, and ring from all the trees
Sweet freedom's song:
Let mortal tongues awake; let all that breathe partake;
Let rocks their silence break, the sound prolong.
Our fathers' God, to Thee, Author of liberty,
To Thee we sing:
Long may our land be bright with freedom's holy light;
Protect us by Thy might, great God our King!

The Star-Spangled Banner

Oh, say, can you see, by the dawn's early light,
What so proudly we hailed at the twilight's last gleaming?
Whose broad stripes and bright stars, thro' the perilous fight,
O'er the ramparts we watched, were so gallantly streaming?
And the rockets' red glare, the bombs bursting in air,
Gave proof thro' the night that our flag was still there.
Oh, say, does that star-spangled banner yet wave
O'er the land of the free, and the home of the brave?
On the shore, dimly seen thro' the mists of the deep,
Where the foe's haughty host in dread silence reposes,
What is that which the breeze, o'er the towering steep,
As it fitfully blows, half conceals, half discloses?
Now it catches the gleam of the morning's first beam,
In full glory reflected, now shines on the stream:

'Tis the star-spangled banner; oh, long may it wave
O'er the land of the free, and the home of the brave.
And where is that band, who so valiantly swore
That the havoc of war and the battle's confusion,
A home and a country should leave us no more?
Their blood has washed out their foul footsteps' pollution;
No refuge could save the hireling and slave
From the terror of flight or the gloom of the grave.
And the star-spangled banner in triumph doth wave
O'er the land of the free and the home of the brave.
Oh, thus be it ever when freemen shall stand
Between their loved homes and war's desolation;
Blest with vict'ry and peace, may the Heav'n-rescued land
Praise the Pow'r that hath made and preserved us a nation!
Then conquer we must, when our cause it is just;
And this be our motto: "In God is our trust!"
And the star-spangled banner in triumph shall wave
O'er the land of the free, and the home of the brave.

God of Our Fathers, Whose Almighty Hand

God of our fathers, whose almighty hand
Leads forth in beauty all the starry band
Of shining worlds in splendor thro' the skies,
Our grateful songs before Thy throne arise.
Thy love divine hath led us in the past,
In this free land by Thee our lot is cast;
Be Thou our ruler, guardian, guide and stay,
Thy word our law, Thy paths our chosen way.
From war's alarms, from deadly pestilence,
Be Thy strong arm our ever strong defense;
Thy true religion in our hearts increase,
Thy bounteous goodness nourish us in peace.
Refresh Thy people on their toilsome way,
Lead us from night to never-ending day;
Fill all our lives with love and grace divine,
And glory, laud, and praise be ever Thine.

Appendix 1

The Founding Fathers Support Natural Moral Law and Religion in America

THE FOUNDING FATHERS SUPPORT NATURAL MORAL LAW

THE FOLLOWING ARE REPRESENTATIVE of a widespread view of the role of Natural Moral Law and religion or virtue in the life of a nation.[1]

Rev. Jonathan Mayhew has already been cited in the text, so only a portion of that election sermon is quoted again here where he assumes Natural Moral Law: " . . . And those times are perilous indeed, wherein men shall be only lovers of their own selves, having no concern for the good of the public. Shall we go to the pagans to learn this god-like virtue? Even they can teach it . . . "

In 1744 Rev. Elisha Williams wrote concerning the religious origin of liberty and law. He noted in his "A Seasonable Plea" that it is a plea primarily for the right to freedom of conscience and private judgment in religious matters.

> Reason teaches that all Men are naturally equal in Respect of Jurisdiction or Dominion one over another. Altho' true it is that Children are not born in this full State of Equality, yet they are born to it . . . [entitled to it . . .]. For God having given Man an Understanding to direct his Actions, has given him therewith a

---

1. See Long, *Yardstick*, viii–ix, xxii–xxiii, 4–6, 22–24, 64, 74–76, 85–86, 94–95, etc. Also see such works as Foster and Swanson, *American Covenant*; Slater, *Christian History*; and Hall, *Christian History*.

Appendix 1

> Freedom of Will and Liberty of Acting, as properly belonging thereto, within the Bounds of that Law he is under ... [Natural Law, God's Law] ... So that we are born Free as we are born Rational ... This natural Freedom is not a Liberty for every one to do what he pleases without any Regard to any Law; for a rational Creature cannot but be made under a Law from its MAKER: But it consists in a Freedom from any superior Power on Earth, and not being under the Will or legislative Authority of Man, and having only the Law of Nature (or in other Words, of its MAKER) for his Rule.

The connection between civil and religious liberty was clearly perceived by Rev. John Witherspoon, a signer of the Declaration of Independence and an evangelical, who later became president of Princeton. In a sermon, May 17, 1776 he wrote, "There is not a single instance in history in which civil liberty was lost, and religious liberty preserved entire. If therefore we yield up our temporal property, we at the same time deliver the conscience into bondage."

The sentiments of the foregoing were expressed in various resolutions of the legislative bodies of the colonies. Those of the House of Representatives of Massachusetts, 1765, are representative: "Resolved, that the inhabitants of this Province are unalienably entitled to those essential rights ["founded in the law of God and of Nature"] in common with all men: and that no law of society can, consistent with the law of God and nature, divest them of those rights."

In 1774, in "Rights of British America," Thomas Jefferson wrote of the divine origin of rights. He said: "The God who gave us life gave us liberty at the same time; the hand of force may destroy, but cannot disjoin them."

Again, in 1782, in "Notes on the State of Virginia," Jefferson said: "And can the liberties of a nation be thought secure when we have removed their only firm basis, a conviction in the minds of the people that these liberties are the gift of God?" Unfortunately, many non-Christians and many Christians are ignorant of the divine source of their liberties, or fail to grasp the significance of the connection. Finally, in 1775, in his essay, "The Farmer Refuted," Alexander Hamilton wrote, "The Sacred Rights of mankind are not to be rummaged for among old parchments or musty records. They are written, as with a sunbeam, in the whole volume

Appendix 1

of human nature, by the Hand of the Divinity itself, and can never be erased or obscured by mortal power."

THE FOUNDING FATHERS SUPPORT RELIGION AS THE BASIS OF MORALITY

Several founding fathers explicitly spoke about the connection of morality to religion or faith. The following are representative. These are their own words.[2]

Samuel Adams wrote of the direct connection between liberty and morality in 1776. He said:

> ... I fully agree in Opinion with a very celebrated Author, that "Freedom or Slavery will prevail in a (City or) Country according as the Disposition & Manners of the People render them fit for the one or the other"; and I have long been convincd (sic) that our Enemies have made it an Object, to eradicate from the Minds of the People in general a Sense of true Religion & Virtue, in hopes thereby the more easily to carry their Point of enslaving them. Indeed my Friend, this is a Subject so important in my Mind, that I know not how to leave it. Revelation assures us that "Righteousness exalteth a Nation"—Communities are dealt with in this World by the wise and just Ruler of the Universe. He rewards or punishes them according to their general Character. The diminution of publick Virtue is usually attended with that of publick Happiness, and the public Liberty will not long survive the total Extinction of Morals. ("[C]onvincd" in the original.)

Benjamin Franklin, at the Federal Framing Convention of 1787, spoke of God's governing among men when he made a motion for prayer:

> I have lived, Sir, a long time, and the longer I live, the more convincing proofs I see of this truth—that God governs in the affairs of men. And if a sparrow cannot fall to the ground without his notice, is it probable that an empire can rise without his aid? ... I also believe that without his concurring aid we shall succeed in this political building no better than the Builders of Babel ...

In his autobiography, Franklin wrote:

---

2. See Long, *Yardstick*, viii–ix, xxii–xxiii, 4–6, 22–24, 64, 74–76, 85–86, 94–95, etc.

Appendix 1

> I never doubted, for instance, the existence of a Deity; that he made the world and governed it by his providence; that the most acceptable service of God was the doing good to man; that our souls are immortal; and that all crimes will be punished, and virtue rewarded, either here or hereafter.

James Madison said at the Virginia Ratifying Convention, in 1788, that only the people's virtue could assure liberty. He wrote:

> But I go on this great republican principle, that the people will have virtue and intelligence to select men of virtue and wisdom. Is there no virtue among us? If there be not, we are in a wretched situation. No theoretical checks—no form of government can render us secure. To suppose that any form of government will secure liberty or happiness without any virtue in the people, is a chimerical idea. If there be sufficient virtue and intelligence in the community, it will be exercised in the selection of these men. So that we do not depend on their virtue, or put confidence in our rulers, but in the people who are to choose them.

Earlier, in his "Memorial and Remonstrance of 1785," Madison wrote:

> It is the duty of every man to render to the Creator such homage and such only as he believes to be acceptable to Him. This duty is precedent, both in order of time and degree of obligation, to the claims of Civil Society. Before any man can be considered as a member of Civil Society, he must be considered as a subject of the Governor of the Universe.

John Adams and Daniel Webster spoke directly to the connection of religion and morality. Adams, in his "Address to Officers of the First Brigade of the 3rd Division of the Militia of Massachusetts," October 11, 1798, wrote: "We have no government armed in power capable of contending in human passions unbridled by morality and religion. Our Constitution was made only for a moral and religious people. It is wholly inadequate for the government of any other." In his "A Discourse Delivered at Plymouth on Dec. 22, 1820," Daniel Webster said:

> Lastly, our ancestors established their system of government on morality and religious sentiment. Moral habits, they believed, cannot safely be trusted on any other foundation than religious principle, nor any government be secure which is not supported by moral habits.

Appendix 1

Finally, in his Farewell Address our first President, George Washington, said that religion and morality are essential to political prosperity:

> Of all the dispositions and habits which lead to political prosperity, Religion and morality are indispensable supports. In vain would that man claim the tribute to Patriotism, who should labour to subvert these great Pillars of human happiness, these firmest props of the duties of Men and citizens. The mere Politician, equally with the pious man ought to respect and to cherish them. A volume could not trace all their connections with private and public felicity. Let it simply be asked where is the security for property, for reputation, for life, if the sense of religious obligation desert the oaths, which are the instruments of investigation in Courts of Justice? And Let us with caution indulge the supposition, that morality can be maintained without religion. Whatever may be conceded to the influence of refined education on minds of peculiar structure, reason and experience both forbid us to expect that National morality can prevail in exclusion of religious principle. 'Tis substantially true, that virtue or morality is a necessary spring of popular government. (Emphasis his.)

Appendix 2

The Reformers on Revolution

MARTIN LUTHER

By his essay, "Secular Authority: To What Extent it Should Be Obeyed," Martin Luther had a significant impact upon subsequent church-state relations.[1] His teaching is briefly set forth here to commend his contribution to this important subject.

Charles Emmerich has sought to interpret Luther again for modern times. According to Emmerich, Luther had a consistent world ethic and theology based upon a foundation which included the centrality of the Cross, the life of faith, and the purpose of law, both divine and positive (legislation). Both kinds of law are legitimate and good, and serve theological, didactic, and political purposes.[2]

The Christian lives "in two realms of responsibility: the Heavenly Kingdom under the direct rule of God, and the Earthly Kingdom under the control of divinely established secular government."[3] These realms of responsibility include four primary stations or "mandates": marriage, labor, government, and church.[4] The first two have existed from creation; the last two came about because of the fall of man and the need for preserving the order and goodness yet remaining. Of the four only the church will endure after Christ returns and history is culminated. In the

---

1. Luther, "Secular Authority," in ch. 4 of Dillenberger, *Martin Luther*, 363–402.
2. Emmerich, "Luther's World Ethic," 1: 10–14.
3. Ibid., 34.
4. Ibid.

Appendix 2

New Heavens and Earth, there will be a radical change from the present form of institutions.

Both kingdoms have a claim upon man's allegiance in all four stations of life. Yet the heavenly kingdom is preeminent over the earthly, since the former preaches a gospel with eternal significance. The secular kingdom is temporal and one day will be abolished. The ethic of the earthly kingdom is retribution or *lex talionis*, since "realistically this is the only ethic that will fulfill the functions of restraining evil and promoting order in the world," writes Emmerich of Luther's view.[5] The ethic of love belongs to the heavenly kingdom among Christians in their relations with one another or with individual unbelievers. Luther's view, it seems, is consistent with the teaching of Scripture—both the Sermon on the Mount and Romans 13:1ff. It would be improper and impossible for either kingdom to operate by the ethic of the other.

Luther believed that Christians should hold the law and government in high esteem, and not because they needed the law to curb their sin. Rather in their desire to do what is profitable for their neighbors who are not Christians, they submit to government and law, pay taxes and do all they can to further government. This is of great benefit and necessary to curb evil and preserve peace.[6] Hence out of love for their neighbors, Christians serve the state, not because they themselves need it but because others need it.

For the same reasons Luther believed that the Christian should participate in government when qualified and when the needs of his neighbor demand it. Such service benefits others; it is for the good of one's neighbor; and it maintains the role of government in society. In this way the Christian may personally suffer evil and injustice, and yet also punish evil and injustice as it affects one's neighbor. If one may serve God by governmental power, who is better equipped to do so than the Christian?

For Luther, Matthew 5:39, "resist not evil," pertains to the individual Christian. He does not avenge himself. For others, however, he should seek vengeance and justice and do whatever he can toward this. The state should help and protect such. If the state does not do this, he should

---

5. Emmerich, "Luther's World Ethic," 36.
6. Luther, "Secular Authority," 373.

permit himself to be robbed and otherwise criminally offended, and not resist evil.[7]

The Christian, Luther believed, is not to use secular power for himself but for the unbeliever. He does not invoke the law for himself but only for others so that wickedness may be hindered.[8] Love of neighbor seeks not its own (1 Corinthians 13:5). The sword or law may be used on behalf of oneself, Luther allowed, but only where there is an "affluence of the Spirit," that is, when one is full of the Spirit.[9]

In approaching ethical decisions in contemporary society, the believer, Luther believed, must live theonomously. This means that one allows his reason and conscience to be under the rule of God.[10] When the two kingdoms conflict, the Christian must determine under which kingdom's jurisdiction he falls and then must act according to its ethics. Always, however, the heavenly kingdom's claims are superior; blind obedience to the state has no place. Therefore there are instances when the state must be resisted, and suffering at its hands may then be the cost of discipleship. The New Testament provides many examples of the latter, Luther believed.

Luther believed that warfare was justifiable on certain grounds, especially wars for self-defense, and also Christian participation in such wars.[11] He rejected the use of violent force in opposition to one's own government; there is no place for rebellion and revolution. Resistance can take only the form of preaching the Gospel.

Some recent Lutheran theologians have rejected this last position and have embraced a contract theory of government whereby a particular regime of government, which grossly misuses its authority, surrenders its right to govern and may be resisted. Emmerich suggests that perhaps Luther himself would have changed his view given the enormity of the evil of Nazi Germany.[12]

Luther's world ethic influenced not only the religious future of Europe but also the political. Both a theocracy, with a national church

---

7. Luther, "Secular Authority," 379.
8. Ibid., 380–381.
9. Ibid., 381–382.
10. Emmerich, "Luther's World Ethic," 14.
11. See Luther, "Secular Authority," 398–399.
12. Emmerich, "Luther's World Ethic," 39.

Appendix 2

governing the state, and caesaropapism, with the earthly kingdom governing the church, must be avoided. Implicit, then, to Luther's division are the seeds of a proper concept of the separation of church and state. Emmerich believes that, without Luther's influence, Henry VIII may never have broken with Rome and established the Church of England.[13] Although this precipitated a church-state union, it in turn brought a new search for religious liberty on the part of the Pilgrims.

Luther, however, was not advocating a secularization or separation between church and state but an "enlightened cooperation."[14] The two kingdoms intersect, as do all four stations of life. It is here that conflict often arises. The government "should encourage the spiritual ministry of the church in much the same way as the church undergirds the temporal authority of the state,"[15] Emmerich interprets Luther. The government should use its sword in a Christian manner.

Emmerich discusses six principles which Luther set forth to address the question of how a Christian ruler should use his temporal authority. In summary these are: (1) he should be dependent upon God; (2) he should act in love as a servant toward his subjects; (3) he should be personally attentive and sensitive to his subjects; (4) he should choose the lesser of two evils in order to promote the greater good; (5) there are exceptions to positive law, and reason must rule in its application (jurisprudential realism); and (6) love and natural law, "a higher ethos," ethically undergird positive law.[16]

Luther's fifth point, a call to jurisprudential realism, is a reminder that it is not always possible to attain justice. Hence mitigating principles must be part of any judicial system. This is especially pertinent for those seeking a ban on all abortions by way of constitutional amendment or legal statute. Exceptions may be allowed as the law of the land, such as in cases of rape, incest or to save the life of the mother, whereas personal preference may not allow such.

The increasingly secular nature of jurisprudence in America must lead inexorably to the growth of government and increased conflict and involvement of the secular kingdom in the affairs of the heavenly

---

13. Emmerich, "Luther's World Ethic," 39.
14. Ibid., 40.
15. Ibid.
16. Ibid., 40–41.

kingdom. This will mean not only rough times for Christians, but a growing threat to the freedom of all citizens.

Luther believed that the Christian has an obligation to speak out regarding current public ethical issues because of a love ethic that considers first the needs of others. What is best for one's neighbor and the viability of a nation in the light of God's plan demands confrontation with a vacillating society.

Luther's view of the two kingdoms with their respective ethical standards of love and retribution commends itself by providing for Christians today a coherent and consistent way to view their role in society.

JOHN CALVIN

Apparently both Luther and Calvin would forbid an individual Christian from participating in resistance to constituted authority. Yet, although private men should not perform an act of civil disobedience, Calvin taught that properly chosen magistrates should take charge and effect change. The individual should act when ordered to do so by the lesser ruler who also is invested with authority. Popular officials may make revolutionary decisions to curb tyranny. In so doing, they make resistance official and acceptable. Note Calvin's words:

> If it is proper that anything in a public ordinance should be corrected, let them not act tumultuously, or put their hands to a work where they ought to feel that their hands are tied, but let them leave it to the cognizance of the magistrate, whose hand alone here is free. My meaning is, let them not dare to do it without being ordered. For when the command of the magistrate is given, they too are invested with authority.
>
> I speak only of private men. For when popular magistrates have been appointed to curb the tyranny of kings . . . [sic] So far am I from forbidding these officially to check the undue license of kings, that if they connive at kings when they tyrannize and insult over the humbler of the people, I affirm that their dissimulation is not free from nefarious perfidy, because they fraudulently betray the liberty of the people, while knowing that, by the ordinance of God, they are its appointed guardians.[17]

---

17. Calvin, *Institutes*, 2: 669, 675.

Appendix 2

Of course, the exception to the above practice of restraint is where obedience to rulers is incompatible with obedience to God. Then God must be obeyed and men disobeyed, Calvin wrote.[18] This disobedience for religious reasons will be civil disobedience in the eyes of the state (cf. 1 Corinthians 7:23).

Another question arises with Calvin's view. If only the lesser, duly appointed magistrate can initiate revolution, but not the individual Christian, what happens if the lesser magistrate is a Christian? Does this violate the idea that Christians should not lead a rebellion? Apparently it would not, since the person is not only a Christian but also a civil authority.

As Gray points out with regard to the influence of Calvin on the French Huguenots, Calvin's ideas had political implications and influenced the adoption of democratic ideals in Switzerland, France, the Low Countries, England, Scotland, and North America. There are seeds of constitutional resistance and legal limitations upon rulers—all arising purely out of religious zeal.[19]

The resistance Calvin and his followers advocated was based on and tested by three things, according to Foster: (1) the written Word of God correctly interpreted; (2) a political covenant or compact, preferably written; and (3) some form of fundamental law.[20]

OTHER REFORMERS

Other reformers and their successors contributed to the issue of the Christian's response to unjust law. William Tyndale and John Bunyan violated the civil law and were willing to pay, even with their lives, the consequences. John Knox, the Scottish reformer, went beyond Luther and Calvin, according to Schaeffer.[21] His contribution was the justification of revolution by the people when leaders ruled contrary to God's law. He influenced Samuel Rutherford, who, in his *Lex Rex*, established the right and duty of lawful Christian resistance when a ruler destroyed the governing structure of a country. John Locke secularized Rutherford and influenced the founders of America with his four basic points (inalienable

18. Calvin, *Institutes*, 2: 675-676..
19. Gray, *French Huguenots*, 47–51.
20. Foster, "Calvin and His Followers," quoted in Gray, *French Huguenots*, 48–49.
21. Schaeffer, *Manifesto*, 93–106.

rights; government by consent; separation of powers; right to revolution or resistance of unlawful authority.)[22]

The influence of Reformation thought on America is unmistakable. When the American revolution took place the Colonies revolted only after the King of England had withdrawn rights or authority of government once granted the Americans. He initiated the revolution by violating his own promises or covenant.

For example, the king removed the authority of the Americans to elect their own governor and assembly. At least fifteen references are made in the Declaration of Independence to the King's abrogation of laws or of *de facto* government. The following are some examples:

> He has combined with others to subject us to a jurisdiction foreign to our constitution, and unacknowledged by our laws; giving his Assent to their Acts of pretended Legislation . . . For taking away our Charters, abolishing our most valuable Laws and altering fundamentally the Forms of our Governments: For suspending our own Legislatures, and declaring themselves invested with power to legislate for us in all cases whatsoever . . .

One could say that the King began the Revolution when by his actions the existing form of government ceased; there was no longer a "power existing," to which alone Paul's and Peter's words seem to apply (see Romans 13:1; 1 Peter 2:13). Conditions were already in a state of transition, and political power was changing hands. The American Revolution was actually a counter Revolution. Christians were in a position of choosing with which side to identify.

The influence of the reformers has been great. Their ideas about government continue to have direct application to the current struggle over moral pluralism in society, and the Christian's response.

---

22. Schaeffer, *Manifesto*, 105.

Bibliography

Aharoni, Yohanan, and Michael Avi-Yonah. *The Macmillan Bible Atlas*. New York: Macmillan, 1968.
Ahlstrom, Sydney E. *A Religious History of the American People*. New Haven: Yale University Press, 1972.
Arnold, Matthew. "Hebraism and Hellenism." In Anderson, George K. and William E. Buckler. *The Literature of England*. Glenview, Illinois: Scott, Foresman and Company, 1967.
Baldwin, Alice M. *The New England Clergy and the American Revolution*. New York: Frederick Ungar Pub. Co., 1965.
Ball, William B. *Moody Monthly* (July/August 1981).
Barrett, C. K. *A Commentary on the Epistle to the Romans*. New York: Harper and Row, 1957.
Basler, Roy P., ed. *The Collected Works of Abraham Lincoln*. New Brunswick: Rutgers University, 1953.
Beane, Rebecca. "Child Pornography on the Newstands." *Moody Monthly*, October 1986.
Bellah, Robert N. "Religion and Polity in America." *Andover Newton Quarterly* 15 (November 1974) :111.
Bernard, J. H. *The Pastoral Epistles*. Cambridge: At the University Press, 1906.
Beverley, James A. "Is Islam a Religion of Peace?" *Christianity Today*, January 2002.
Bigg, Charles. *Critical and Exegetical Commentary on the Epistles of St. Peter and St. Jude*. Edinburgh: T. and T. Clark, rep. 1969.
Billington, Ray Allen. "Northwest Ordinance." In *The World Book Encyclopedia*, 14: 408. Chicago: Field Enterprises Educational Corp., 1967.
Bird, Wendell R. "U.S. Supreme Court Decisions on Freedom of Religion." Special ed. *Religious Freedom Reporter* (June/July 1985): 5:1–52.
Blackstone, Sir William. *Commentaries on the Law of England*. 1803.
Blankenhorn, David. *The Future of Marriage*. New York: Encounter Books, 2007.
Boa, Kenneth D. "What is Behind Morality?" *Bibliotheca Sacra* 133 (April/June 1976): 154–156.
Brabner-Smith, John. "The Prudent Pursuit of Happiness." *Christian Legal Society Quarterly* (Fall 1980): 1:8.
Brackney, W.H. "Backus, Isaac." In *Biographical Dictionary of Evangelicals*, edited by Timothy Larsen. Downers Grove: InterVarsity Press, 2003.
Brimelow, Peter, and Stephen J. Markman. "Supreme Irony." *Harper's Magazine*, October 1981.
Calvin, John. *Commentaries on the Epistles to Timothy, Titus, and Philemon*. Translated by William Pringle. Grand Rapids: Baker, rep. 1979.

Bibliography

Calvin, John. *Institutes of the Christian Religion*. Translated by Henry Beveridge. Grand Rapids: Eerdmans, 1970.

Clouse, Robert G., ed. *War: Four Christian Views*. Downers Grove, Illinois: InterVarsity, 1981.

Cohen, F. S. *Law, Language and Ethics*. Quoted by Charles J. Emmerich in "Luther's World Ethic: A Christian Call to Confront Culture." *Christian Legal Society Quarterly* (Fall 1980): 1:10.

Cranfield, C. E. B. *A Critical and Exegetical Commentary on the Epistle to the Romans*. Edinburgh: T. and T. Clark Ltd., 1979.

Culver, Robert Duncan. *The Peace Mongers*. Wheaton: Tyndale, 1985.

Curry, Dayna and Heather Mercer. *Prisoners of Hope*. New York: Doubleday, 2002.

Daly, Robert J., ed. *Christians and the Military*. Philadelphia: Fortress Press, 1985.

Deissmann, Adolf. *Light from the Ancient East*. Grand Rapids: Baker, rep. 1978.

DeYoung, James B. *Burning Down the Shack: How the "Christian" Bestseller is Deceiving Millions*. Washington, D.C.: WND Books, 2010.

———. *Homosexuality: Contemporary Claims Examined in Light of the Bible and Other Ancient Literature and Law*. Grand Rapids: Kregel, 2000.

———. "The Meaning of 'the Law' in 1 Corinthians 14:34: With Implications for the Role of Women in Ministry and for General and Special Revelation." Paper presented to the Evangelical Theological Society, San Diego, California, November 15, 2007.

Durant, Will and Ariel Durant. *The Lessons of History*. New York: Simon and Schuster, 1968.

Durant, Will. *The Story of Civilization*. Vol. 1: *Our Oriental Heritage*. New York: Simon and Schuster, 1935.

Emmerich, Charles J. "Luther's World Ethic: A Christian Call to Confront Culture." *Christian Legal Society Quarterly* (Fall 1980): 1:10.

Foster, Herbert Darling. "Calvin and His Followers Championed Representative Government." In Janet Glenn Gray, *The French Huguenots: Anatomy of Courage*, pp. 48–49. Grand Rapids: Baker, 1981.

Foster, Marshall and Mary-Elaine Swanson. *The American Covenant*. Thousand Oaks: Foundation for Christian Self-Government, 1981.

Fuller, Michael. "Science, Religion and Ethics: Charting beyond Critical Realism." *Expository Times* (2002): 114:2.

Gifford, E. H. *The Epistle of St. Paul to the Romans*. Minneapolis: Klock and Klock, rep. 1977.

Gould, Stephen Jay. *Rocks of Ages*. London: Johathan Cape, 2001.

Gray, Janet Glenn. *The French Huguenots: Anatomy of Courage*. Grand Rapids: Baker, 1981.

Gwatkin, Melvill, ed. *Selections from Early Writers*. Westwood: Fleming H. Revell, 1893.

Hall, Verna M. *The Christian History of the Constitution of the United States of America*. San Franciso: Foundation for American Christian Education, 1966.

Hendriksen, William. *New Testament Commentary: Exposition of the Pastoral Epistles*. Grand Rapids: Baker, 1957.

Henry, Carl F.H. "Insights on Liberation Theology." *Action*, March/April 1986.

Hitchcock, James. "Competing Ethical Systems." *Imprimis*, April 1981.

Holmes, Michael W., ed. *The Apostolic Fathers*. Grand Rapids: Baker, 2002.

Horn, Carl. "Taking God to Court." *Christianity Today* (January 2, 1981).

Bibliography

Johnson, Alan F. "Is There a Biblical Warrant for Natural-law Theories?" *JETS* 2 (June, 1982): 185-199.

Johnstone, Robert. *The First Epistle of Peter*. Minneapolis: James Family Publishing Co., rep. 1978.

Josephus, *The Jewish War*. Trans. H. St. J. Thackeray. Loeb Classical Library. Cambridge, MA: Harvard, 1967, 1968.

Kaiser, Jr., Walter C. *Toward Old Testament Ethics*. Grand Rapids: Zondervan, 1983.

Kelly, J. N. D. *A Commentary on the Pastoral Epistles*. London: Adam and Charles Black, 1963.

Kirk, Russell. "Simplicity and Audacity in Reform: A Call for Reactionary Radicalism." *Modern Age* (Summer 1979): 232.

Kirsopp Lake, *The Apostolic Fathers* (Cambridge: Harvard University Press, 1965), 1:311-312.

Kline, Meredith G. "*Lex Talionis* and the Human Fetus." *JETS* 20 (September 1977): 200-201.

Leighton, Robert. *Commentary on First Peter*. Grand Rapids: Kregel, rep. 1972.

"Liberation Theology's Curious Contradiction," *Christianity Today* (July 10, 1987), 54-55.

Liddell, H.G. and R. Scott. *A Greek-English Lexicon*, 9th ed. Oxford: Clarendon, 1940.

Liddon, H. P. *Explanatory Analysis of St. Paul's Epistle to the Romans*. Minneapolis: James and Klock, rep. 1977.

Lillie, John. *Lectures on the First and Second Epistles of Peter*. Minneapolis: Klock and Klock, rep. 1978.

Lipscomb, Wyatt W. and M.B. Dunn. *War in the Spiritual Realm, the Ultimate Field of Battle*. Garland, Texas: Support for Action, Inc., 1980.

Lock, Walter. *A Critical and Exegetical Commentary on the Pastoral Epistles*. Edinburgh: T. and T. Clark, 1966.

Long, Hamilton Albert. *Your American Yardstick*. Philadelphia: Your Heritage Books, Inc., 1963.

Luther, Martin. "Secular Authority: To What Extent It should be Obeyed." In *Martin Luther: Selections from His Writings*, edited by John Dillenberger. Garden City: Doubleday & Co., Inc., 1961.

Madison, James. "Memorial and Remonstrance." In Robert A. Rutland et al, eds., *The Papers of James Madison*, 20 vols. (Chicago: The University of Chicago Press, 1973), 8: 299.

Malik, Charles H. "The Two Tasks." *JETS* 23 (December 1980): 289.

McLoughlin, William G. *Isaac Backus and the American Pietistic Tradition*. Boston: Little, Brown and Company, 1967.

Minson, Douglas C. "Ordered Liberty Under God." *Intercollegiate Review* (Fall 2002): 38:55.v.

Munoz, Vincent P. "Religious Liberty and the American Founding." *Intercollegiate Review* (Spring/Summer 2003): 34.

Murray, John. *The Epistle to the Romans*. Grand Rapids: Eerdmans, 1968.

Nederhood, Joel. "The Demise of Justice." *Christian Legal Society Quarterly* (Spring, 1980): 1:11.

Niemeyer, Gerhart. "Beyond 'Democratic Disorder.'" *Intercollegiate Review* (Spring/Summer, 1981): 16: 73.

Novak, David. "Law of Moses, Law of Nature." *First Things* (February 1996): 48.

Bibliography

Pavlischek, Keith. "Just and Unjust War in the Terrorist Age." *Intercollegiate Review* (Spring 2002): 37:29.

Payne, Keith B. and Karl I. Payne. *A Just Defense: The Use of Force, Nuclear Weapons and Our Conscience*. Portland: Multnomah Press, 1987.

Philo, *On Abraham*. Trans. F. H. Colson. Loeb Classical Library. Cambridge, MA: Harvard, 1966.

———, *On the Special Laws*. Trans. F. H. Colson. Loeb Classical Library. Cambridge, MA: Harvard, rep. 1968.

Plato, *The Laws*. Trans. R. G. Bury. Loeb Classical Library. Cambridge, MA: Harvard, 1967.

Poythress, Vern. "Why Scientists Must Believe in God: Divine Attributes of Scientific Law." *JETS* 46/1 (March 2003): 111–23.

Price, David M. "An Historical Interpretation of the Establishment Clause." Th.M. thesis, Western Seminary, 1987.

Rehwinkel, Alfred M. *The Wonders of Creation*. Minneapolis: Bethany Fellowship, 1974.

"Revolution." *Webster's New Collegiate Dictionary*. Springfield: G. & C. Merriam Co., 1960.

Robertson, Archibald Thomas. *Word Pictures in the New Testament*. Nashville: Broadman, 1931.

Ross, Allen P. "The Dispersion of the Nations in Genesis 11:1–9." *Bibliotheca Sacra* 138 (April/June 1981): 120.

Rushdoony, Rousas John. *Law and Liberty*. Fairfax, Virginia: Thoburn Press, 1977.

Sanday, William and Arthur C. Headlam. *A Critical and Exegetical Commentary on the Epistle to the Romans*. Edinburgh: T. and T. Clark, rep. 1968.

Schaeffer, Francis A. *A Christian Manifesto*. Westchester: Crossway Books, 1981.

Scruton, Roger. "The Political Problem of Islam." *Intercollegiate Review* (Fall 2002): 38:3–15.

Selwyn, Edward Gordon. *The First Epistle of St. Peter*. New York: St. Martin's Press, 1969.

Shedd, William G. T. *A Critical and Doctrinal Commentary on the Epistle of St. Paul to the Romans*. Minneapolis: Klock and Klock, rep. 1978.

Sherwin-White, A. N. *Roman Society and Roman Law in the New Testament*. Oxford: Clarendon Press, 1963.

Singer, C. Gregg. *A Theological Interpretation of American History*. Nutley, N.J.: The Craig Press, 1964: 284–285. Quoted by Edward Rowe in "Why Christians Must Become Active As Citizens." Religious Roundtable (n.p., n.d.), 7.

Slater, Rosalie J. *Teaching and Learning America's Christian History*. San Francisco: Foundation for American Christian Education, 1965.

Sobran, Joseph. "National Church Council Bible Censorship Plan—Liberation Run Amok." *Conservative Digest* (January 1981): 7:44.

Solzhenitsyn, Alexander. "Solzhenitsyn on Communism." *Time*, February 18, 1980.

Stifler, James M. *The Epistle to the Romans*. Chicago: Moody Press, 1960.

The Sunday Oregonian, June 7, 1981, A 20.

Swartzwalder, Robert F. "An Evaluation of Evangelical Perspectives on Nuclear War." Master's thesis, Western Conservative Baptist Seminary, 1983.

Swift, Louis J. *The Early Fathers on War and Military Service*. Wilmington: Michael Glazier, Inc., 1983.

Titus, Herbert W. "Moses, Blackstone and the Law of the Land." *Christian Legal Society Quarterly* (Fall 1980): 1:6.

Bibliography

Toynbee, Arnold. *America and the World Revolution.* New York: Oxford University Press, 1962.

———. *Civilization on Trial and the World and the West.* New York: World Publishing Co., 1971.

Wallace, Daniel B. "Granville Sharp: A Model of Evangelical Scholarship and Social Activism." *JETS* 41/4 (December 1998): 591–613.

Wasson, R. Gordon, et al. *The Road to Eleusis.* New York: Harcourt Brace Jovanovich, 1978.

Webster, Douglas D. "Liberation Theology." *Evangelical Dictionary of Theology.* Edited by Walter A. Elwell. Grand Rapids: Baker, 1984.

"What Hath Roe Wrought?" *The Healing Ethic* (Fall 1987), 1: 1–2.

Whitehead, John W. "The Secularizing of America." *Moody Monthly* (July/August 1981): 18–21.

www.ingramcontent.com/pod-product-compliance
Lightning Source LLC
Chambersburg PA
CBHW070404240426
43661CB00056B/2537